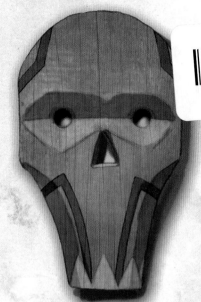

BRUTAL
NATURE
FURY

COVER ART BY
ARIEL OLIVETTI

COLLECTION EDITS BY
JUSTIN EISINGER AND ALONZO SIMON

COLLECTION DESIGN BY
NEIL UYETAKE

PUBLISHER
TED ADAMS

ISBN: 978-1-63140-975-2   20 19 18 17   1 2 3 4

Become our fan on Facebook **facebook.com/idwpublishing**
Follow us on Twitter **@idwpublishing**
Subscribe to us on YouTube **youtube.com/idwpublishing**
See what's new on Tumblr **tumblr.idwpublishing.com**
Check us out on Instagram **instagram.com/idwpublishing**

Ted Adams, CEO & Publisher
Greg Goldstein, President & COO
Robbie Robbins, EVP/Sr. Graphic Artist
Chris Ryall, Chief Creative Officer
David Hedgecock, Editor-in-Chief
Laurie Windrow, Senior VP of Sales & Marketing
Matthew Ruzicka, CPA, Chief Financial Officer
Lorelei Bunjes, VP of Digital Services
Jerry Bennington, VP of New Product Development

For international rights, please contact
licensing@idwpublishing.com

WRITTEN BY
LUCIANO SARACINO

ART BY
ARIEL OLIVETTI

LETTERS BY
SHAWN LEE

TRANSLATION AND SERIES EDITS BY
CARLOS GUZMAN

PUBLISHER
TED ADAMS

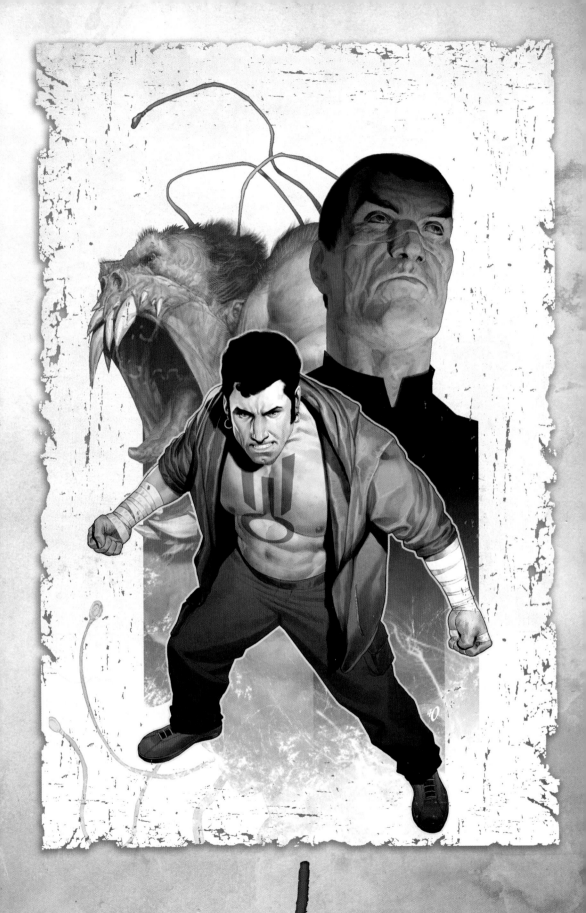

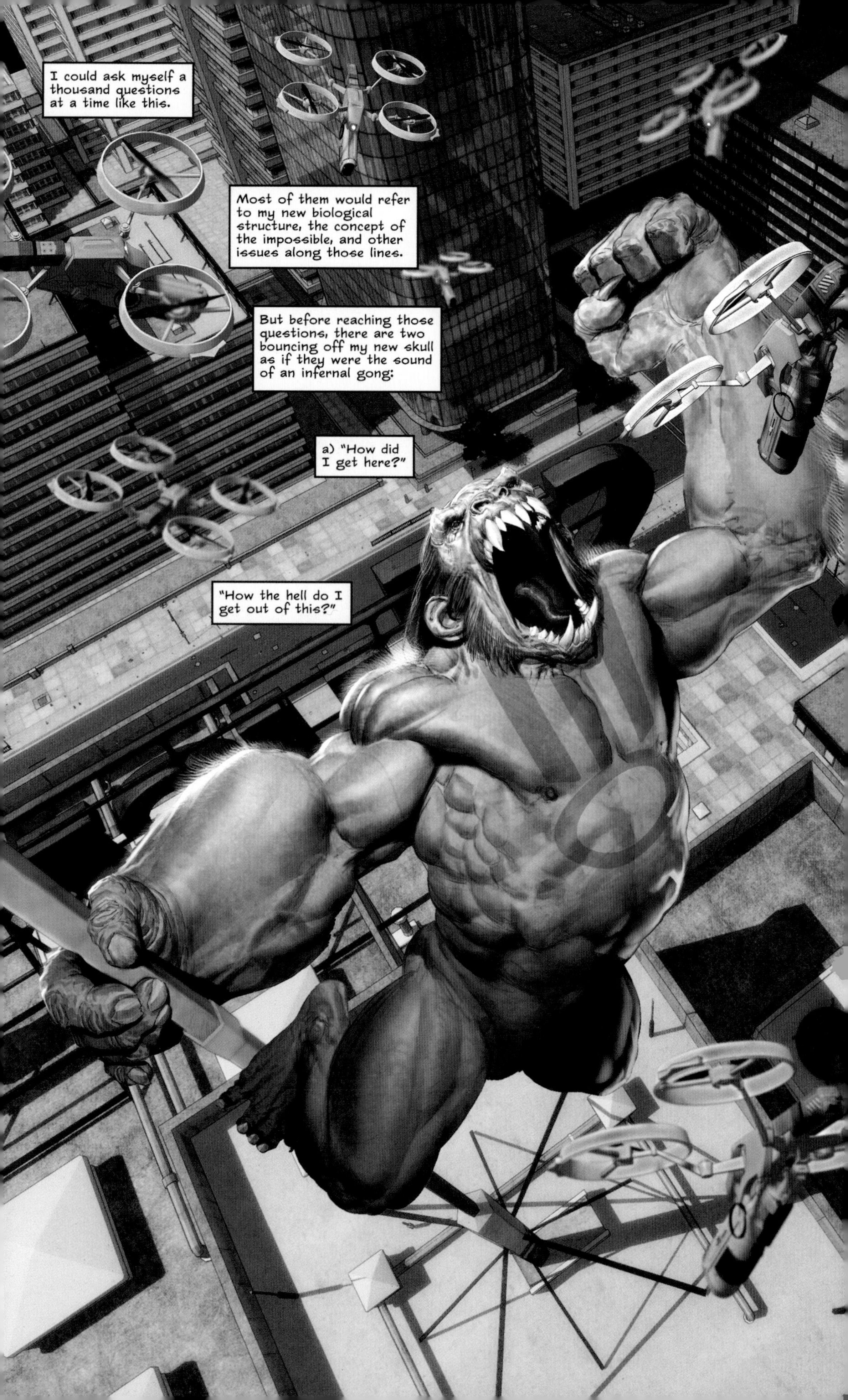
I could ask myself a thousand questions at a time like this.
Most of them would refer to my new biological structure, the concept of the impossible, and other issues along those lines.
But before reaching those questions, there are two bouncing off my new skull as if they were the sound of an infernal gong:
a) "How did I get here?"
"How the hell do I get out of this?"

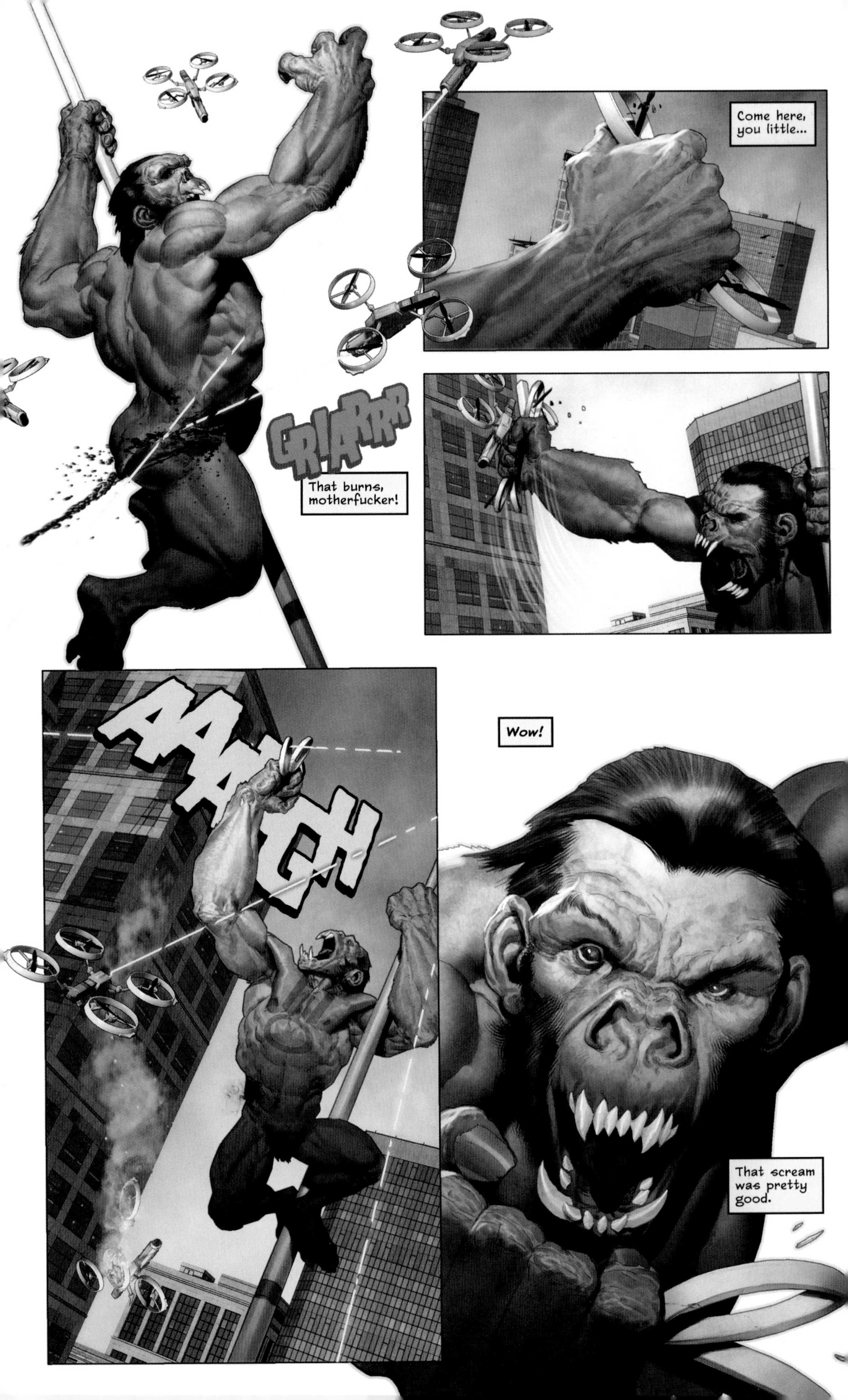

Come here,
you little...
GRIARRR
That burns,
motherfucker!
AAAGH
Wow!
That scream
was pretty
good.

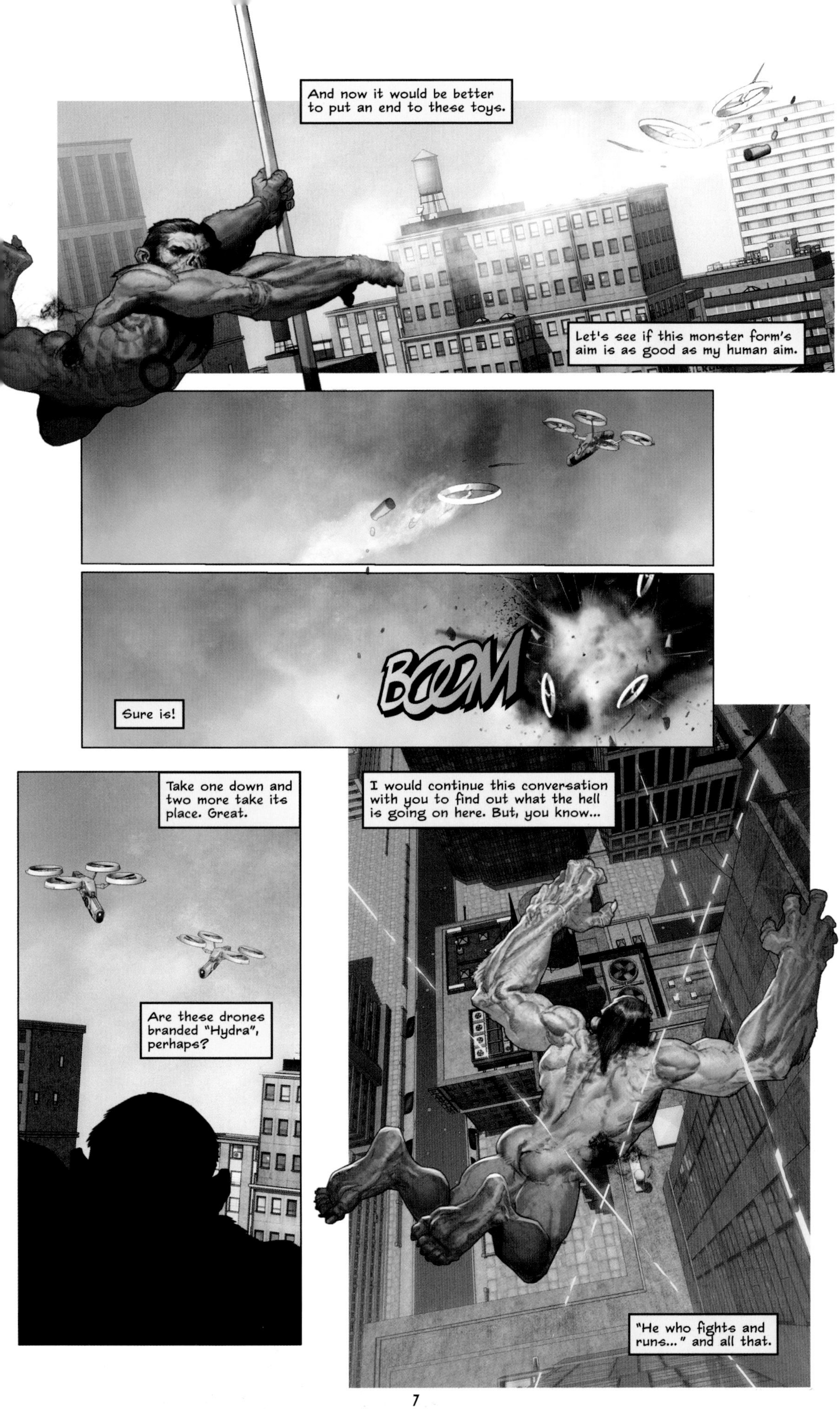

And now it would be better to put an end to these toys.
Let's see if this monster form's aim is as good as my human aim.
BOOM
Sure is!
Take one down and two more take its place. Great.
Are these drones branded "Hydra", perhaps?
I would continue this conversation with you to find out what the hell is going on here. But, you know...
"He who fights and runs..." and all that.

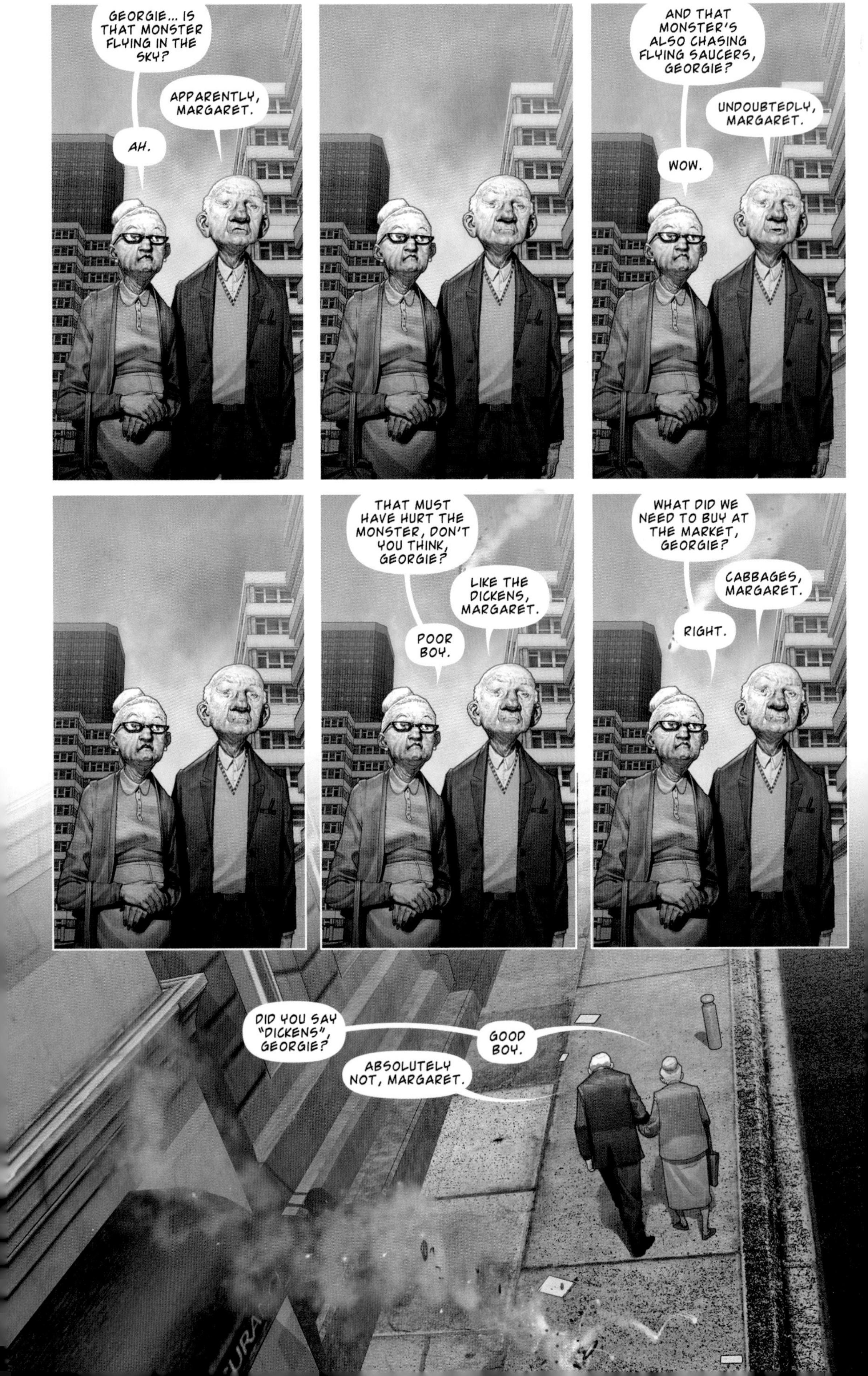
GEORGIE... IS THAT MONSTER FLYING IN THE SKY?
APPARENTLY, MARGARET.
AH.
AND THAT MONSTER'S ALSO CHASING FLYING SAUCERS, GEORGIE?
UNDOUBTEDLY, MARGARET.
WOW.
THAT MUST HAVE HURT THE MONSTER, DON'T YOU THINK, GEORGIE?
LIKE THE DICKENS, MARGARET.
POOR BOY.
WHAT DID WE NEED TO BUY AT THE MARKET, GEORGIE?
CABBAGES, MARGARET.
RIGHT.
DID YOU SAY "DICKENS", GEORGIE?
ABSOLUTELY NOT, MARGARET.
GOOD BOY.

AAARGHHH

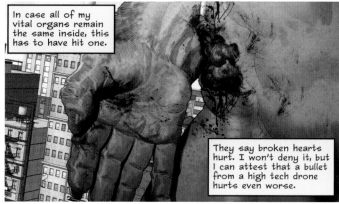

In case all of my vital organs remain the same inside, this has to have hit one.

They say broken hearts hurt. I won't deny it, but I can attest that a bullet from a high tech drone hurts even worse.

Desperate times...

GRRRAARHHH

...call for desperate measures.

CRASH

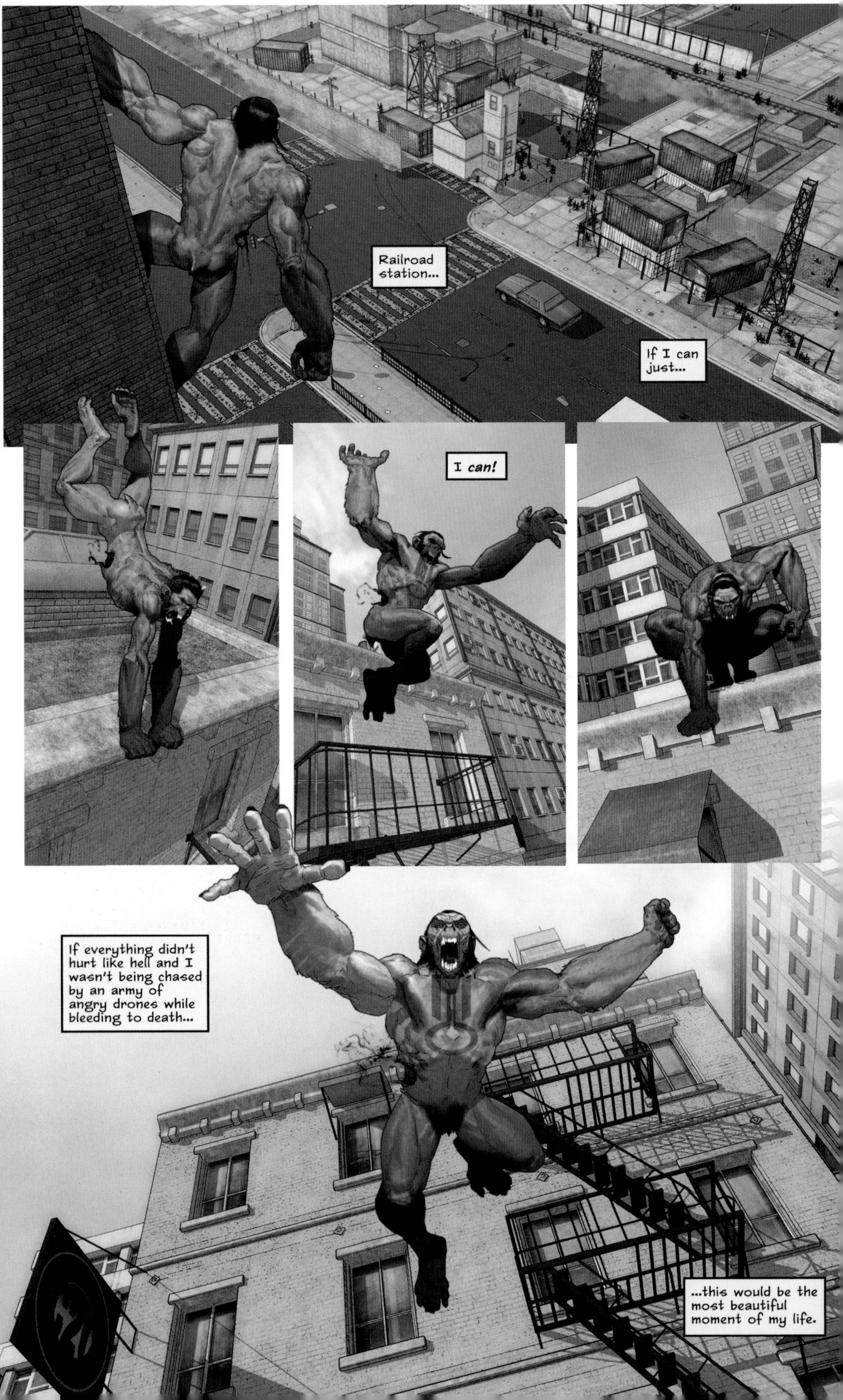
Railroad station...
If I can just...
I *can!*
If everything didn't hurt like hell and I wasn't being chased by an army of angry drones while bleeding to death...
...this would be the most beautiful moment of my life.

THE SUBJECT IS HEADING TO THE RAILROAD AREA.

IF HE GETS THERE, WE LOSE HIM. THERE ARE TUNNELS THAT...

HE WON'T MAKE IT.

HOW CAN YOU KNOW THAT?

CALL IT FEMININE INTUITION, MR. WOLF.

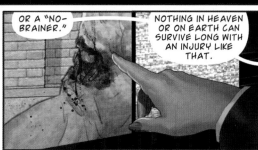

OR A "NO-BRAINER."

NOTHING IN HEAVEN OR ON EARTH CAN SURVIVE LONG WITH AN INJURY LIKE THAT.

"THERE ARE MORE THINGS IN HEAVEN AND EARTH, HORATIO, THAN ARE DREAMT OF IN YOUR PHILOSOPHY."

EXCUSE ME, MR. WOLF?

SHAKESPEARE, EDITH. THE GREATEST WRITER OF TRAGEDIES OF ALL TIME.

AND IF YOU'LL ALLOW ME A CONFESSION, I LOOK FORWARD TO THIS TRAGEDY TILTING IN FAVOR OF THE RIGHTEOUS.

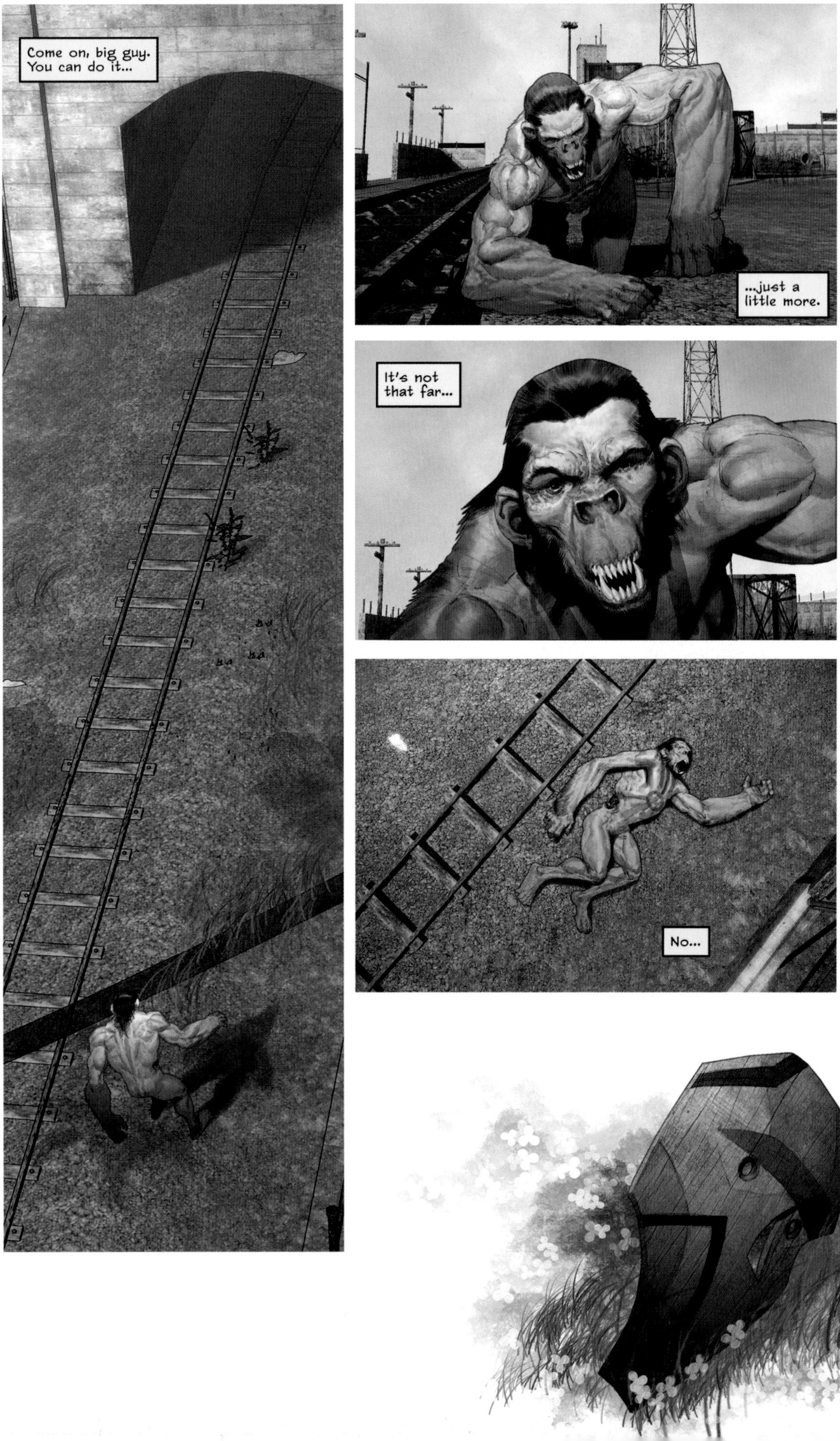
Come on, big guy. You can do it...
...just a little more.
It's not that far...
No...

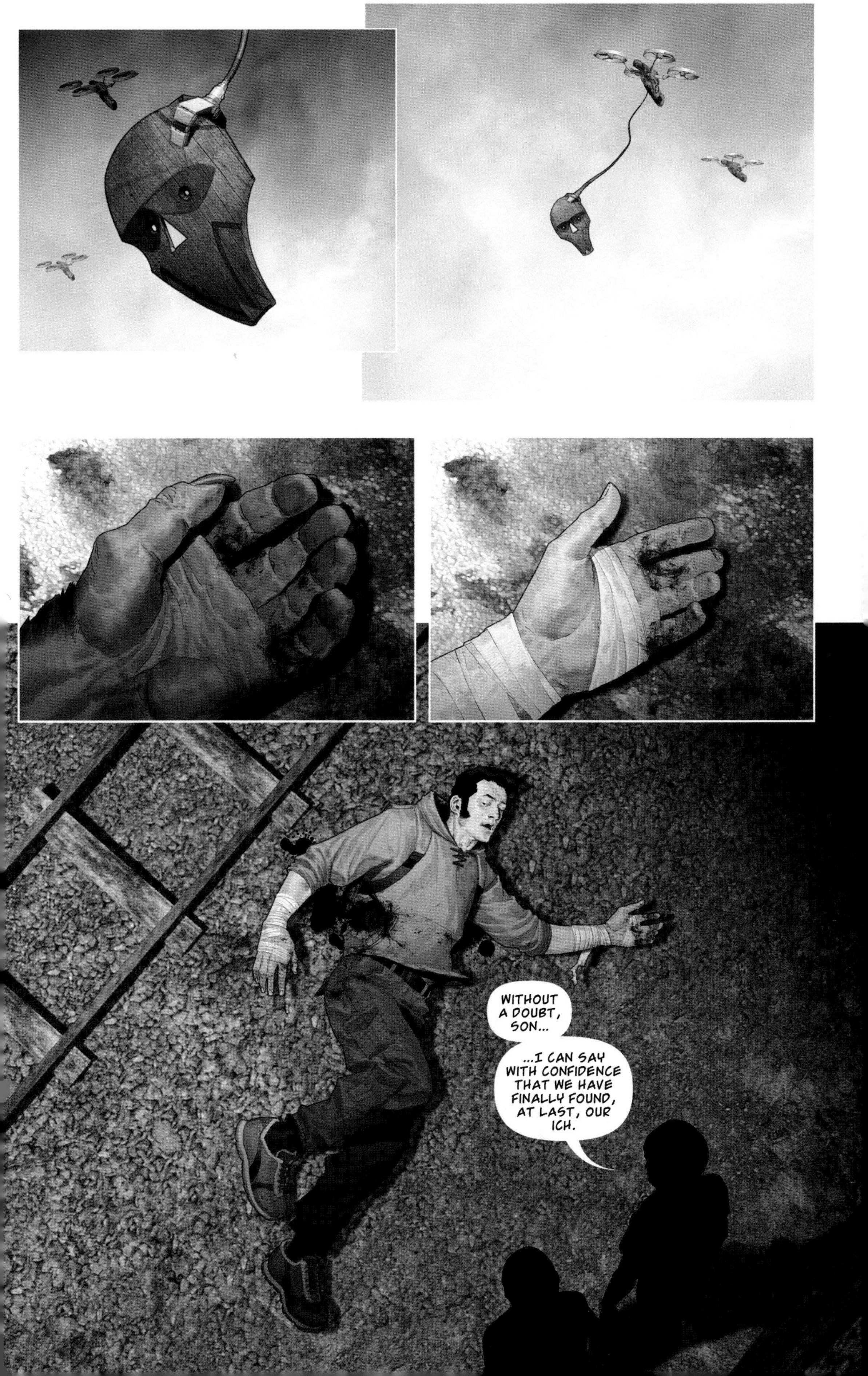
WITHOUT A DOUBT, SON...
...I CAN SAY WITH CONFIDENCE THAT WE HAVE FINALLY FOUND, AT LAST, OUR ICH.

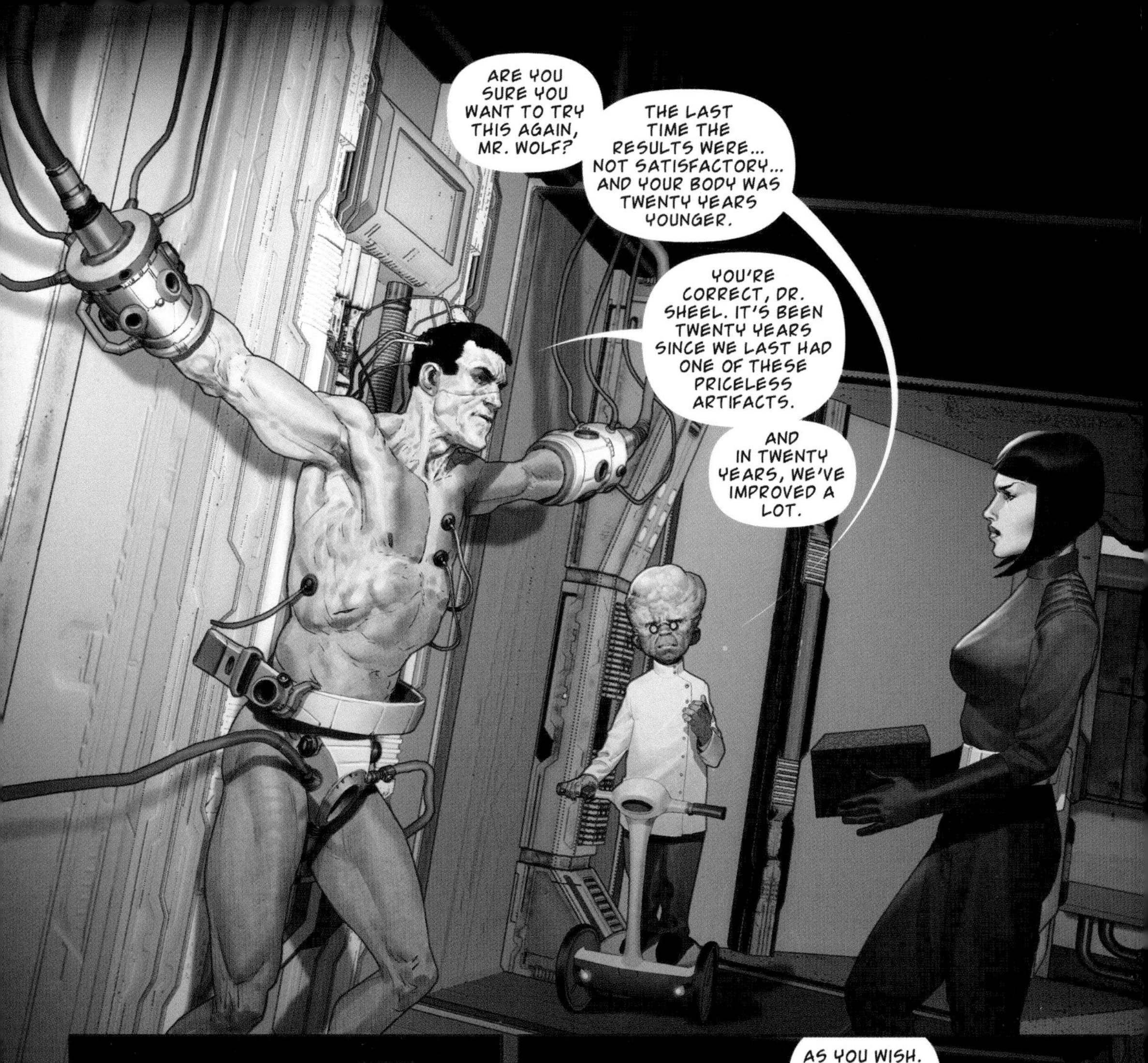
ARE YOU SURE YOU WANT TO TRY THIS AGAIN, MR. WOLF?
THE LAST TIME THE RESULTS WERE... NOT SATISFACTORY... AND YOUR BODY WAS TWENTY YEARS YOUNGER.
YOU'RE CORRECT, DR. SHEEL. IT'S BEEN TWENTY YEARS SINCE WE LAST HAD ONE OF THESE PRICELESS ARTIFACTS.
AND IN TWENTY YEARS, WE'VE IMPROVED A LOT.

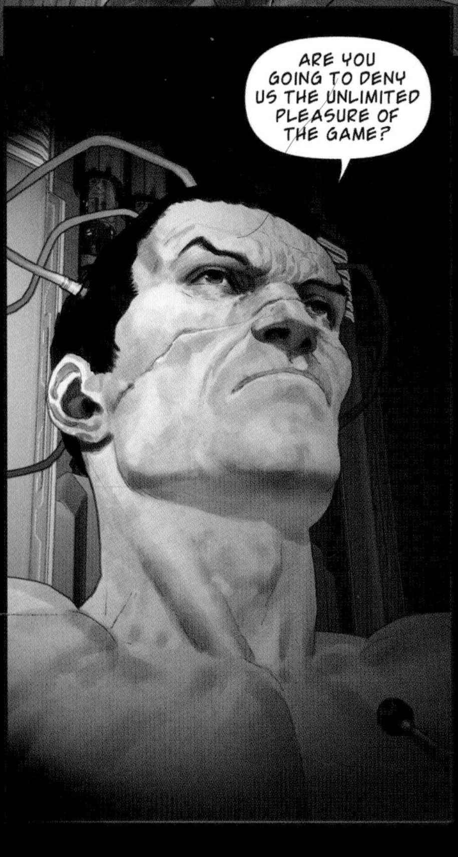
ARE YOU GOING TO DENY US THE UNLIMITED PLEASURE OF THE GAME?

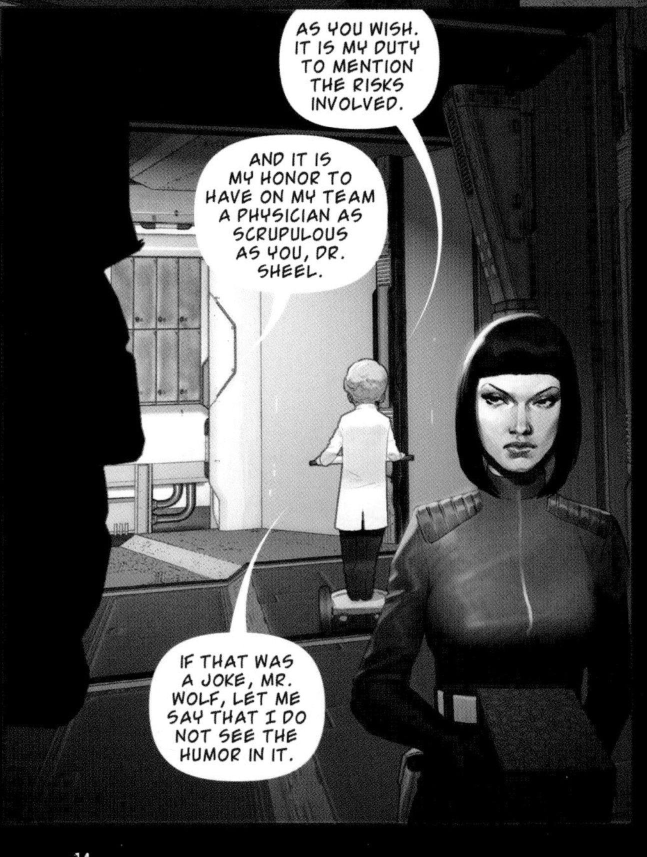
AS YOU WISH. IT IS MY DUTY TO MENTION THE RISKS INVOLVED.
AND IT IS MY HONOR TO HAVE ON MY TEAM A PHYSICIAN AS SCRUPULOUS AS YOU, DR. SHEEL.
IF THAT WAS A JOKE, MR. WOLF, LET ME SAY THAT I DO NOT SEE THE HUMOR IN IT.

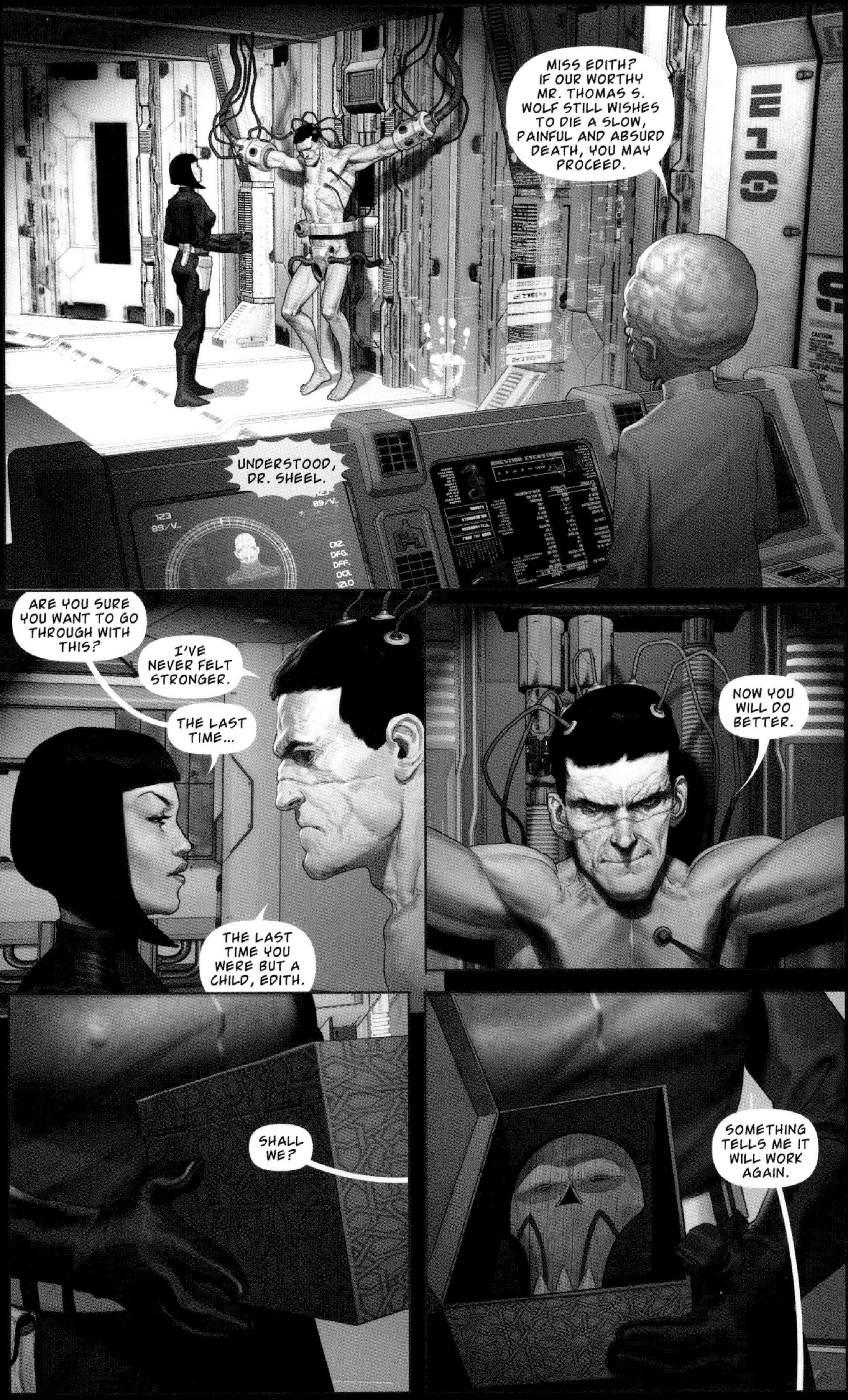
MISS EDITH? IF OUR WORTHY MR. THOMAS S. WOLF STILL WISHES TO DIE A SLOW, PAINFUL AND ABSURD DEATH, YOU MAY PROCEED.
UNDERSTOOD, DR. SHEEL.
ARE YOU SURE YOU WANT TO GO THROUGH WITH THIS?
I'VE NEVER FELT STRONGER.
THE LAST TIME...
THE LAST TIME YOU WERE BUT A CHILD, EDITH.
NOW YOU WILL DO BETTER.
SHALL WE?
SOMETHING TELLS ME IT WILL WORK AGAIN.

HHHH...

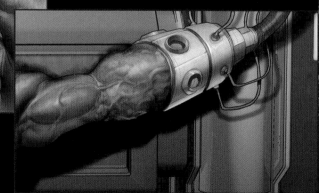

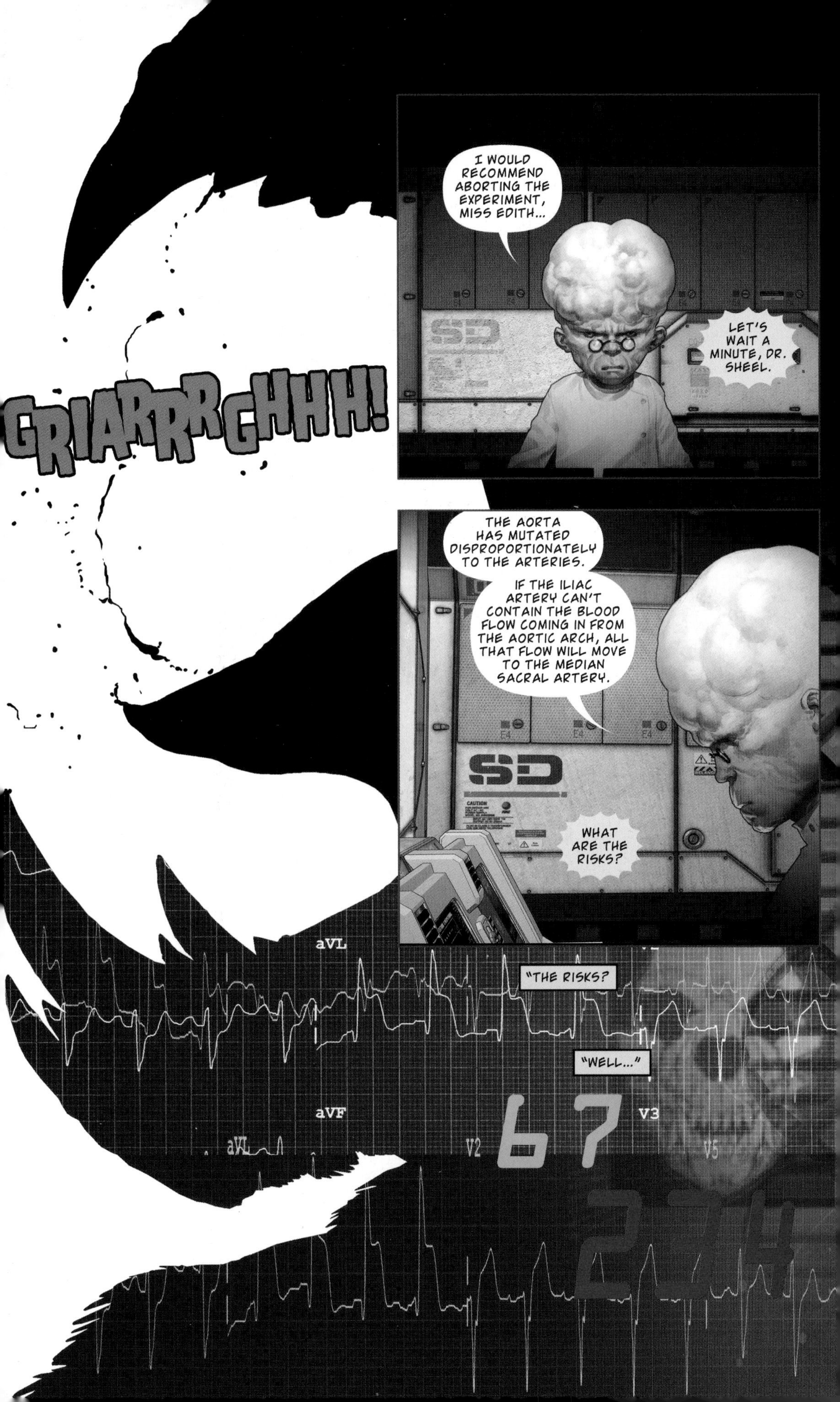

GRIARRRGHHH!
I WOULD RECOMMEND ABORTING THE EXPERIMENT, MISS EDITH...
LET'S WAIT A MINUTE, DR. SHEEL.
THE AORTA HAS MUTATED DISPROPORTIONATELY TO THE ARTERIES.
IF THE ILIAC ARTERY CAN'T CONTAIN THE BLOOD FLOW COMING IN FROM THE AORTIC ARCH, ALL THAT FLOW WILL MOVE TO THE MEDIAN SACRAL ARTERY.
WHAT ARE THE RISKS?
"THE RISKS?
"WELL..."

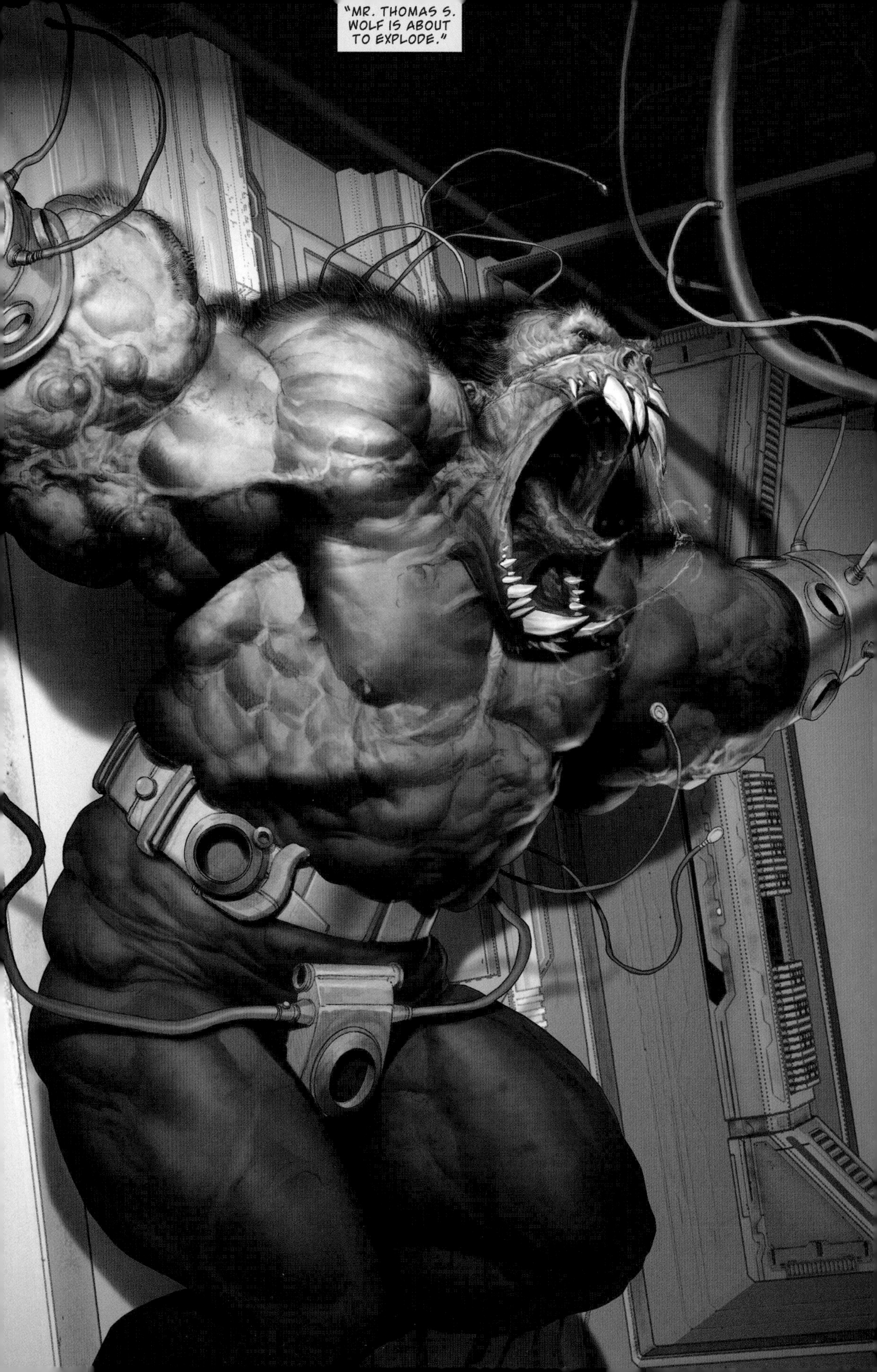
"MR. THOMAS S. WOLF IS ABOUT TO EXPLODE."

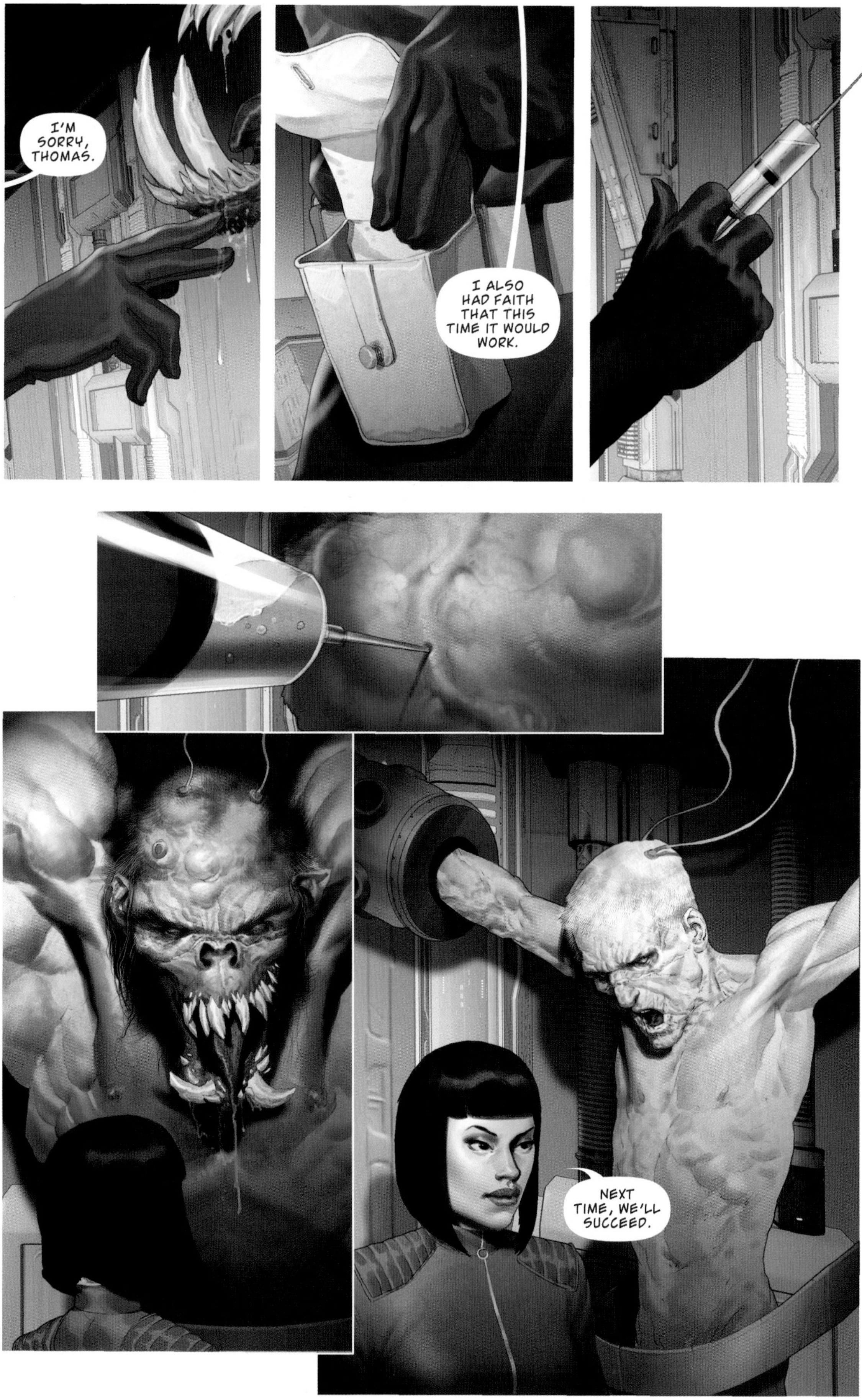

I'M SORRY, THOMAS.
I ALSO HAD FAITH THAT THIS TIME IT WOULD WORK.
NEXT TIME, WE'LL SUCCEED.

This time I dreamed of dreams that did not belong to me.

The dreams of hundreds of souls dreaming within my own soul.

Dreams of all the stories in the world within my own story.

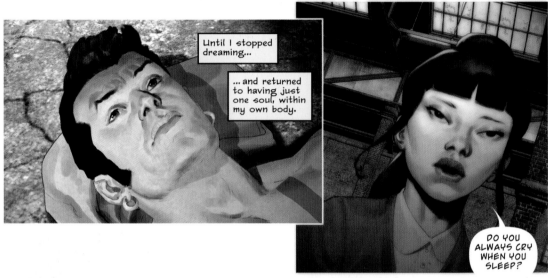

Until I stopped dreaming...

...and returned to having just one soul, within my own body.

DO YOU ALWAYS CRY WHEN YOU SLEEP?

WHERE AM I? AND WHO ARE YOU SUPPOSED TO BE?

DO NOT PUSH YOURSELF. THE WOUND WAS DEEP.

WOUND? MY HOUSE... I...

MY NAME IS XUE.

IT MEANS "SNOW."

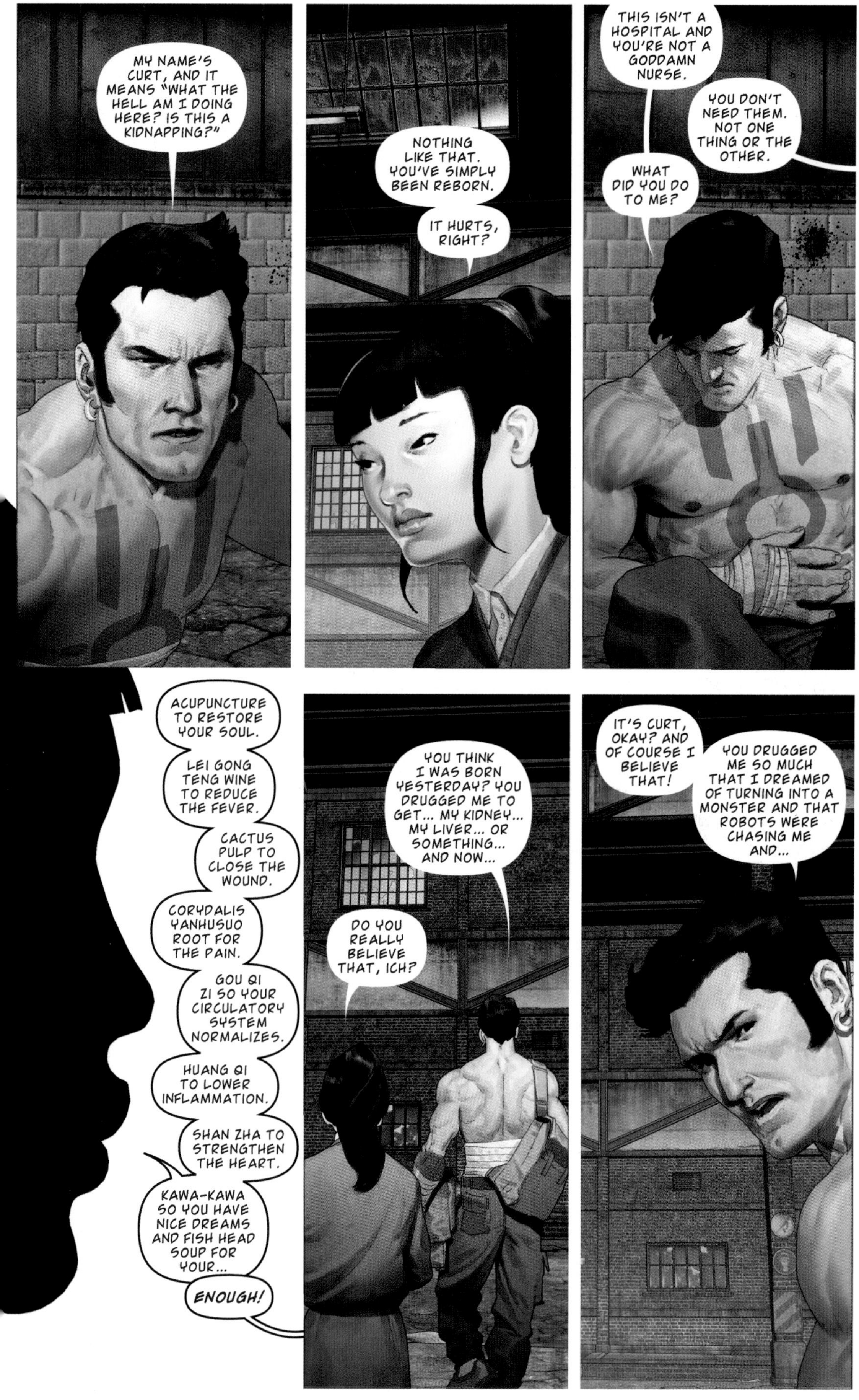
MY NAME'S CURT, AND IT MEANS "WHAT THE HELL AM I DOING HERE? IS THIS A KIDNAPPING?"
NOTHING LIKE THAT. YOU'VE SIMPLY BEEN REBORN.
IT HURTS, RIGHT?
THIS ISN'T A HOSPITAL AND YOU'RE NOT A GODDAMN NURSE.
WHAT DID YOU DO TO ME?
YOU DON'T NEED THEM. NOT ONE THING OR THE OTHER.
ACUPUNCTURE TO RESTORE YOUR SOUL.
LEI GONG TENG WINE TO REDUCE THE FEVER.
CACTUS PULP TO CLOSE THE WOUND.
CORYDALIS YANHUSUO ROOT FOR THE PAIN.
GOU QI ZI SO YOUR CIRCULATORY SYSTEM NORMALIZES.
HUANG QI TO LOWER INFLAMMATION.
SHAN ZHA TO STRENGTHEN THE HEART.
KAWA-KAWA SO YOU HAVE NICE DREAMS AND FISH HEAD SOUP FOR YOUR...
ENOUGH!
YOU THINK I WAS BORN YESTERDAY? YOU DRUGGED ME TO GET... MY KIDNEY... MY LIVER... OR SOMETHING... AND NOW...
DO YOU REALLY BELIEVE THAT, ICH?
IT'S CURT, OKAY? AND OF COURSE I BELIEVE THAT!
YOU DRUGGED ME SO MUCH THAT I DREAMED OF TURNING INTO A MONSTER AND THAT ROBOTS WERE CHASING ME AND...

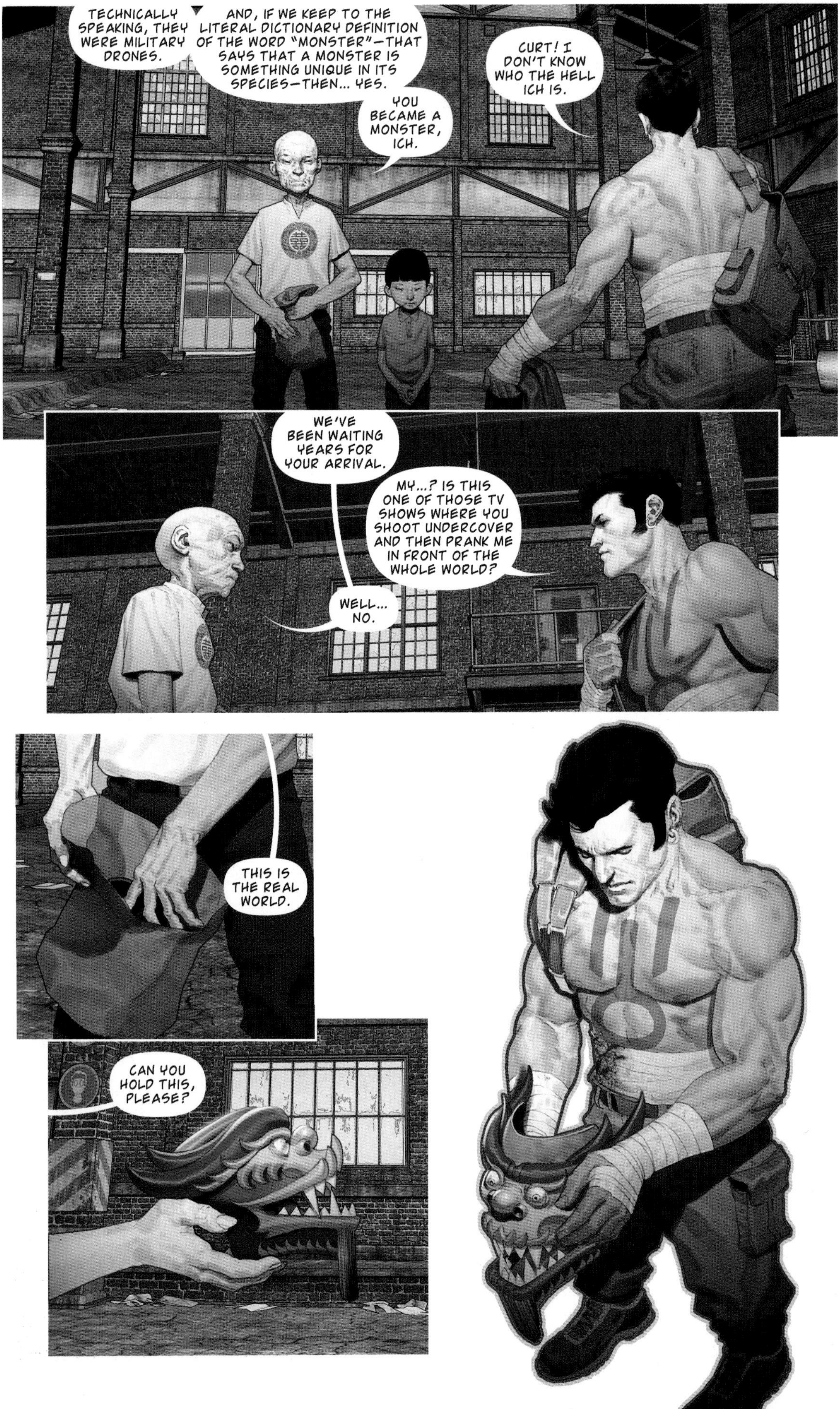
TECHNICALLY SPEAKING, THEY WERE MILITARY DRONES.
AND, IF WE KEEP TO THE LITERAL DICTIONARY DEFINITION OF THE WORD "MONSTER"—THAT SAYS THAT A MONSTER IS SOMETHING UNIQUE IN ITS SPECIES—THEN... YES.
YOU BECAME A MONSTER, ICH.
CURT! I DON'T KNOW WHO THE HELL ICH IS.
WE'VE BEEN WAITING YEARS FOR YOUR ARRIVAL.
MY...? IS THIS ONE OF THOSE TV SHOWS WHERE YOU SHOOT UNDERCOVER AND THEN PRANK ME IN FRONT OF THE WHOLE WORLD?
WELL... NO.
THIS IS THE REAL WORLD.
CAN YOU HOLD THIS, PLEASE?

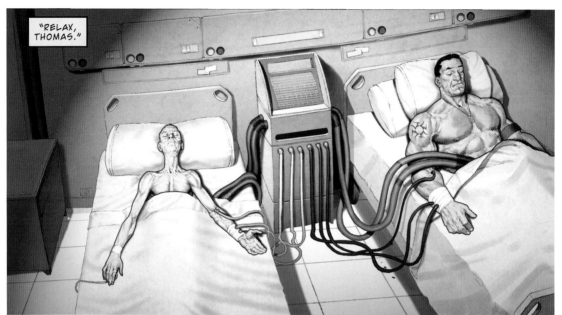

"RELAX, THOMAS."

I IMAGINE YOU HAD A HARD DAY.

NOTHING THAT CAN'T BE SOLVED WITH A SOFT TOUCH, DON'T YOU THINK?

IS THERE A PLACE FOR ME ON THAT BED?

"AND PROPER MEDICAL TREATMENT, OF COURSE."

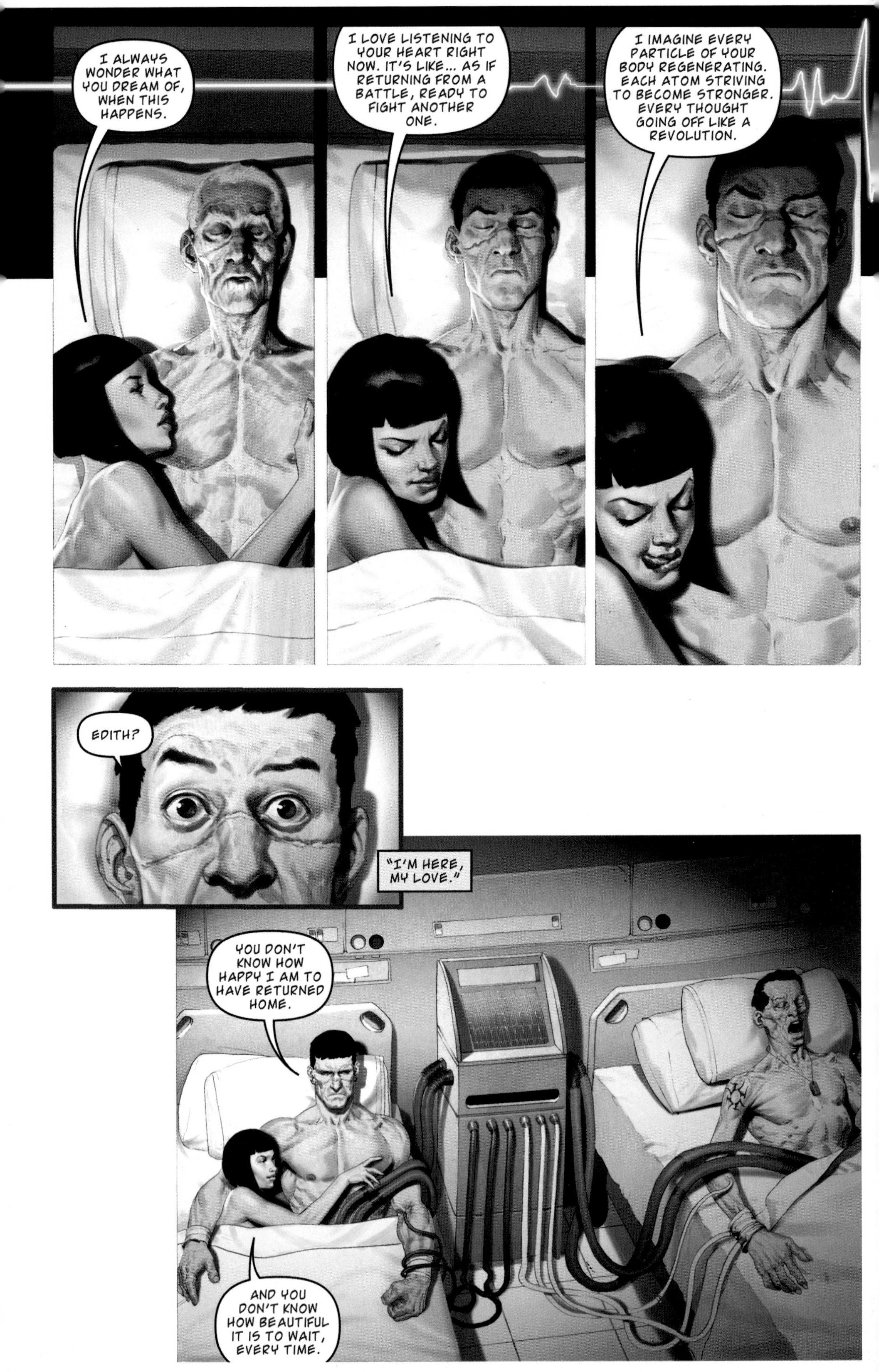
I ALWAYS WONDER WHAT YOU DREAM OF, WHEN THIS HAPPENS.
I LOVE LISTENING TO YOUR HEART RIGHT NOW. IT'S LIKE... AS IF RETURNING FROM A BATTLE, READY TO FIGHT ANOTHER ONE.
I IMAGINE EVERY PARTICLE OF YOUR BODY REGENERATING. EACH ATOM STRIVING TO BECOME STRONGER. EVERY THOUGHT GOING OFF LIKE A REVOLUTION.
EDITH?
"I'M HERE, MY LOVE."
YOU DON'T KNOW HOW HAPPY I AM TO HAVE RETURNED HOME.
AND YOU DON'T KNOW HOW BEAUTIFUL IT IS TO WAIT, EVERY TIME.

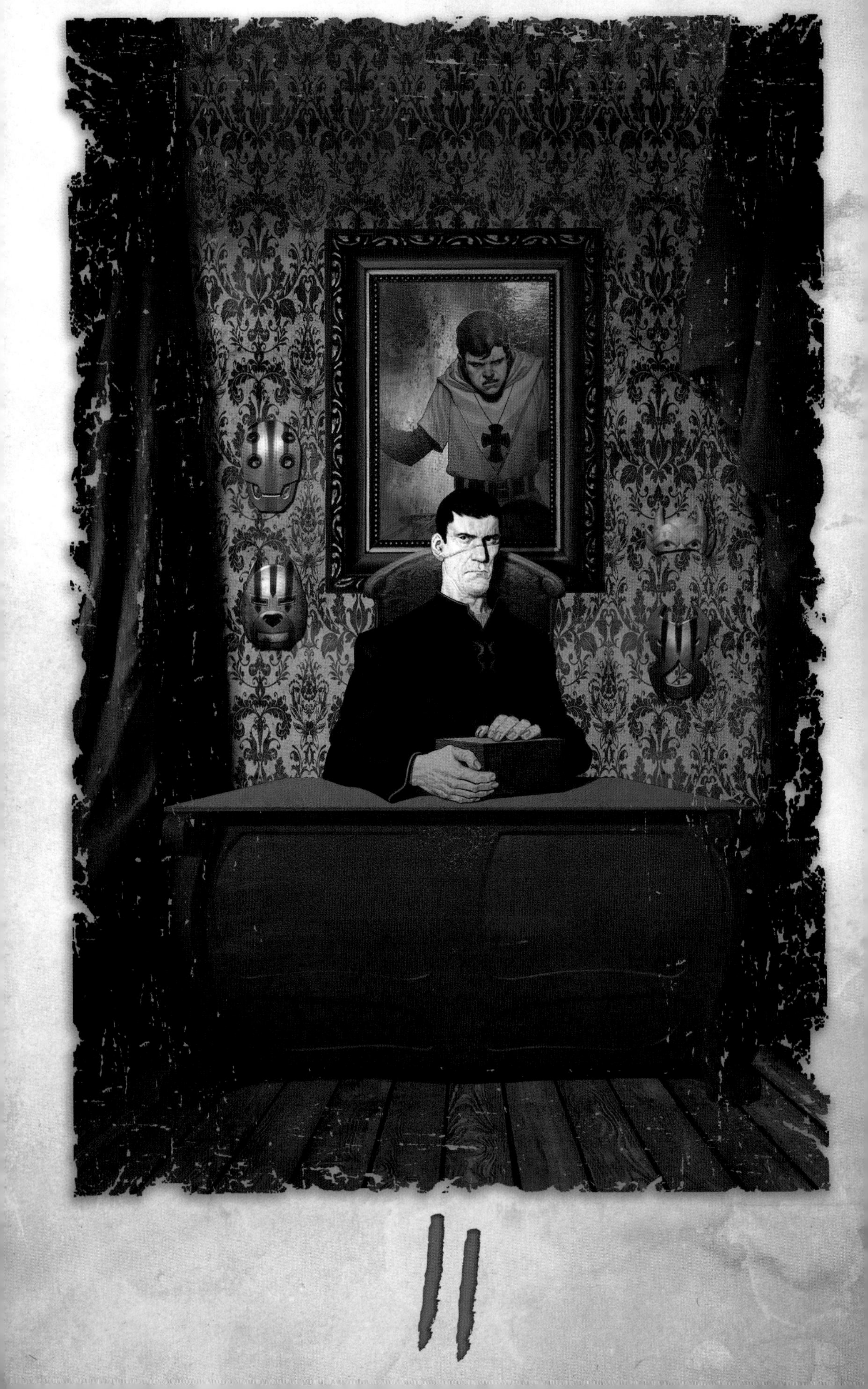

II

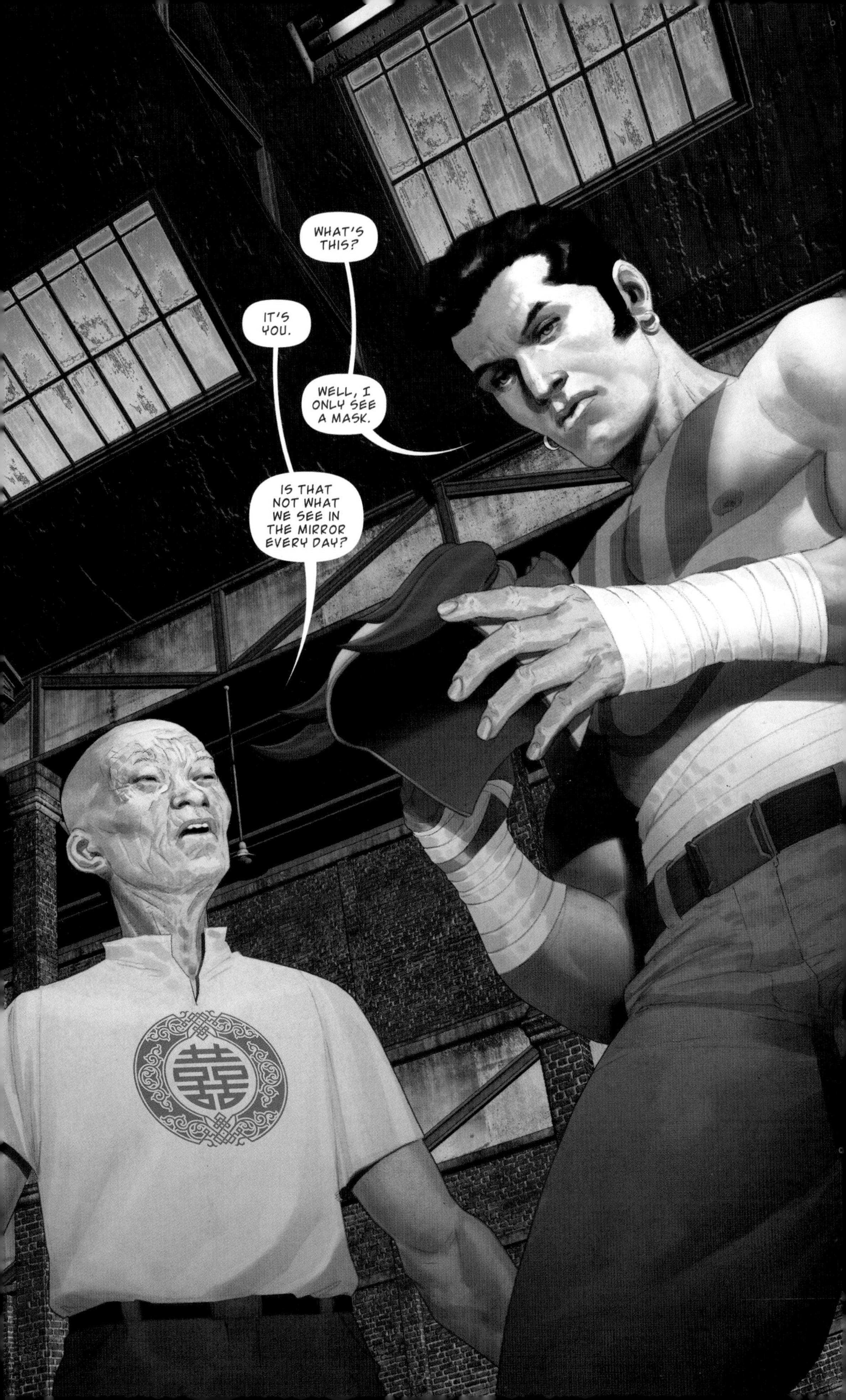
WHAT'S THIS?
IT'S YOU.
WELL, I ONLY SEE A MASK.
IS THAT NOT WHAT WE SEE IN THE MIRROR EVERY DAY?

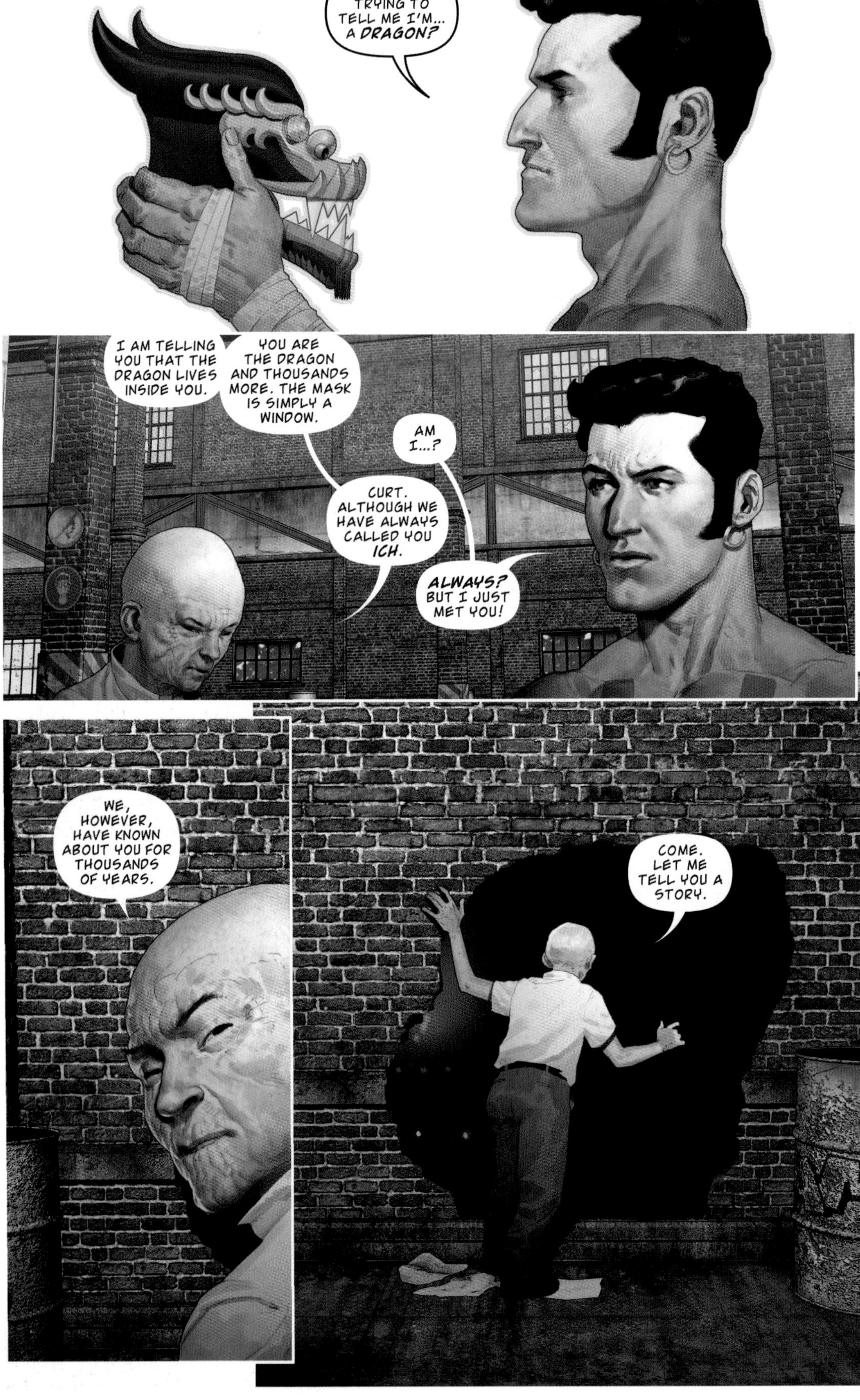
ARE YOU TRYING TO TELL ME I'M... A DRAGON?
I AM TELLING YOU THAT THE DRAGON LIVES INSIDE YOU.
YOU ARE THE DRAGON AND THOUSANDS MORE. THE MASK IS SIMPLY A WINDOW.
AM I...?
CURT. ALTHOUGH WE HAVE ALWAYS CALLED YOU ICH.
ALWAYS? BUT I JUST MET YOU!
WE, HOWEVER, HAVE KNOWN ABOUT YOU FOR THOUSANDS OF YEARS.
COME. LET ME TELL YOU A STORY.

IN THE BEGINNING, THERE WAS NOTHING, YOU KNOW? THERE'S AN IRREFUTABLE TRUTH IN THAT PHRASE.

THIS THE PART WHERE YOU RECITE THE BIBLE, OLD MAN?

NO. THIS IS THE PART WHERE I TELL YOU THE TRUTH.

THEN, THE MASKS WERE MADE. WITH FIRE, EARTH, AIR, WATER. WITH MAGIC.

A MASK FOR EVERY LIVING BEING.

A MASK FOR EVERY CREATURE BORN.

A MASK TO GIVE LIFE TO THE FIRST OF EACH SPECIES.

"THESE MASKS HAVE BEEN SCATTERED BY THE GREATER FORCES IN PLACES WHERE THE CREATURES FIRST EXISTED.

"NATURALLY, MANY MASKS HAVE BEEN LOST OVER THE AGES. YOU KNOW... FLOODS, EARTHQUAKES. THE LAW OF ETERNAL CHANGE SOMETIMES BURIES THEM AND OTHERS GET GROUND UP SO THAT THE FLOWER CAN REGROW."

IF EVERY CREATURE WAS CREATED FROM A MASK, THEN HOUSTON, WE HAVE A PROBLEM.

DRAGONS DO NOT EXIST.

"DON'T THEY?"

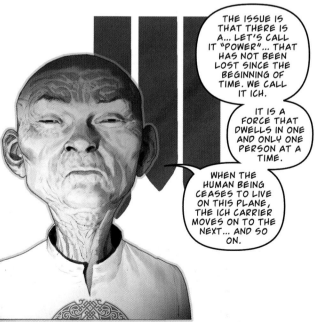

THE ISSUE IS THAT THERE IS A... LET'S CALL IT "POWER"... THAT HAS NOT BEEN LOST SINCE THE BEGINNING OF TIME. WE CALL IT ICH.

IT IS A FORCE THAT DWELLS IN ONE AND ONLY ONE PERSON AT A TIME.

WHEN THE HUMAN BEING CEASES TO LIVE ON THIS PLANE, THE ICH CARRIER MOVES ON TO THE NEXT... AND SO ON.

IF I'M FOLLOWING YOUR DELIRIOUS RAMBLING, OLD MAN, YOU'RE SUGGESTING THAT I HAVE THIS ICH INSIDE MY BODY AT THIS TIME.

I'M TELLING YOU THAT YOU ARE ICH, BOY.

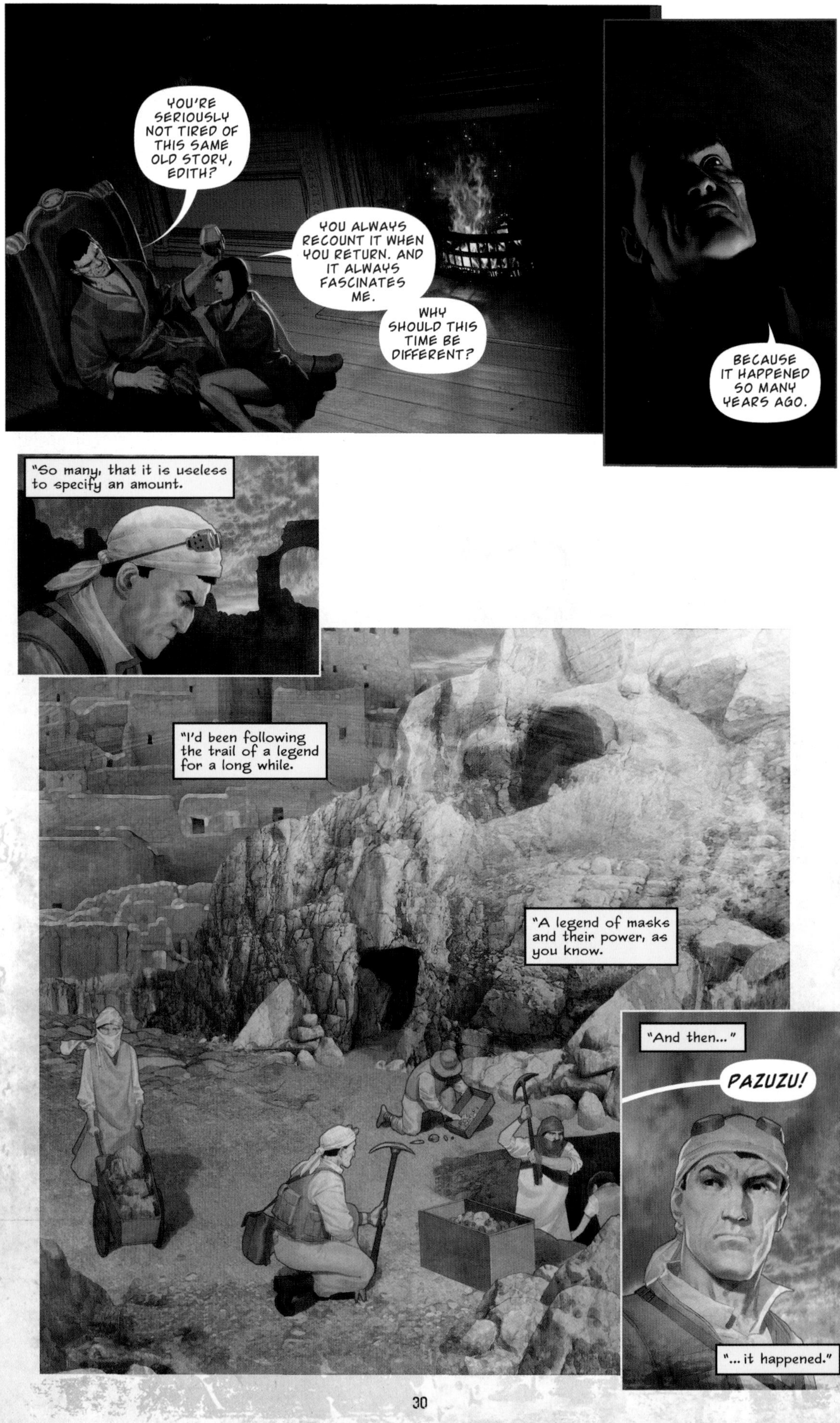
YOU'RE SERIOUSLY NOT TIRED OF THIS SAME OLD STORY, EDITH?
YOU ALWAYS RECOUNT IT WHEN YOU RETURN. AND IT ALWAYS FASCINATES ME.
WHY SHOULD THIS TIME BE DIFFERENT?
BECAUSE IT HAPPENED SO MANY YEARS AGO.
"So many, that it is useless to specify an amount.
"I'd been following the trail of a legend for a long while.
"A legend of masks and their power, as you know.
"And then..."
PAZUZU!
"... it happened."

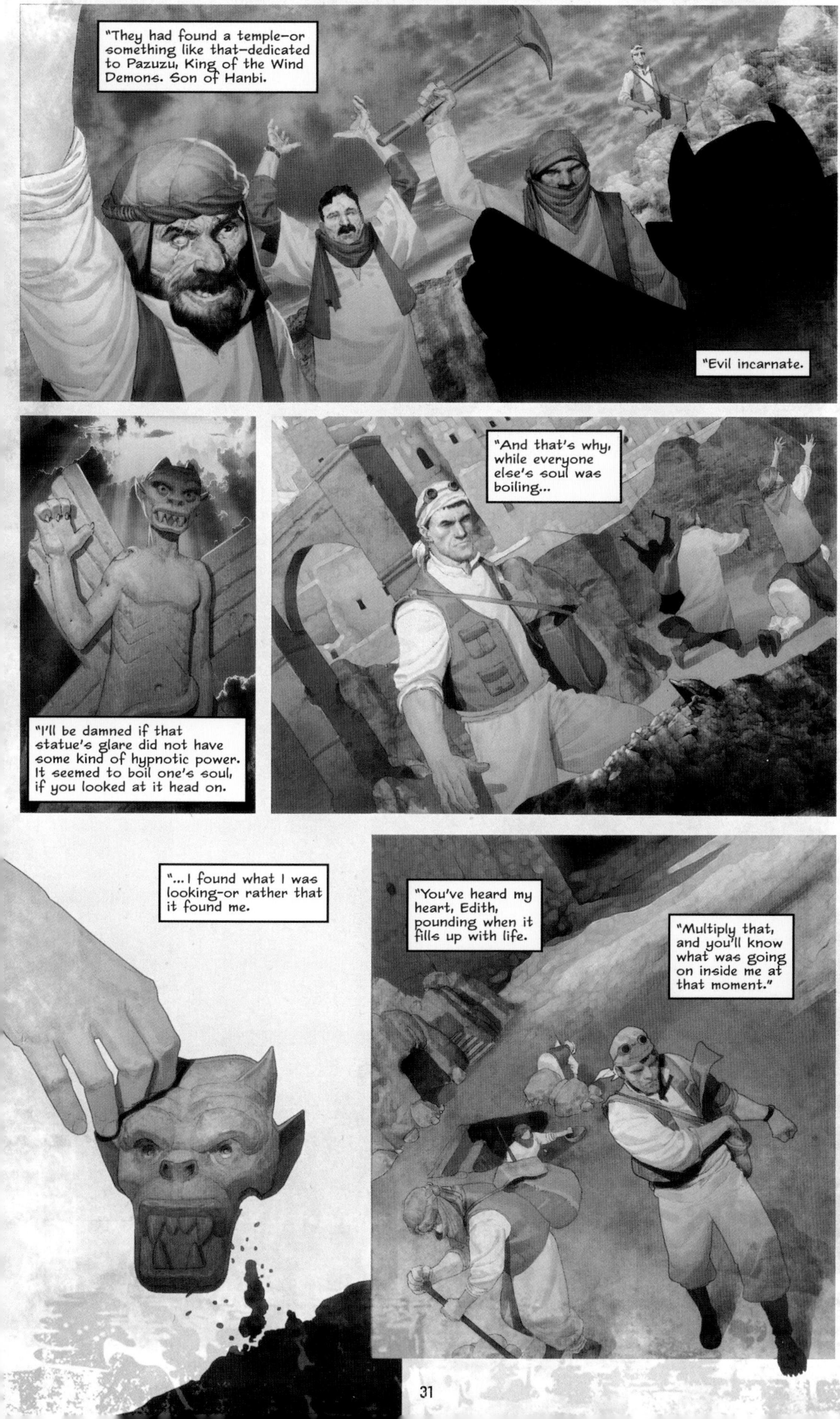
"They had found a temple—or something like that—dedicated to Pazuzu, King of the Wind Demons. Son of Hanbi.
"Evil incarnate.
"I'll be damned if that statue's glare did not have some kind of hypnotic power. It seemed to boil one's soul, if you looked at it head on.
"And that's why, while everyone else's soul was boiling...
"...I found what I was looking—or rather that it found me.
"You've heard my heart, Edith, pounding when it fills up with life.
"Multiply that, and you'll know what was going on inside me at that moment."

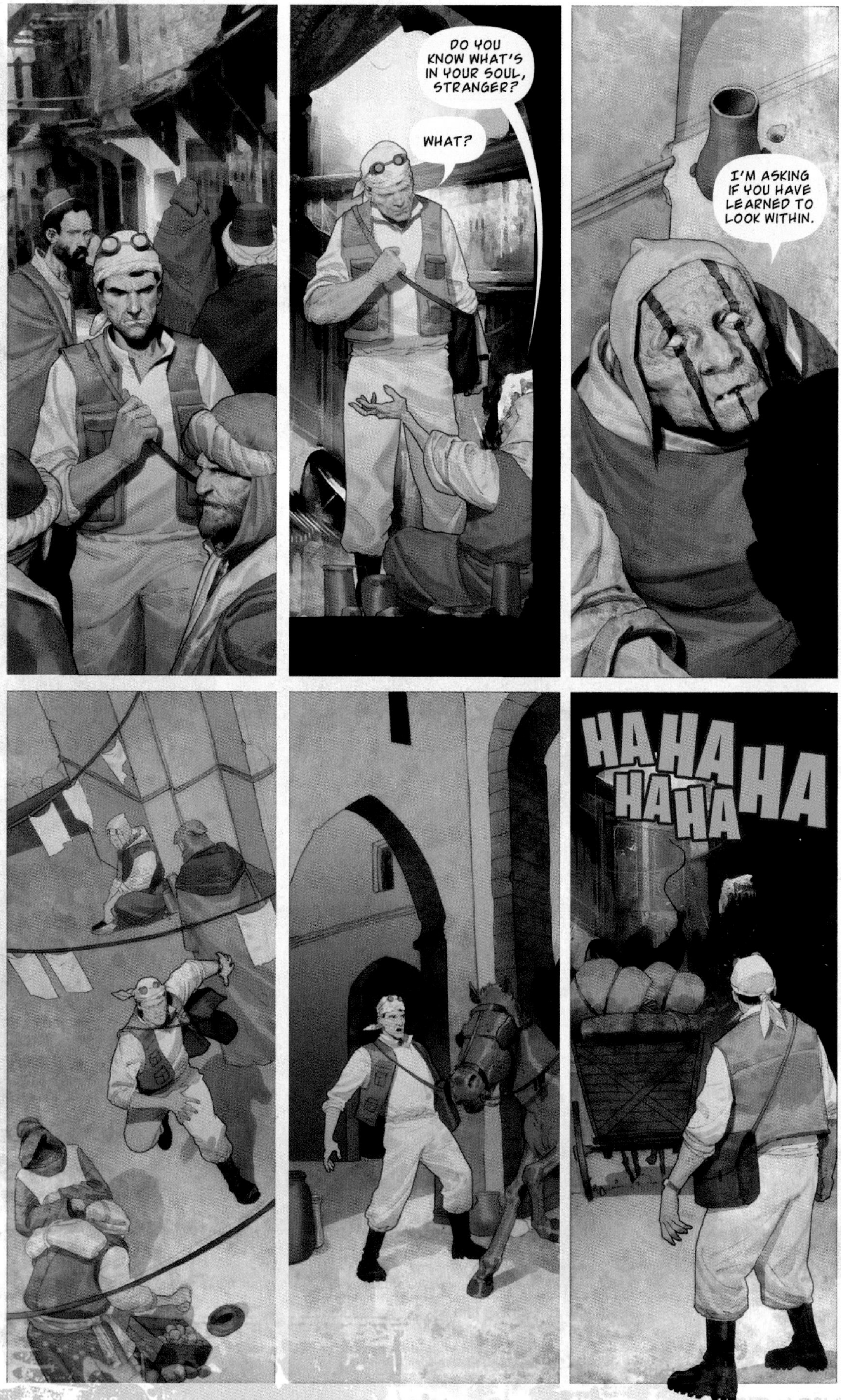
DO YOU KNOW WHAT'S IN YOUR SOUL, STRANGER?
WHAT?
I'M ASKING IF YOU HAVE LEARNED TO LOOK WITHIN.
HAHAHA
HAHAHA

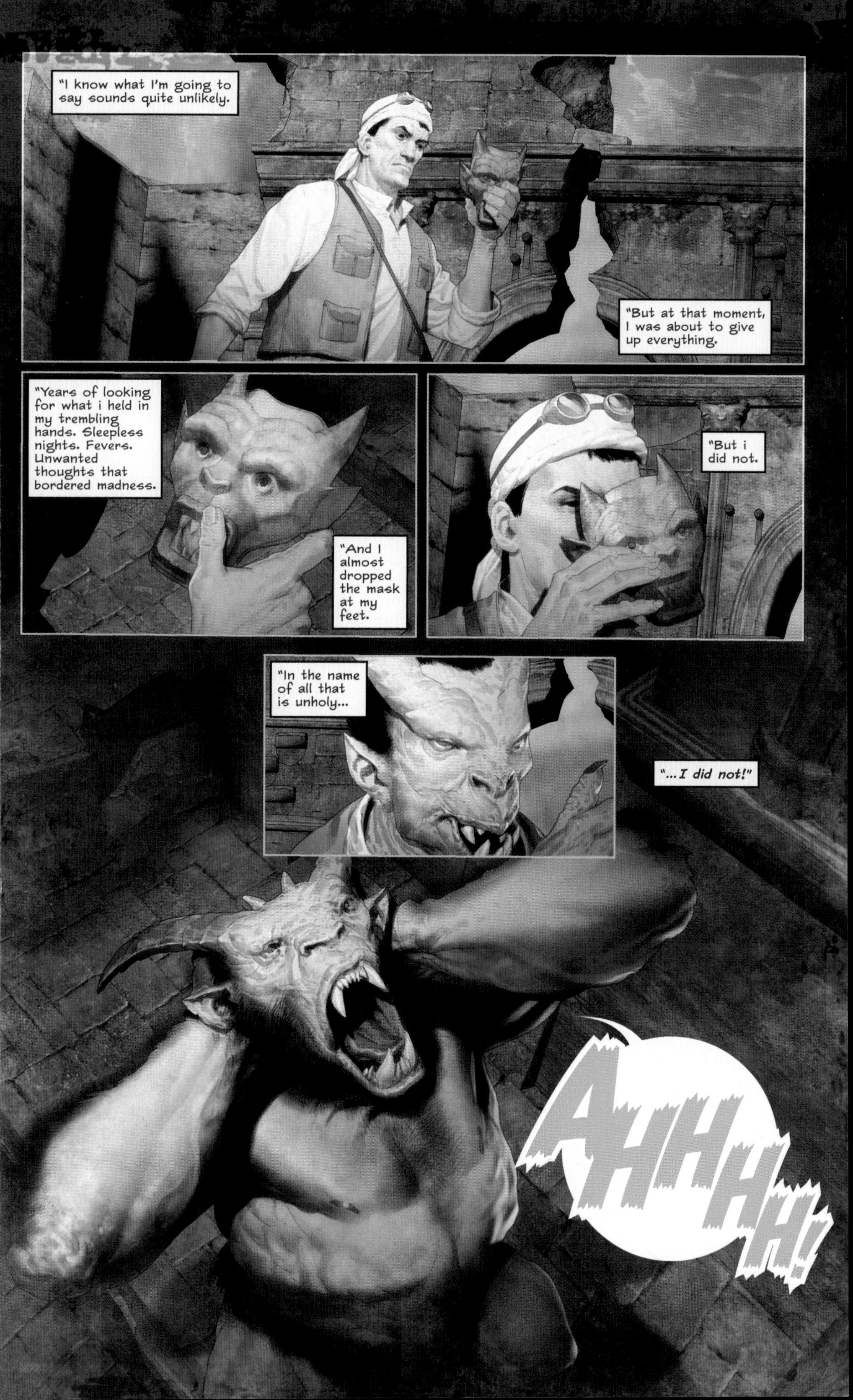
"I know what I'm going to say sounds quite unlikely.
"But at that moment, I was about to give up everything.
"Years of looking for what i held in my trembling hands. Sleepless nights. Fevers. Unwanted thoughts that bordered madness.
"And I almost dropped the mask at my feet.
"But i did not.
"In the name of all that is unholy...
"...I did not!"
AHHHH!

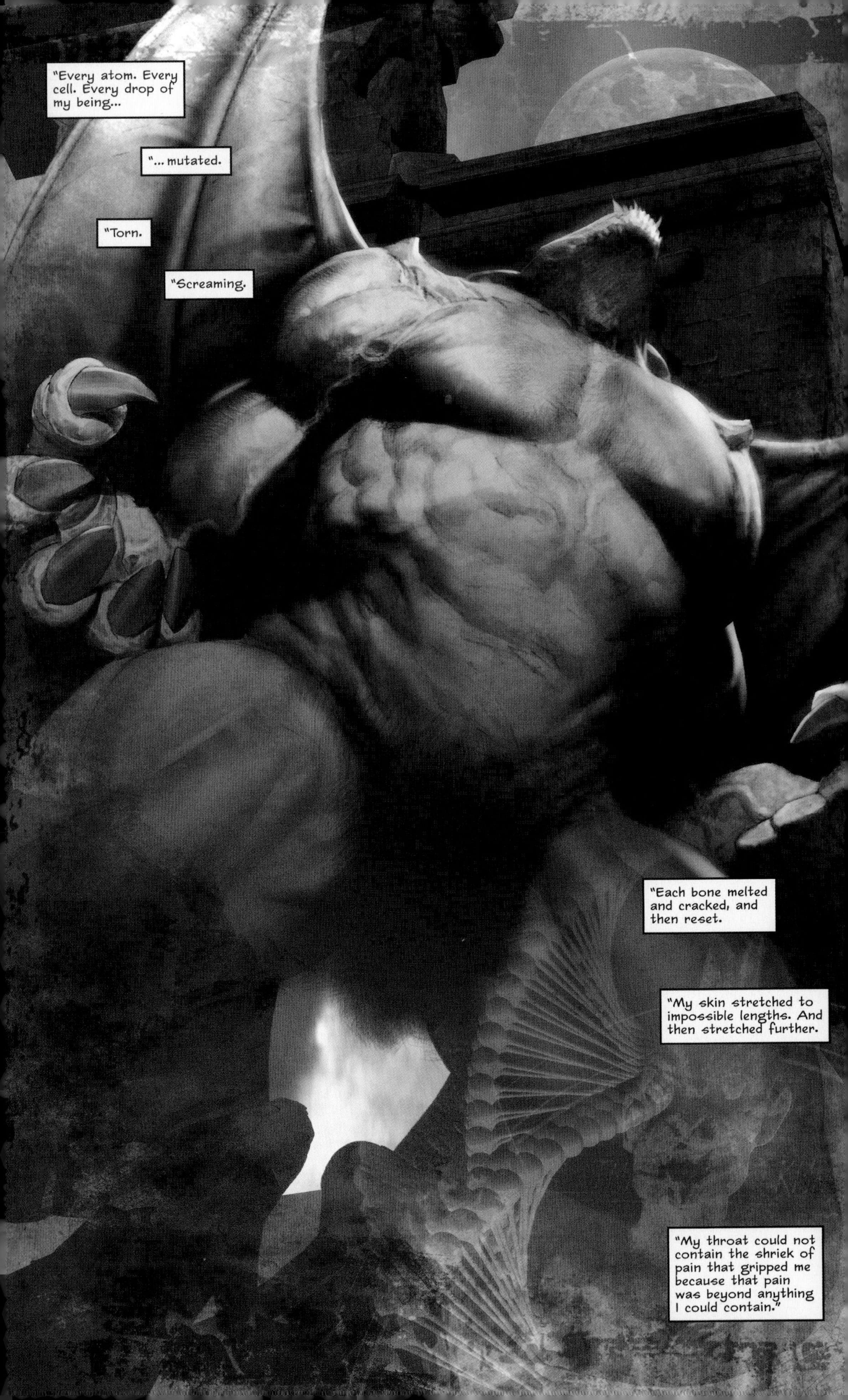
"Every atom. Every cell. Every drop of my being...
"... mutated.
"Torn.
"Screaming.
"Each bone melted and cracked, and then reset.
"My skin stretched to impossible lengths. And then stretched further.
"My throat could not contain the shriek of pain that gripped me because that pain was beyond anything I could contain."

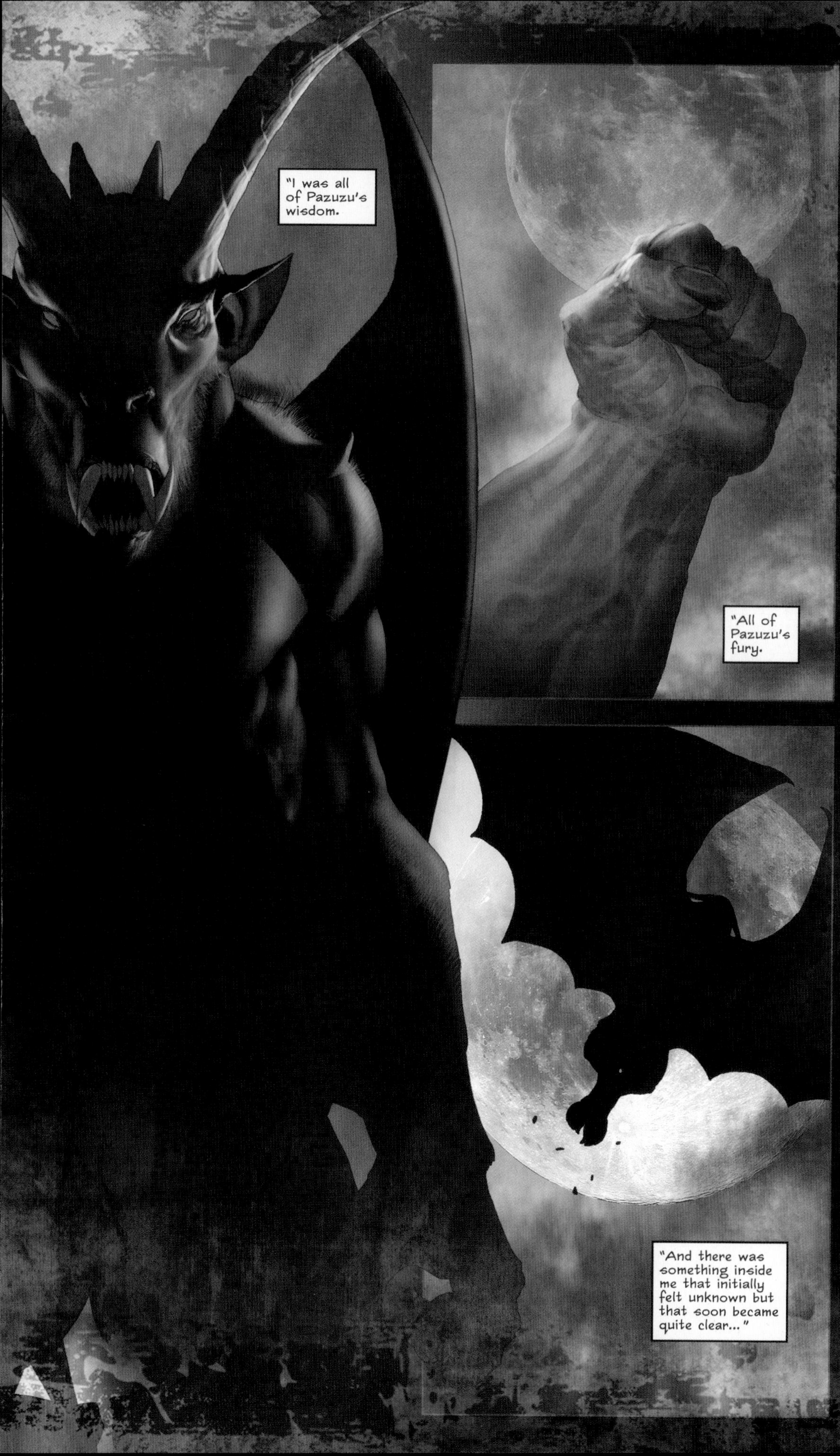
"I was all of Pazuzu's wisdom.
"All of Pazuzu's fury.
"And there was something inside me that initially felt unknown but that soon became quite clear..."

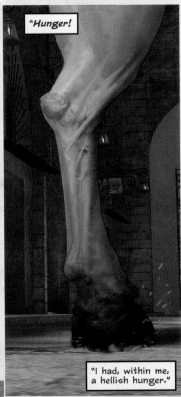

"Hunger!

"I had, within me, a hellish hunger."

HEIN?

HA HA HA!

AHHHH!

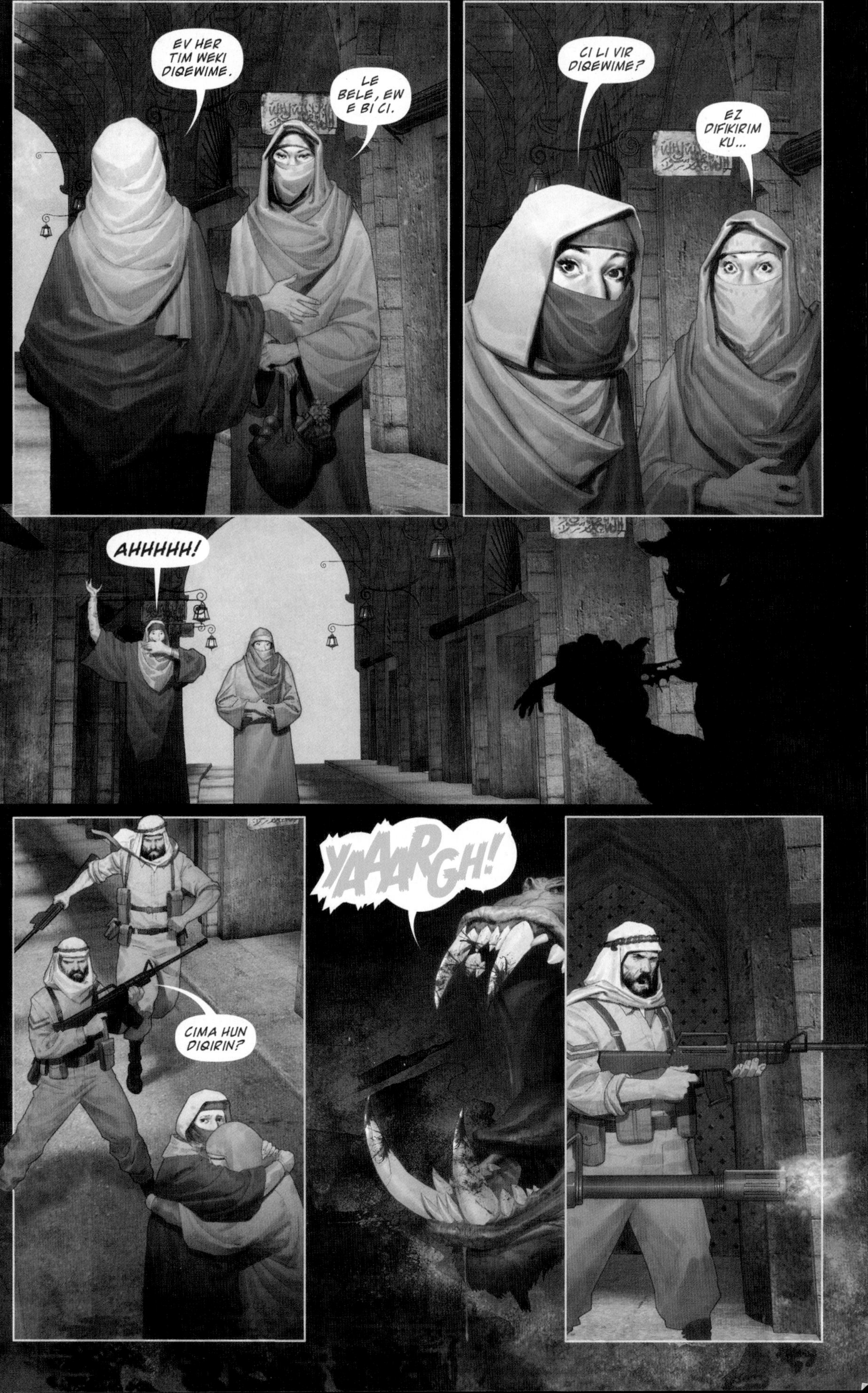
EV HER TIM WEKI DIQEWIME.
LE BELE, EW E BI CI.
CI LI VIR DIQEWIME?
EZ DIFIKIRIM KU...
AHHHHH!
CIMA HUN DIQIRIN?
YAAARGH!

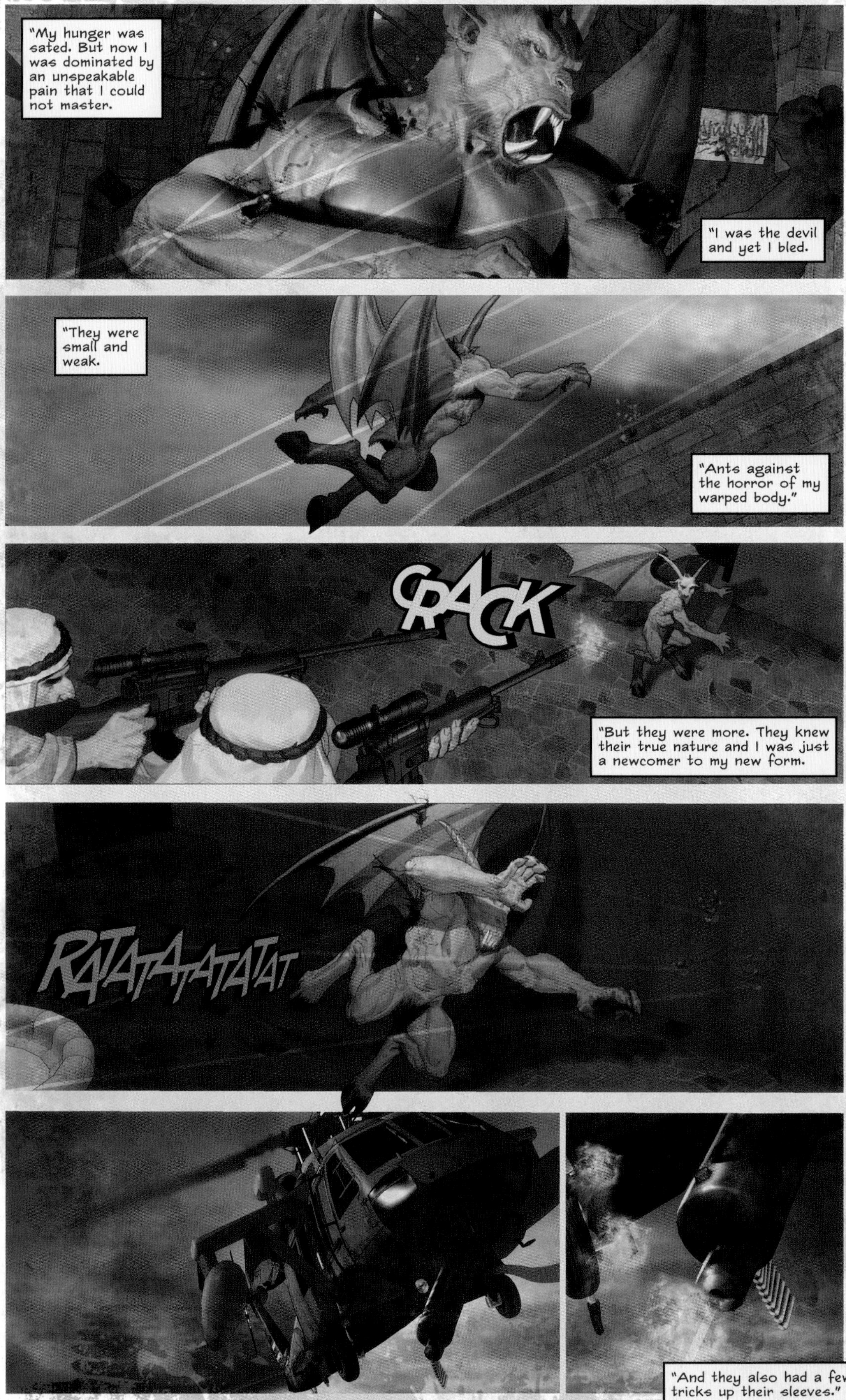
"My hunger was sated. But now I was dominated by an unspeakable pain that I could not master.
"I was the devil and yet I bled.
"They were small and weak.
"Ants against the horror of my warped body."
CRACK
"But they were more. They knew their true nature and I was just a newcomer to my new form.
RATATATATATAT
"And they also had a few tricks up their sleeves."

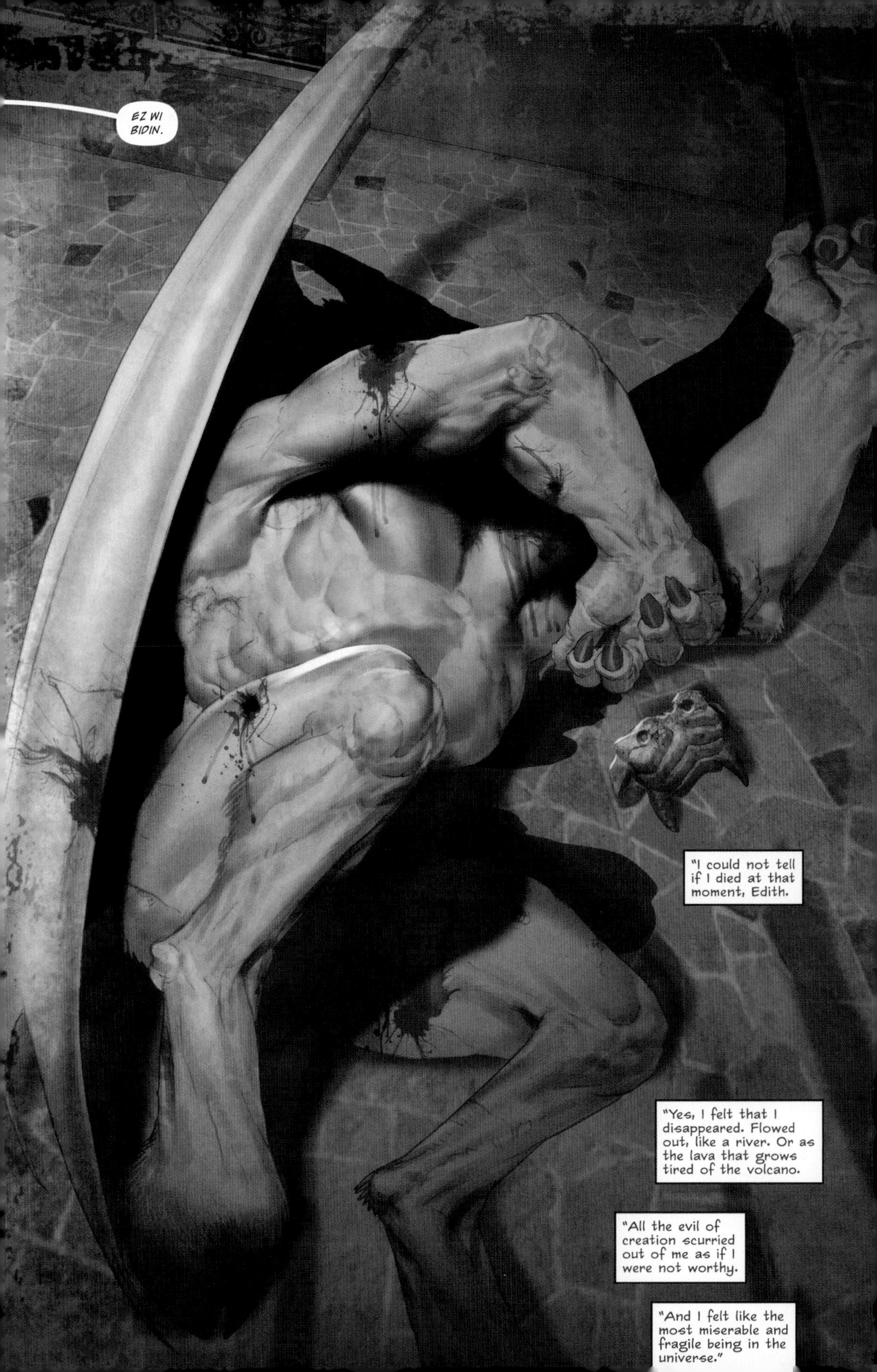
EZ WI BIDIN.
"I could not tell if I died at that moment, Edith.
"Yes, I felt that I disappeared. Flowed out, like a river. Or as the lava that grows tired of the volcano.
"All the evil of creation scurried out of me as if I were not worthy.
"And I felt like the most miserable and fragile being in the universe."

"To explain how I came to be sitting inside the plane that would bring me back home would be to bore you with stories of hospitals, favors between governments, and even more stupefying things.

"The truth is that no one asked questions about it.

"All that witnessed this madness were silenced, forever.

"I guess these things happen all the time.

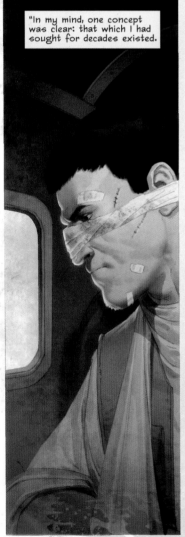

"In my mind, one concept was clear: that which I had sought for decades existed.

"To this day, I could never find the other half of the mask of Pazuzu."

BUT I HAVE NOT TIRED OF SEARCHING, EDITH.

NEITHER THIS MASK NOR THE OTHERS.

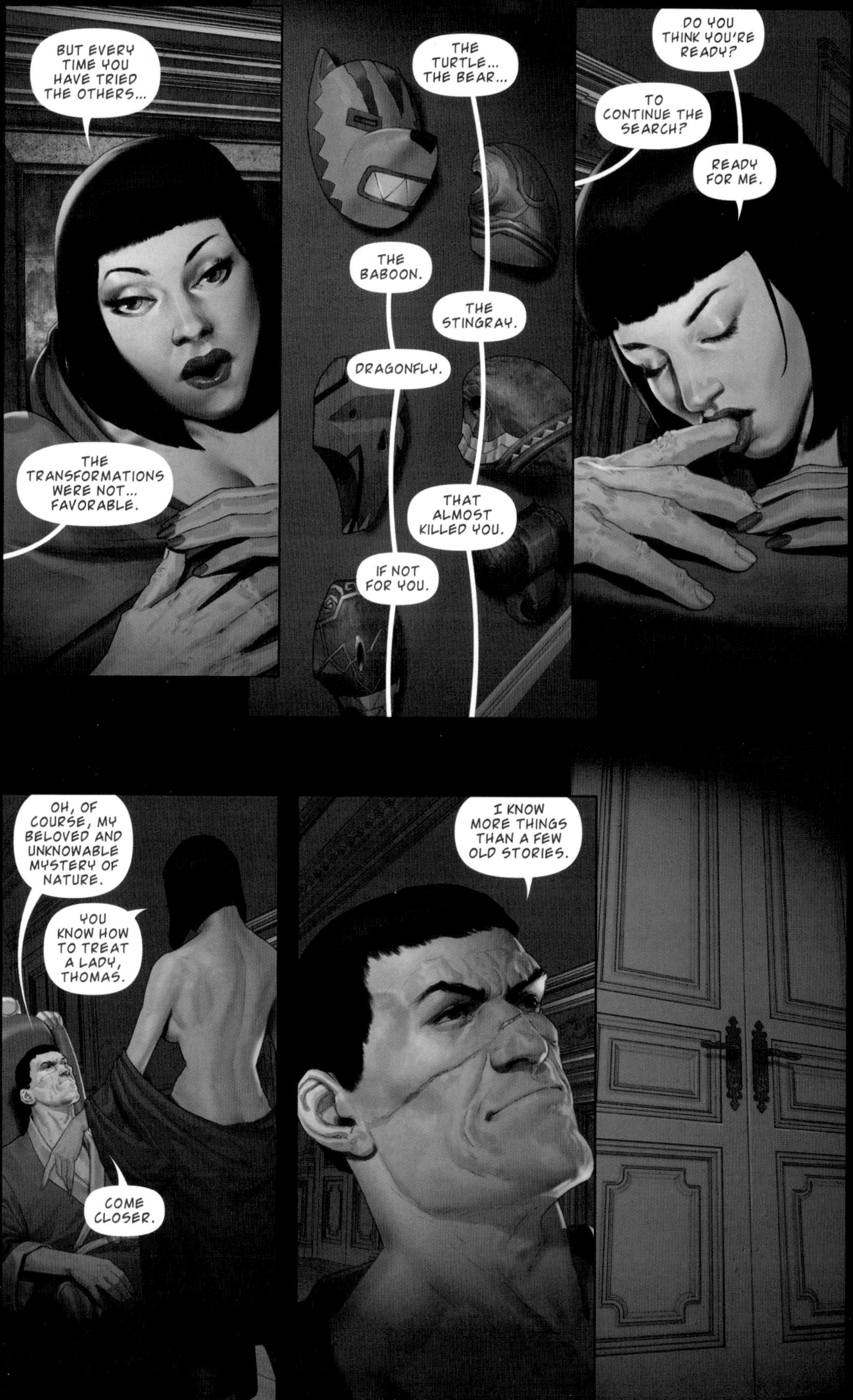
BUT EVERY TIME YOU HAVE TRIED THE OTHERS...
THE TRANSFORMATIONS WERE NOT... FAVORABLE.
THE TURTLE... THE BEAR...
THE BABOON.
THE STINGRAY.
DRAGONFLY.
THAT ALMOST KILLED YOU.
IF NOT FOR YOU.
DO YOU THINK YOU'RE READY?
TO CONTINUE THE SEARCH?
READY FOR ME.
OH, OF COURSE, MY BELOVED AND UNKNOWABLE MYSTERY OF NATURE.
YOU KNOW HOW TO TREAT A LADY, THOMAS.
COME CLOSER.
I KNOW MORE THINGS THAN A FEW OLD STORIES.

YOU KNOW WHAT YOU JUST TOLD ME CONTRADICTS EVERY REASONABLE IDEA ABOUT THE WORLD ITSELF, RIGHT?

I KNOW MANY THINGS, BOY.

BUT YOU KNOW THAT SPECIFICALLY, RIGHT?

YES.

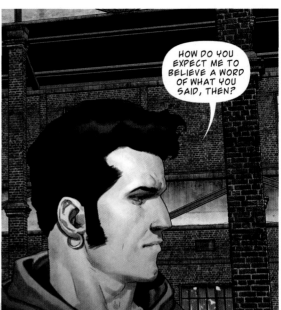

HOW DO YOU EXPECT ME TO BELIEVE A WORD OF WHAT YOU SAID, THEN?

YOU KNOW IT'S BEEN NO MORE THAN A DAY SINCE YOU WERE A CREATURE THAT JUMPED ALL ACROSS THE SKYLINE AND LEFT MILLIONS OF DOLLARS WORTH OF PROPERTY DAMAGE, RIGHT?

THAT WAS... A DREAM.

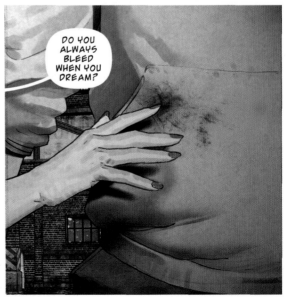

DO YOU ALWAYS BLEED WHEN YOU DREAM?

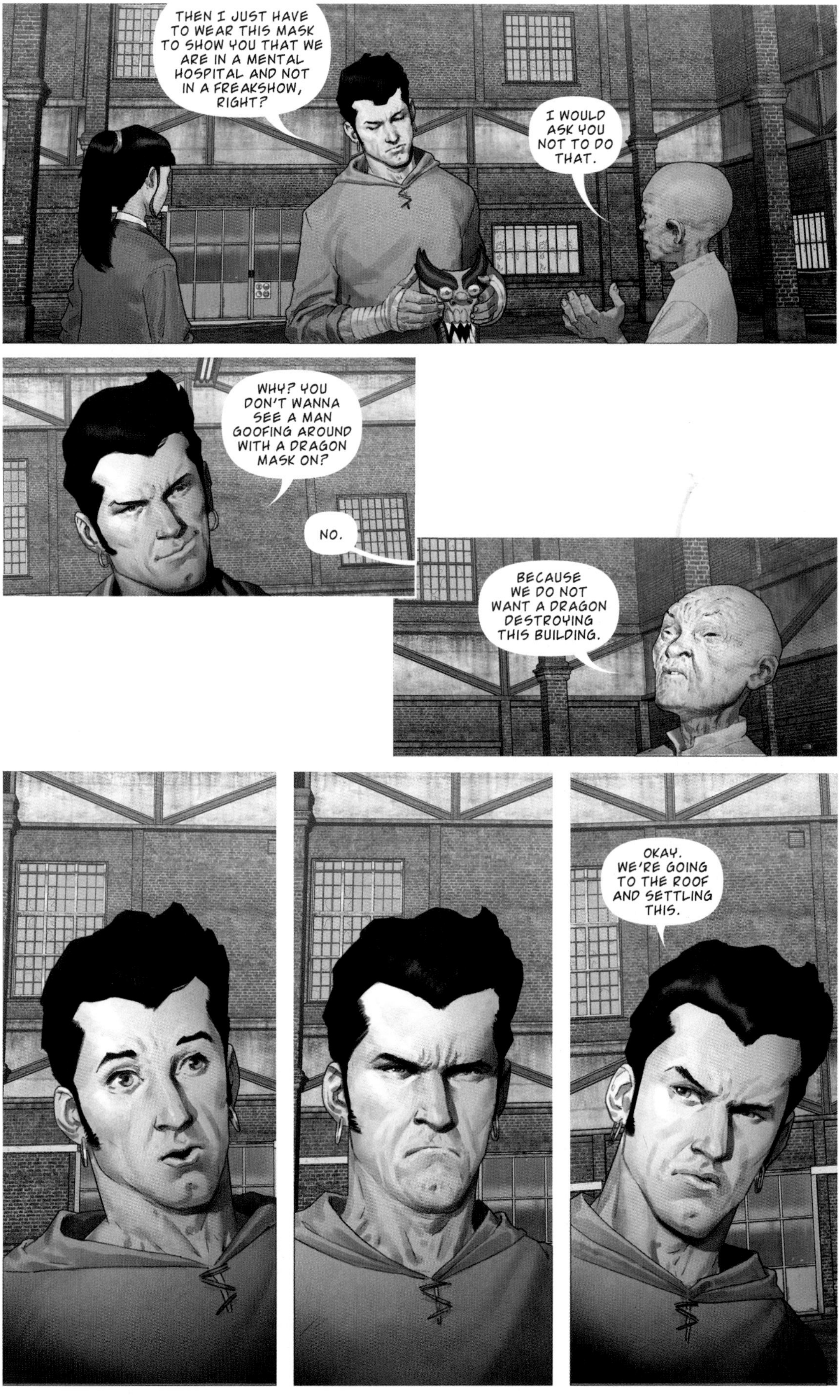
THEN I JUST HAVE TO WEAR THIS MASK TO SHOW YOU THAT WE ARE IN A MENTAL HOSPITAL AND NOT IN A FREAKSHOW, RIGHT?
I WOULD ASK YOU NOT TO DO THAT.
WHY? YOU DON'T WANNA SEE A MAN GOOFING AROUND WITH A DRAGON MASK ON?
NO.
BECAUSE WE DO NOT WANT A DRAGON DESTROYING THIS BUILDING.
OKAY. WE'RE GOING TO THE ROOF AND SETTLING THIS.

IN THE COURSE OF MANY GENERATIONS, WE HAVE COME ACROSS SOME PRIMORDIAL MASKS. THEY SUIT YOU.

THIS, FOR EXAMPLE, IS CALLED CHUNCHU.

THE LAST ONE WHO USED IT BECAME A GOD.

AND IT IS THE ONLY ONE, EVER, THAT HAS FACED THE DEVIL.

WE ASK, FOR HEAVEN'S SAKE, YOU USE EACH OF THESE MASKS WITH THE RESPONSIBILITY THAT YOUR SOUL DEMANDS.

BUT WHEN NOTHING HAPPENS, YOU'LL LET ME GO HOME. DEAL?

YOU WERE NEVER HELD HERE, BOY.

WE HEALED YOUR WOUND. WE OPENED YOUR EYES. BUT WE NEVER FORCED YOU TO STAY WITH US.

IF THE BOYS COULD SEE ME RIGHT NOW...

And then...

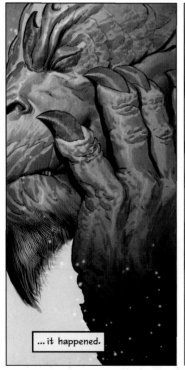

...it happened.

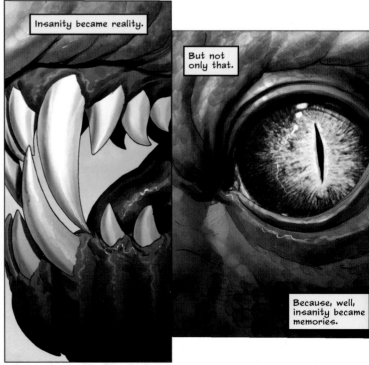

Insanity became reality.

But not only that.

Because, well, insanity became memories.

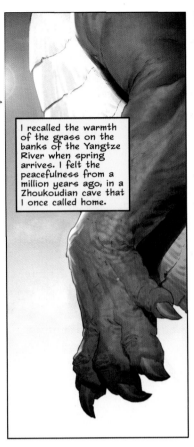

I recalled the warmth of the grass on the banks of the Yangtze River when spring arrives. I felt the peacefulness from a million years ago, in a Zhoukoudian cave that I once called home.

I recalled the first time I saw a human in Liujiang. The smell was not unlike the smell of those watching me now.

But his gaze was unique.

I recalled what it means to have a thousand souls within my soul.

FLY... ICH.

And I flew!

45

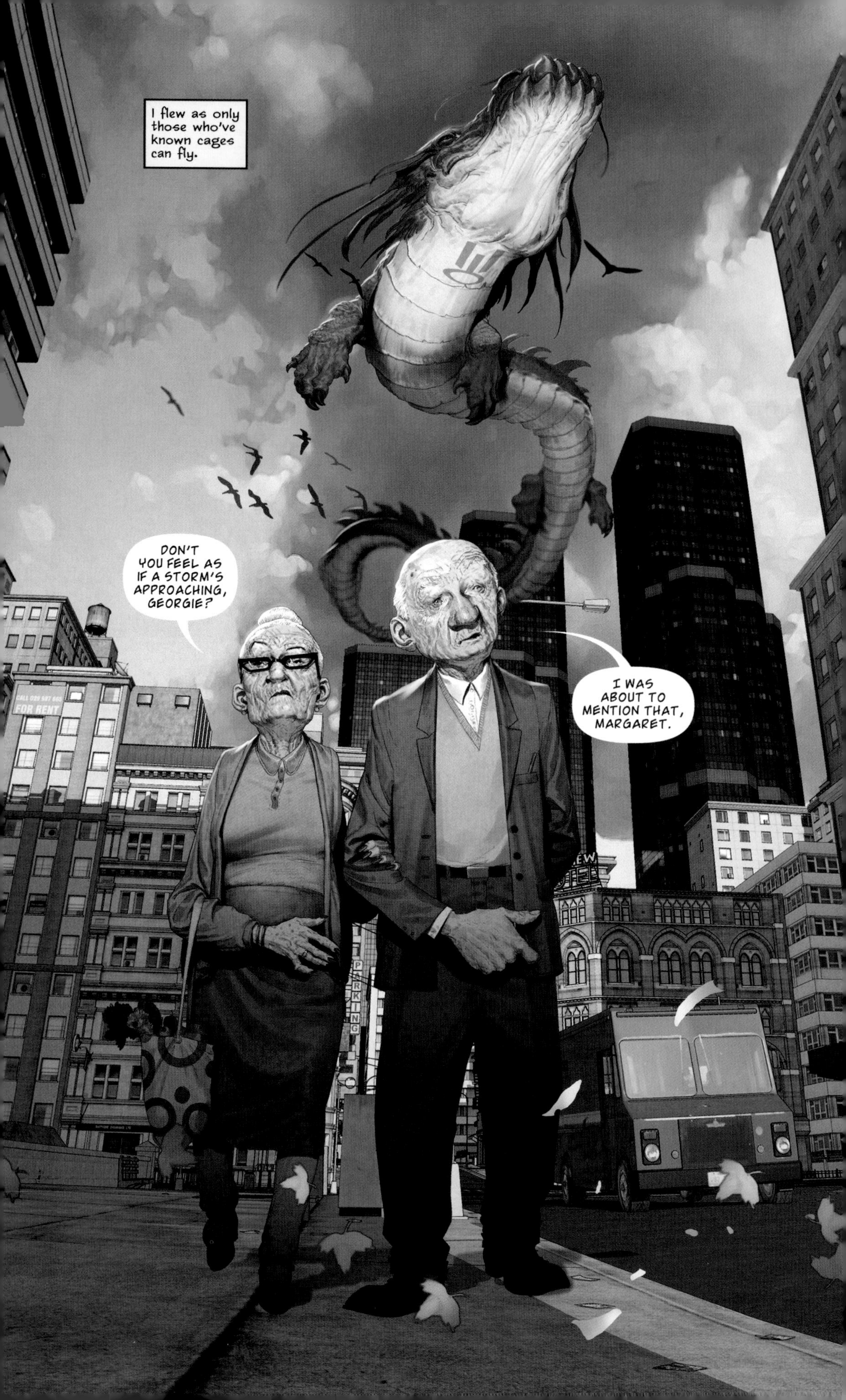
I flew as only those who've known cages can fly.
DON'T YOU FEEL AS IF A STORM'S APPROACHING, GEORGIE?
I WAS ABOUT TO MENTION THAT, MARGARET.
FOR RENT
PARKING

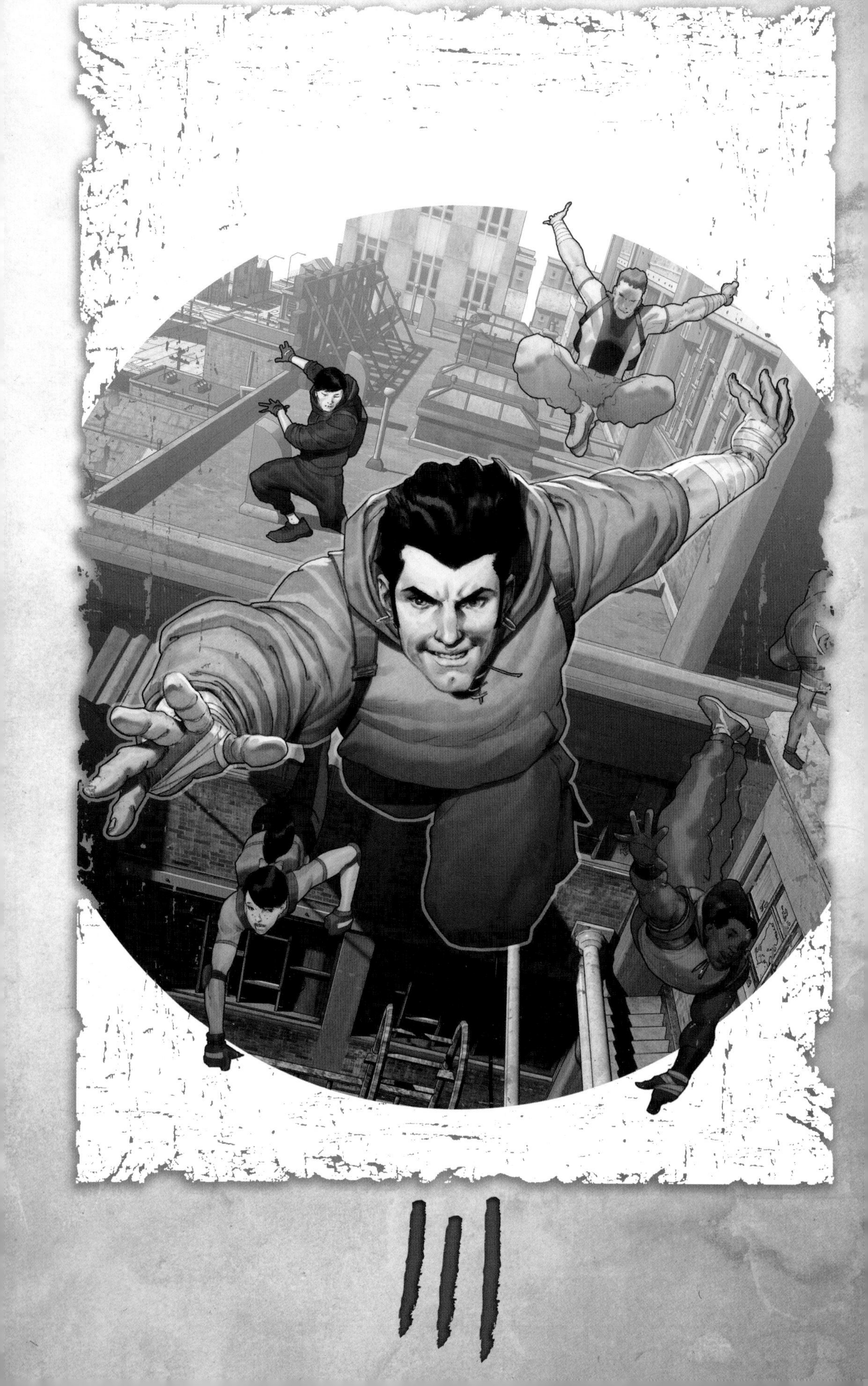

III

"I TOLD YOU NOT TO WORRY, SAMMY. THERE'S NO REASON FOR ALARM.

"DADDY IS... SPECIAL. BUT HE'S NOT BAD PEOPLE. AND YOU'LL GET USED TO THAT, YOU KNOW?

"SOMETIMES HE GOES OUT ON HIS OWN AND FORGETS ABOUT US FOR A MOMENT. BUT HE ALWAYS COMES BACK.

"EVERY SO OFTEN, HE EVEN BRINGS GIFTS.

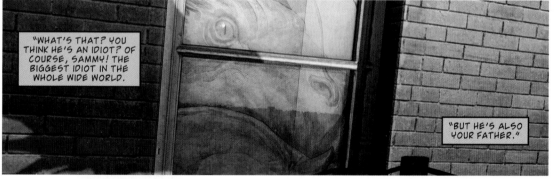

"WHAT'S THAT? YOU THINK HE'S AN IDIOT? OF COURSE, SAMMY! THE BIGGEST IDIOT IN THE WHOLE WIDE WORLD.

"BUT HE'S ALSO YOUR FATHER."

SO LET'S NOT LET ON HOW MUCH WE AGREE ON THAT LITTLE MATTER OF HIS IDIOCY, OKAY?

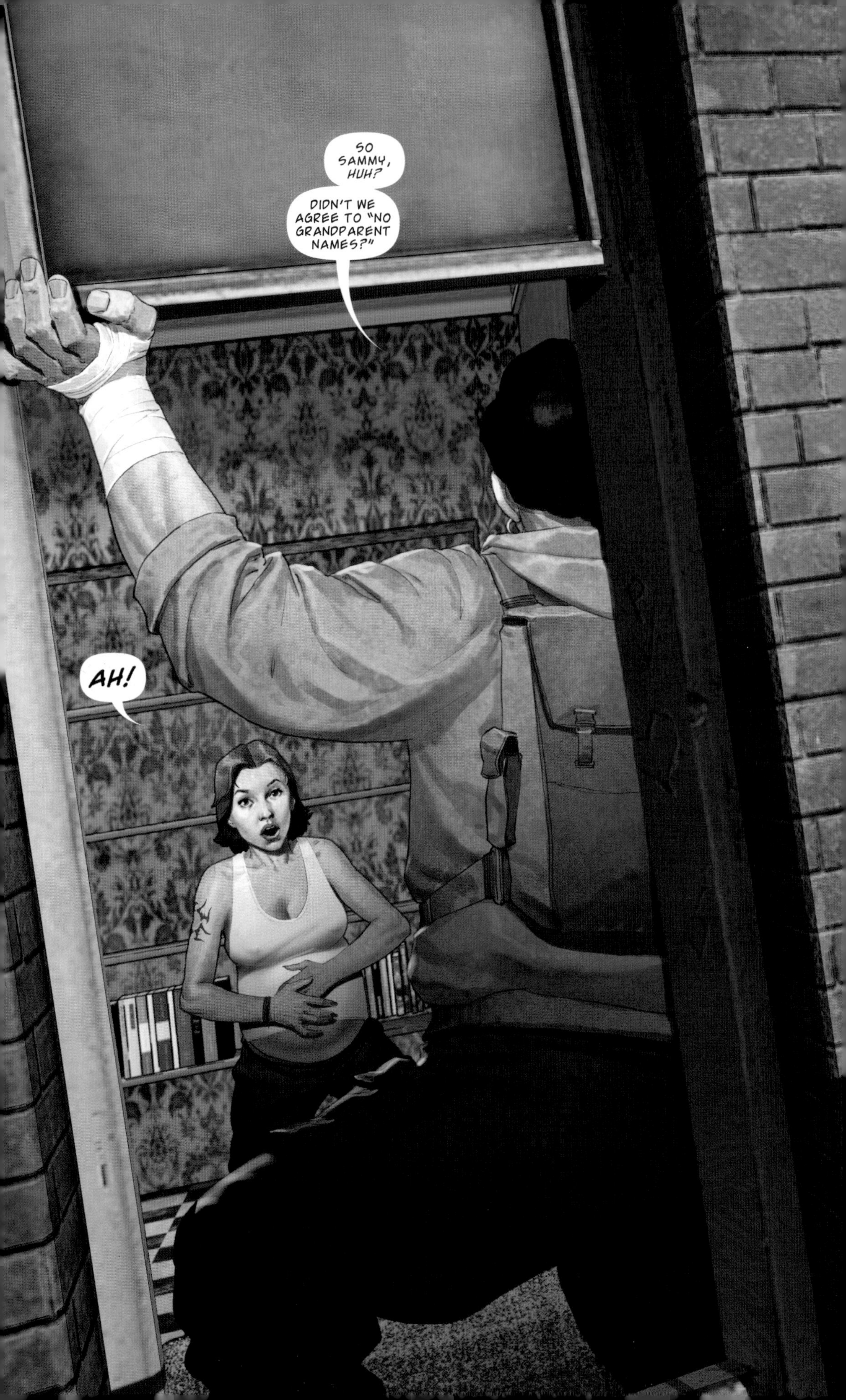
SO SAMMY, HUH?
DIDN'T WE AGREE TO "NO GRANDPARENT NAMES?"
AH!

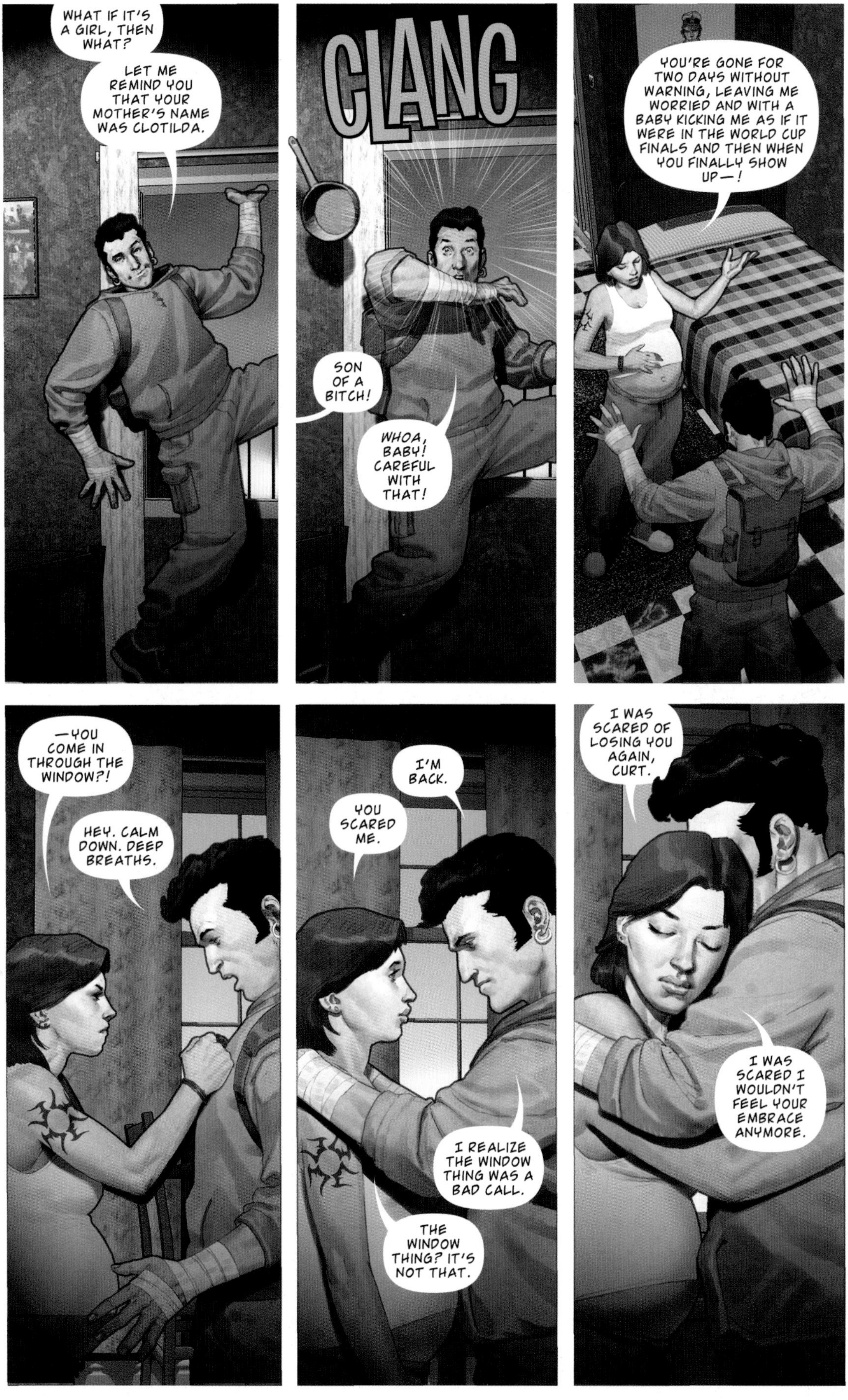
WHAT IF IT'S A GIRL, THEN WHAT?
LET ME REMIND YOU THAT YOUR MOTHER'S NAME WAS CLOTILDA.
CLANG
SON OF A BITCH!
WHOA, BABY! CAREFUL WITH THAT!
YOU'RE GONE FOR TWO DAYS WITHOUT WARNING, LEAVING ME WORRIED AND WITH A BABY KICKING ME AS IF IT WERE IN THE WORLD CUP FINALS AND THEN WHEN YOU FINALLY SHOW UP—!
—YOU COME IN THROUGH THE WINDOW?!
HEY. CALM DOWN. DEEP BREATHS.
I'M BACK.
YOU SCARED ME.
I REALIZE THE WINDOW THING WAS A BAD CALL.
THE WINDOW THING? IT'S NOT THAT.
I WAS SCARED OF LOSING YOU AGAIN, CURT.
I WAS SCARED I WOULDN'T FEEL YOUR EMBRACE ANYMORE.

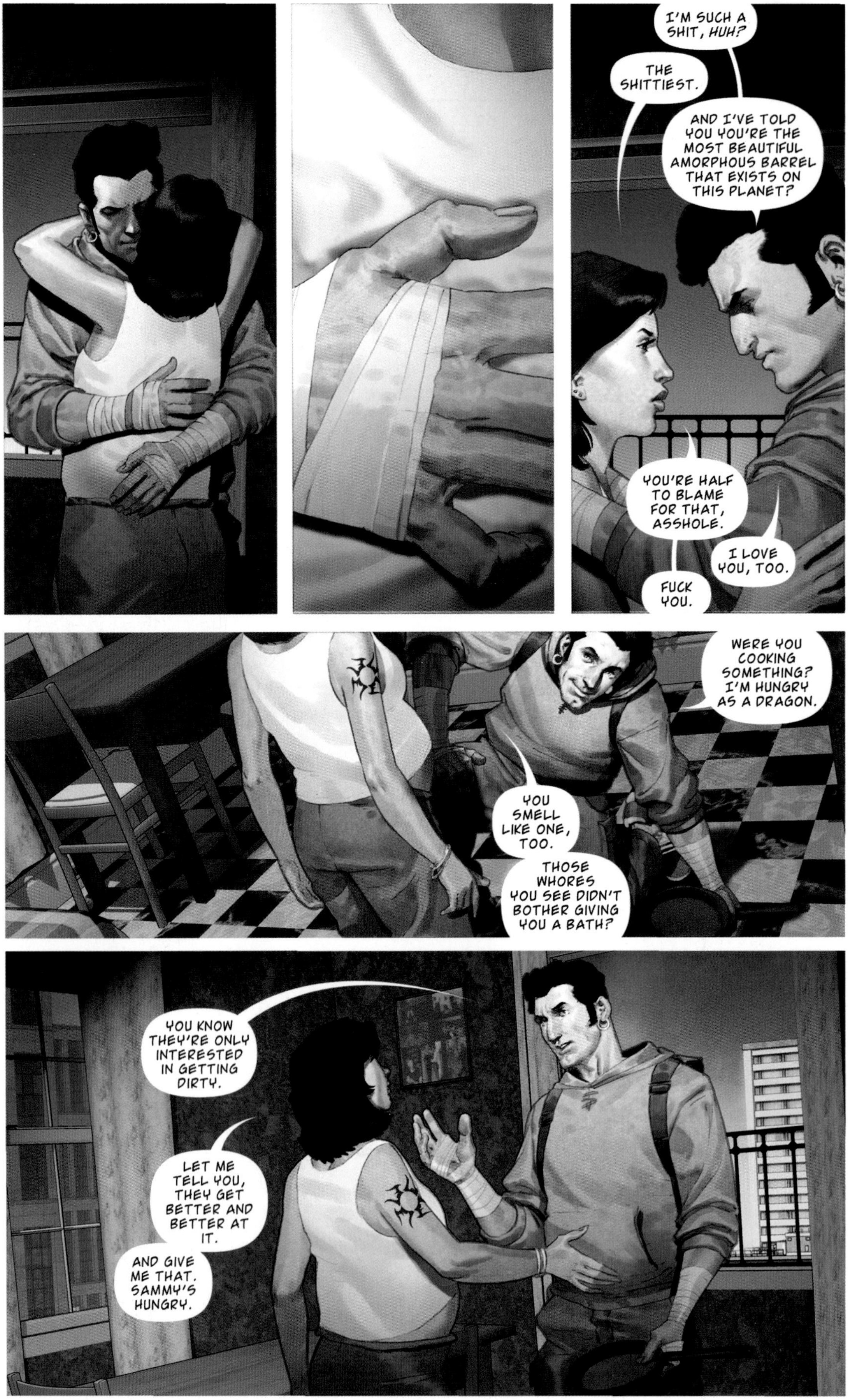
I'M SUCH A SHIT, HUH?
THE SHITTIEST.
AND I'VE TOLD YOU YOU'RE THE MOST BEAUTIFUL AMORPHOUS BARREL THAT EXISTS ON THIS PLANET?
YOU'RE HALF TO BLAME FOR THAT, ASSHOLE.
I LOVE YOU, TOO.
FUCK YOU.
WERE YOU COOKING SOMETHING? I'M HUNGRY AS A DRAGON.
YOU SMELL LIKE ONE, TOO.
THOSE WHORES YOU SEE DIDN'T BOTHER GIVING YOU A BATH?
YOU KNOW THEY'RE ONLY INTERESTED IN GETTING DIRTY.
LET ME TELL YOU, THEY GET BETTER AND BETTER AT IT.
AND GIVE ME THAT. SAMMY'S HUNGRY.

DID YOU BRING SOME MONEY, AT LEAST? OR SOME FOOD?

WELL...

CRAP.

LOVE! WHAT DID YOU DO? WHAT HAPPENED?

LEAVE IT, KATHERINE. IT'S NOTHING. IT'S...

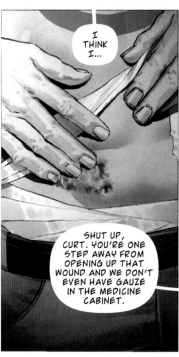

I THINK I...

SHUT UP, CURT. YOU'RE ONE STEP AWAY FROM OPENING UP THAT WOUND AND WE DON'T EVEN HAVE GAUZE IN THE MEDICINE CABINET.

LOVE...

COME HERE, HONEY. AND DON'T MAKE THE SLIGHTEST EFFORT. YOU'LL SEE HOW MOMMY'S GOT CUDDLES THAT WILL CURE WHAT AILS YOU.

YOU'RE PERFECT.

TELL ME ALL ABOUT IT LATER. AND THEN I'LL KILL YOU.

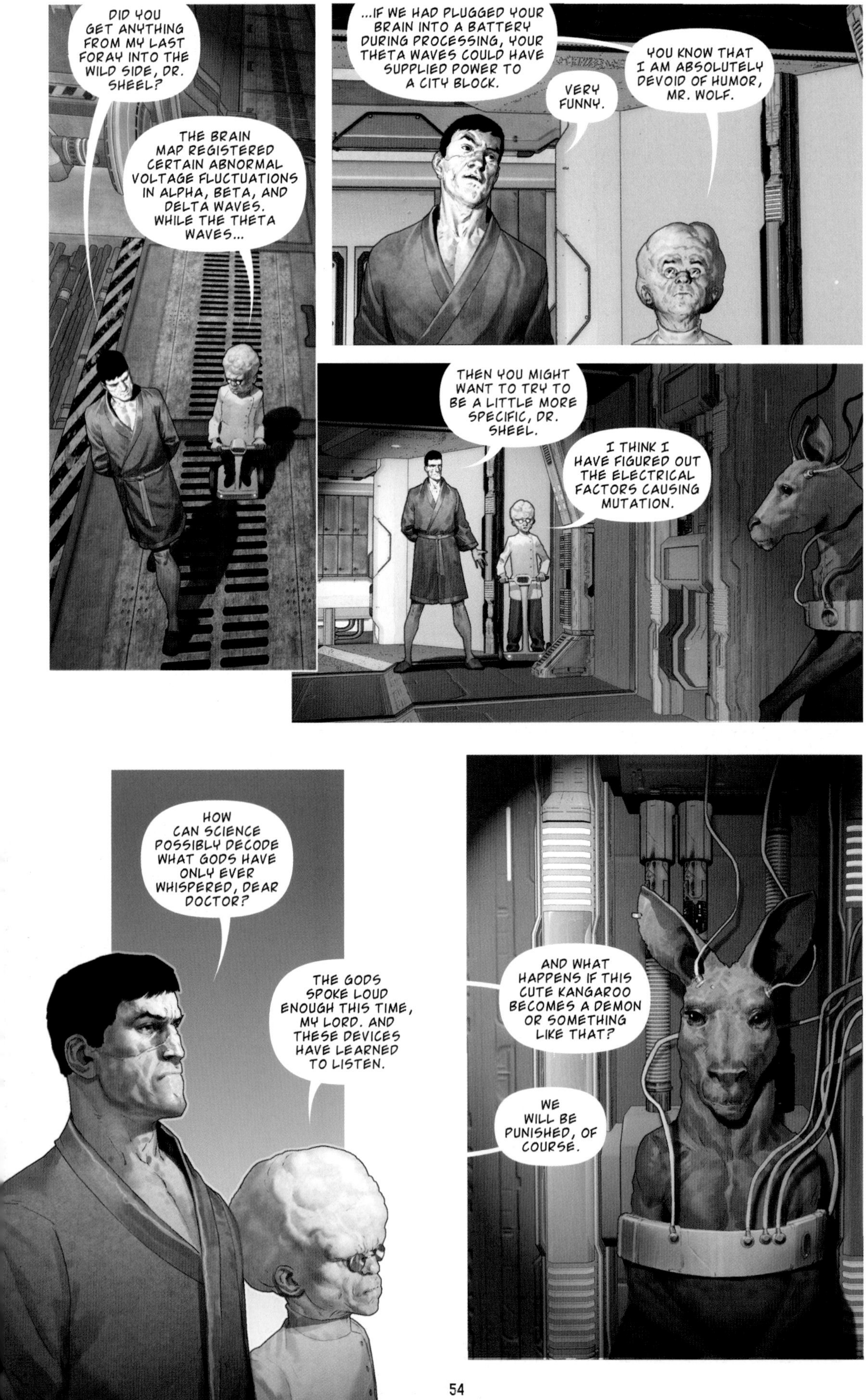

DID YOU GET ANYTHING FROM MY LAST FORAY INTO THE WILD SIDE, DR. SHEEL?
THE BRAIN MAP REGISTERED CERTAIN ABNORMAL VOLTAGE FLUCTUATIONS IN ALPHA, BETA, AND DELTA WAVES. WHILE THE THETA WAVES...
...IF WE HAD PLUGGED YOUR BRAIN INTO A BATTERY DURING PROCESSING, YOUR THETA WAVES COULD HAVE SUPPLIED POWER TO A CITY BLOCK.
VERY FUNNY.
YOU KNOW THAT I AM ABSOLUTELY DEVOID OF HUMOR, MR. WOLF.
THEN YOU MIGHT WANT TO TRY TO BE A LITTLE MORE SPECIFIC, DR. SHEEL.
I THINK I HAVE FIGURED OUT THE ELECTRICAL FACTORS CAUSING MUTATION.
HOW CAN SCIENCE POSSIBLY DECODE WHAT GODS HAVE ONLY EVER WHISPERED, DEAR DOCTOR?
THE GODS SPOKE LOUD ENOUGH THIS TIME, MY LORD. AND THESE DEVICES HAVE LEARNED TO LISTEN.
AND WHAT HAPPENS IF THIS CUTE KANGAROO BECOMES A DEMON OR SOMETHING LIKE THAT?
WE WILL BE PUNISHED, OF COURSE.

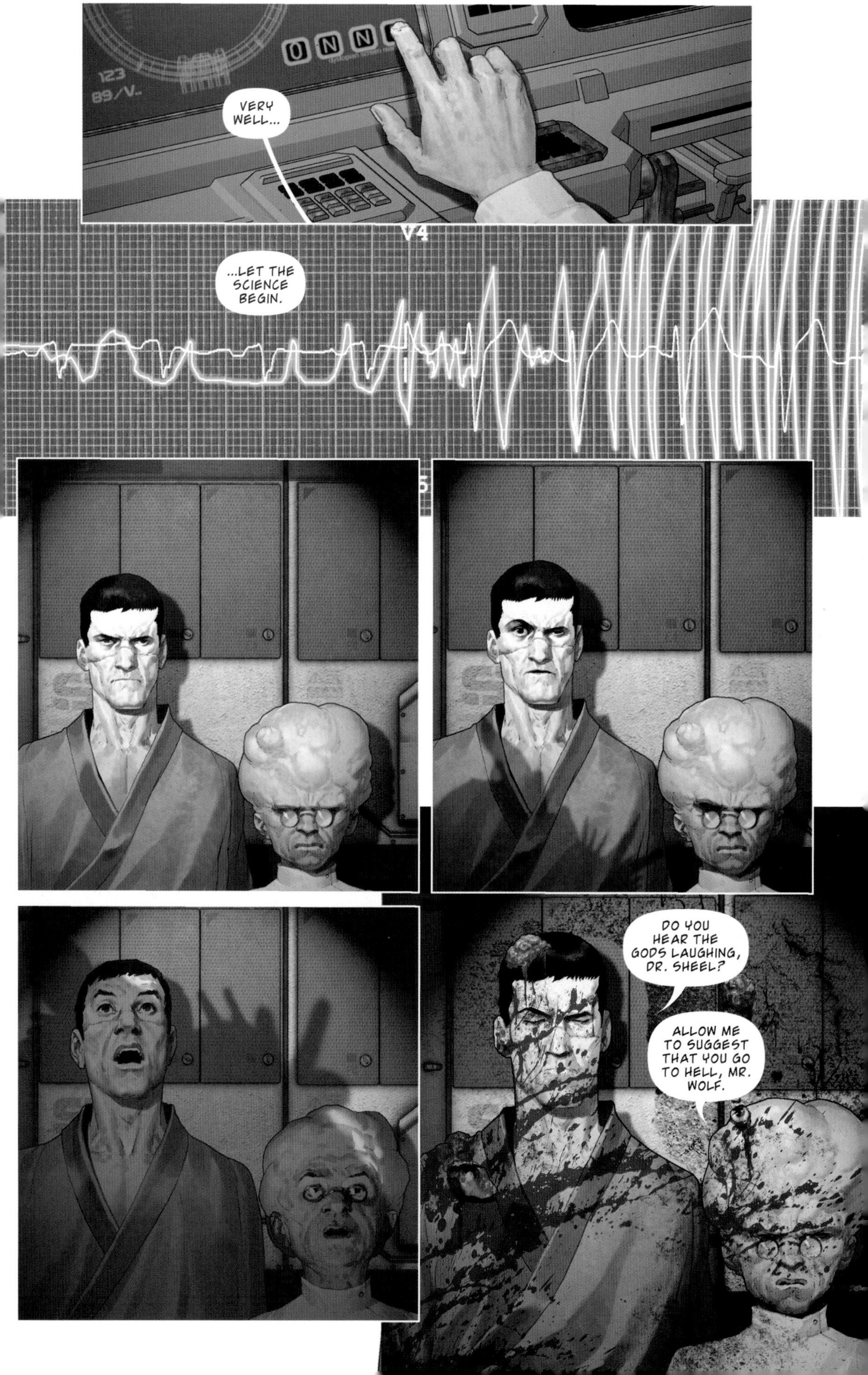
VERY WELL...
...LET THE SCIENCE BEGIN.
DO YOU HEAR THE GODS LAUGHING, DR. SHEEL?
ALLOW ME TO SUGGEST THAT YOU GO TO HELL, MR. WOLF.

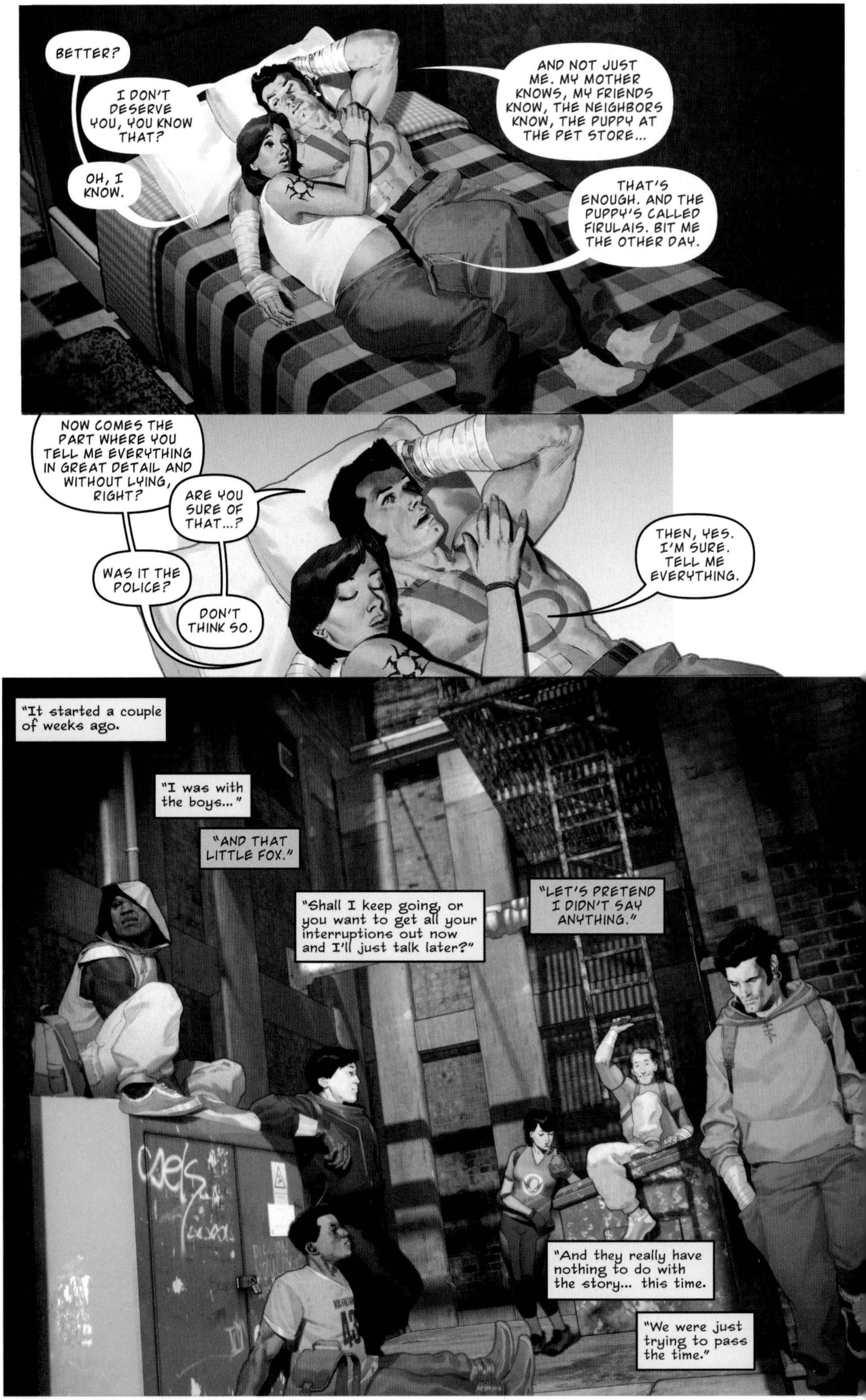
BETTER?
I DON'T DESERVE YOU, YOU KNOW THAT?
OH, I KNOW.
AND NOT JUST ME. MY MOTHER KNOWS, MY FRIENDS KNOW, THE NEIGHBORS KNOW, THE PUPPY AT THE PET STORE...
THAT'S ENOUGH. AND THE PUPPY'S CALLED FIRULAIS. BIT ME THE OTHER DAY.
NOW COMES THE PART WHERE YOU TELL ME EVERYTHING IN GREAT DETAIL AND WITHOUT LYING, RIGHT?
ARE YOU SURE OF THAT...?
WAS IT THE POLICE?
DON'T THINK SO.
THEN, YES. I'M SURE. TELL ME EVERYTHING.
"It started a couple of weeks ago.
"I was with the boys..."
"AND THAT LITTLE FOX."
"Shall I keep going, or you want to get all your interruptions out now and I'll just talk later?"
"LET'S PRETEND I DIDN'T SAY ANYTHING."
"And they really have nothing to do with the story... this time.
"We were just trying to pass the time."

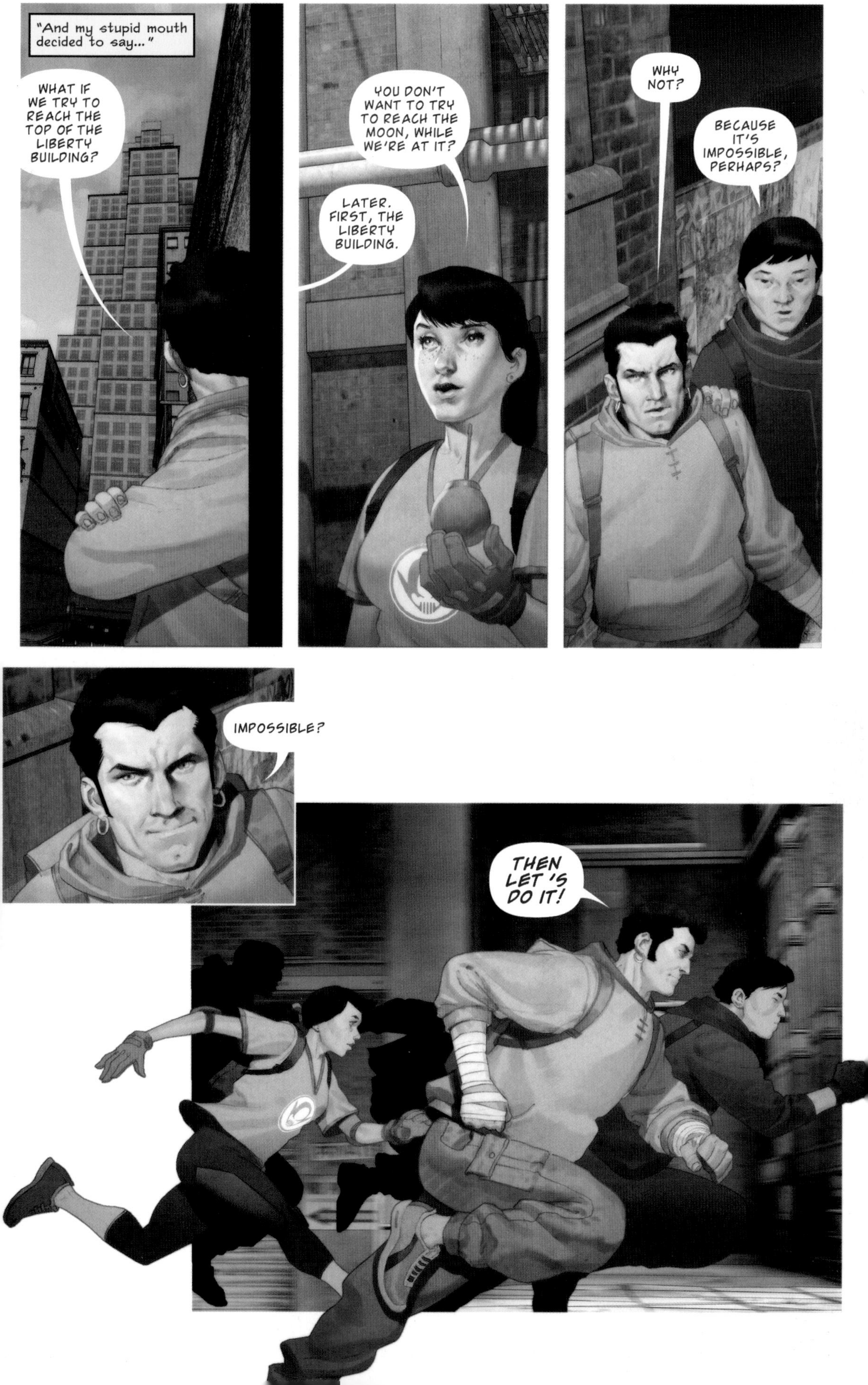
"And my stupid mouth decided to say..."
WHAT IF WE TRY TO REACH THE TOP OF THE LIBERTY BUILDING?
YOU DON'T WANT TO TRY TO REACH THE MOON, WHILE WE'RE AT IT?
LATER. FIRST, THE LIBERTY BUILDING.
WHY NOT?
BECAUSE IT'S IMPOSSIBLE, PERHAPS?
IMPOSSIBLE?
THEN LET'S DO IT!

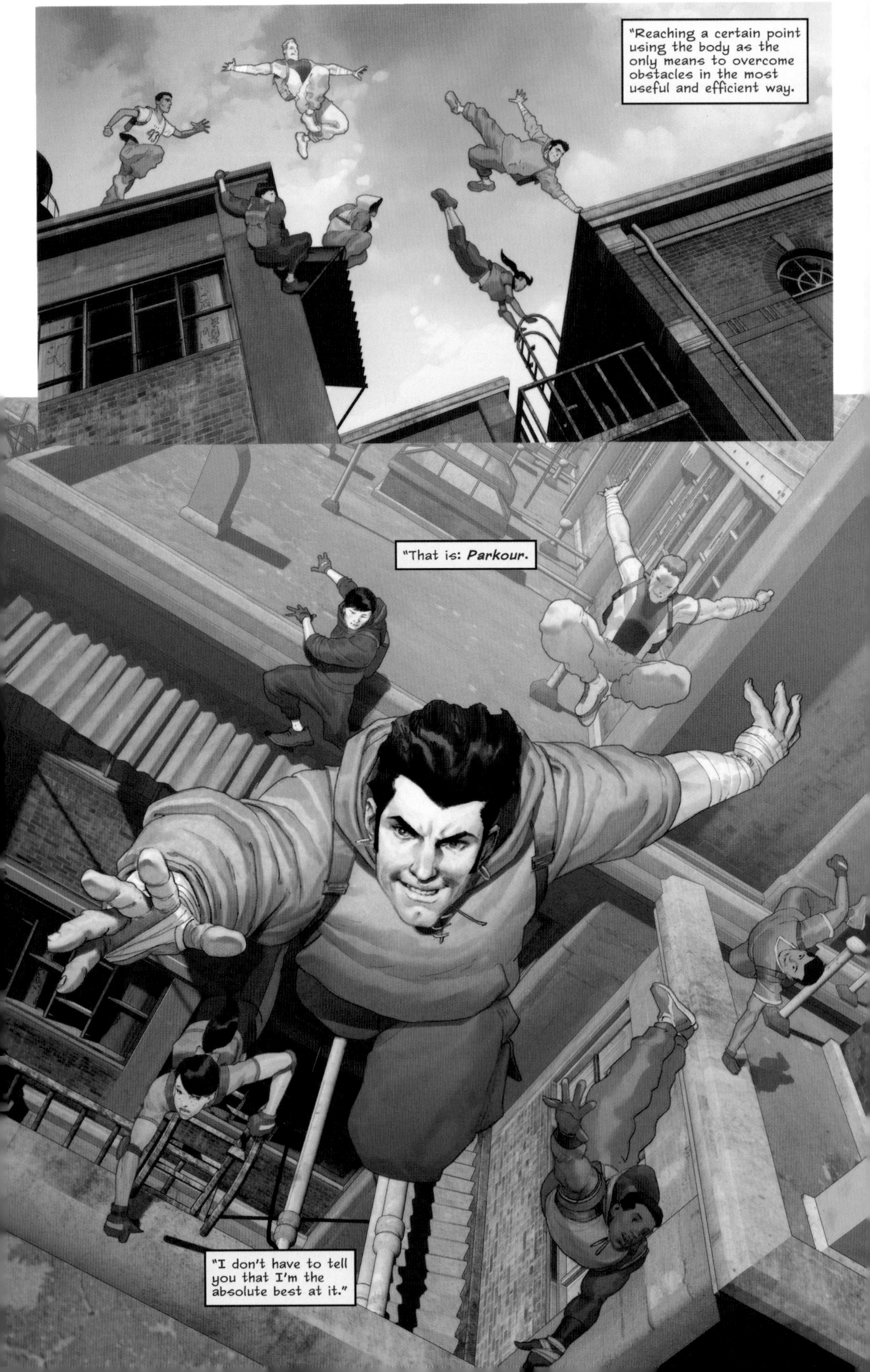
"Reaching a certain point using the body as the only means to overcome obstacles in the most useful and efficient way.
"That is: *Parkour.*
"I don't have to tell you that I'm the absolute best at it."

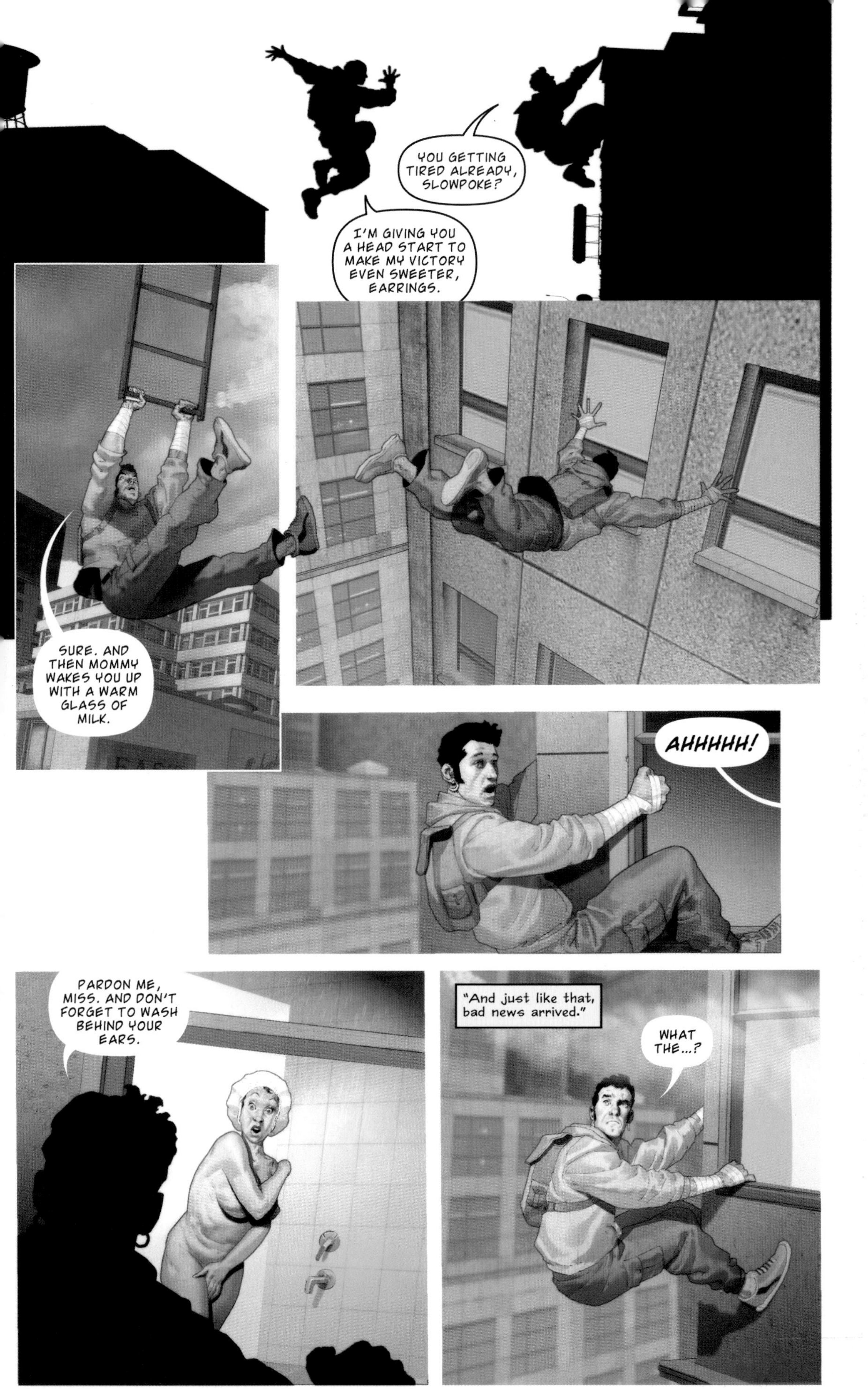
YOU GETTING TIRED ALREADY, SLOWPOKE?
I'M GIVING YOU A HEAD START TO MAKE MY VICTORY EVEN SWEETER, EARRINGS.
SURE. AND THEN MOMMY WAKES YOU UP WITH A WARM GLASS OF MILK.
AHHHHH!
PARDON ME, MISS. AND DON'T FORGET TO WASH BEHIND YOUR EARS.
"And just like that, bad news arrived."
WHAT THE...?

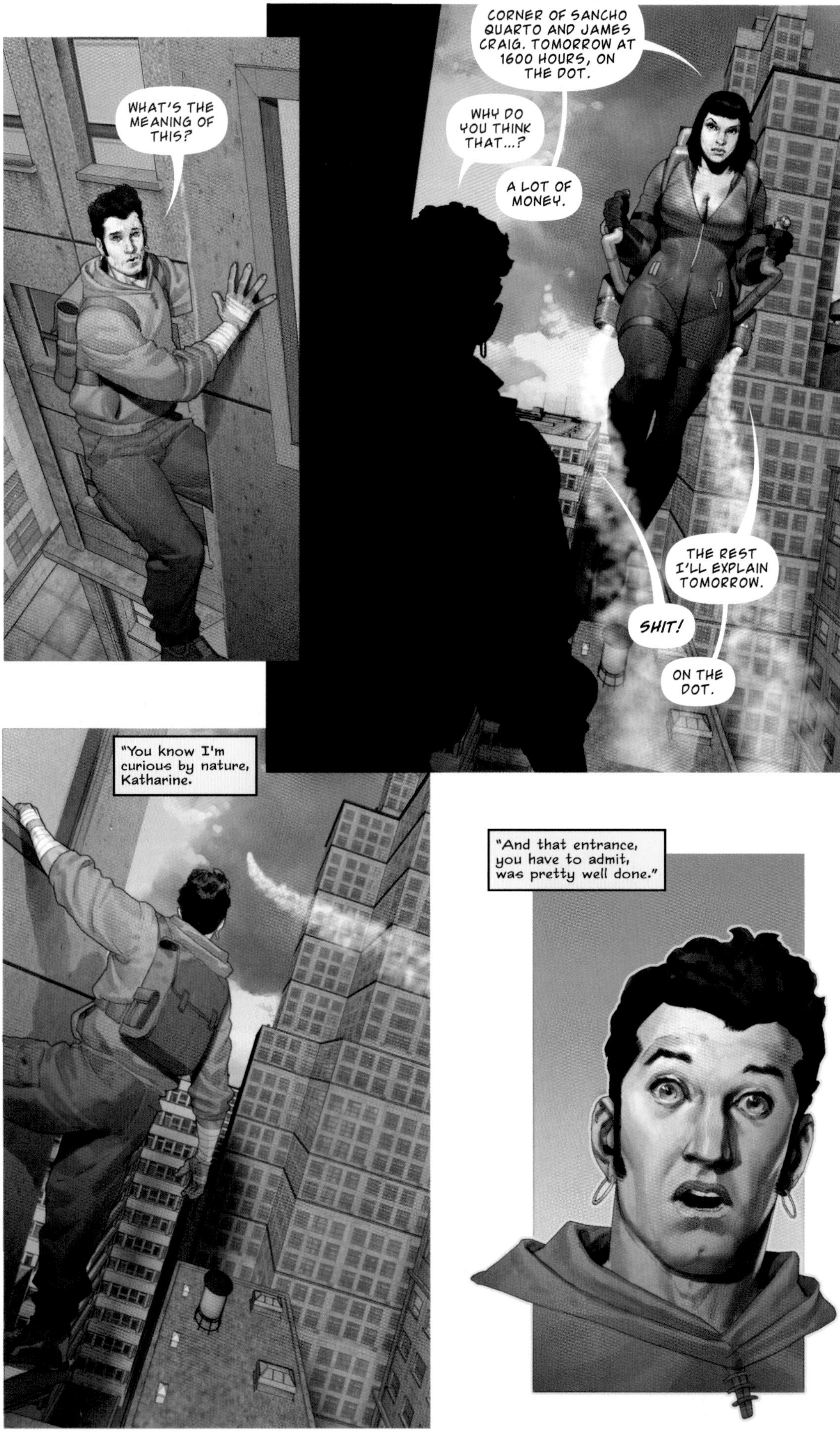
WHAT'S THE MEANING OF THIS?
CORNER OF SANCHO QUARTO AND JAMES CRAIG. TOMORROW AT 1600 HOURS, ON THE DOT.
WHY DO YOU THINK THAT...?
A LOT OF MONEY.
THE REST I'LL EXPLAIN TOMORROW.
SHIT!
ON THE DOT.
"You know I'm curious by nature, Katharine.
"And that entrance, you have to admit, was pretty well done."

"They say curiosity killed the cat.

"In my case, the promise of big money did the trick. The following day, I was there."

STEP IN.

BUT...

STEP IN.

I SUPPOSE ANY QUESTIONS I MIGHT HAVE...

PLEASE WAIT. EVERYTHING WILL BE EXPLAINED IN DUE TIME.

THAT'S WHAT I THOUGHT.

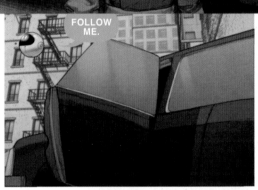

FOLLOW ME.

"So I followed him."

"Have you ever followed a floating toaster down a red carpet?"

"CURT..."

"I swear I'm not lying, not a single word! It happened exactly as I'm telling you."

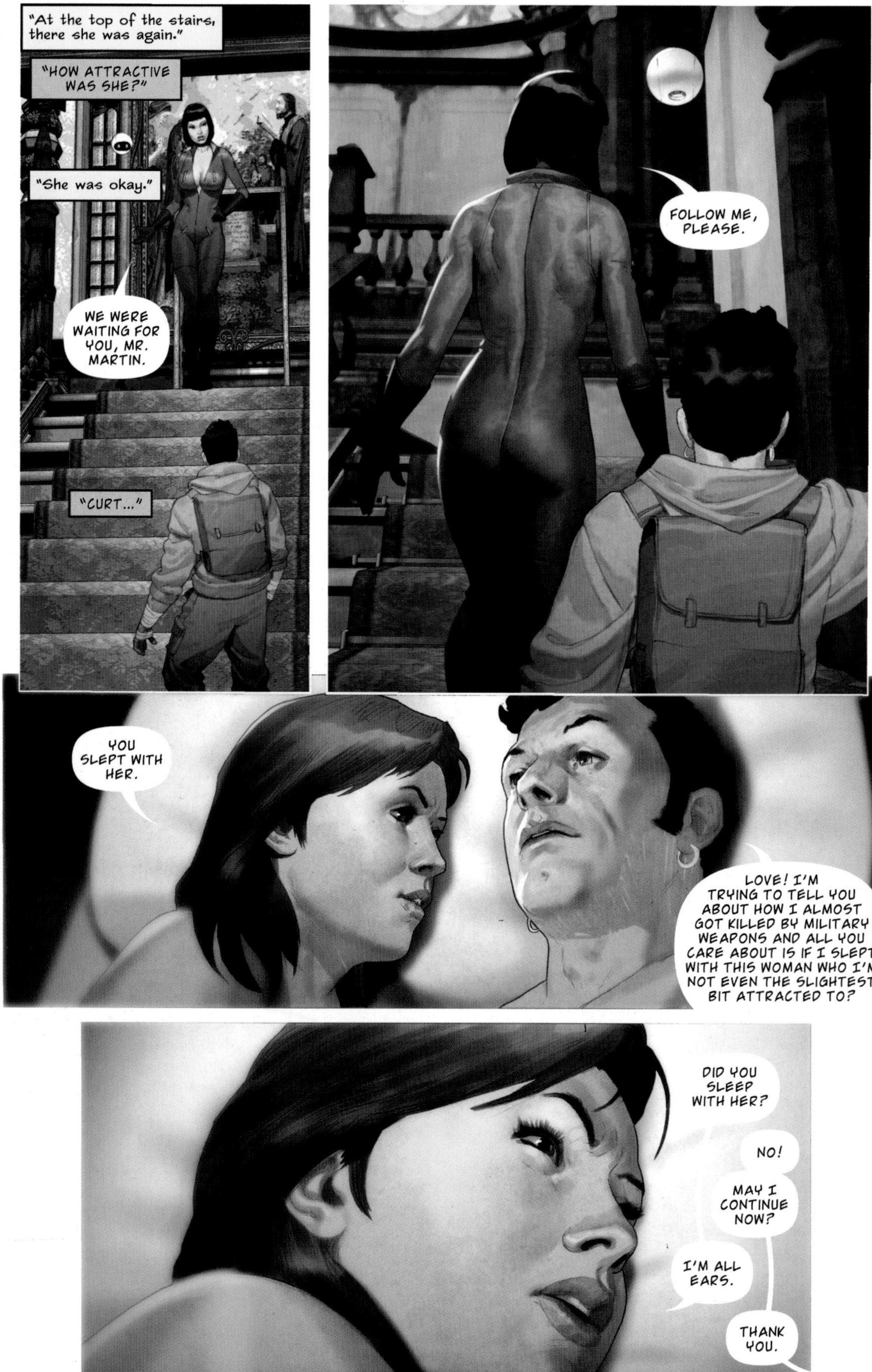
"At the top of the stairs, there she was again."
"HOW ATTRACTIVE WAS SHE?"
"She was okay."
WE WERE WAITING FOR YOU, MR. MARTIN.
"CURT..."
FOLLOW ME, PLEASE.
YOU SLEPT WITH HER.
LOVE! I'M TRYING TO TELL YOU ABOUT HOW I ALMOST GOT KILLED BY MILITARY WEAPONS AND ALL YOU CARE ABOUT IS IF I SLEPT WITH THIS WOMAN WHO I'M NOT EVEN THE SLIGHTEST BIT ATTRACTED TO?
DID YOU SLEEP WITH HER?
NO!
MAY I CONTINUE NOW?
I'M ALL EARS.
THANK YOU.

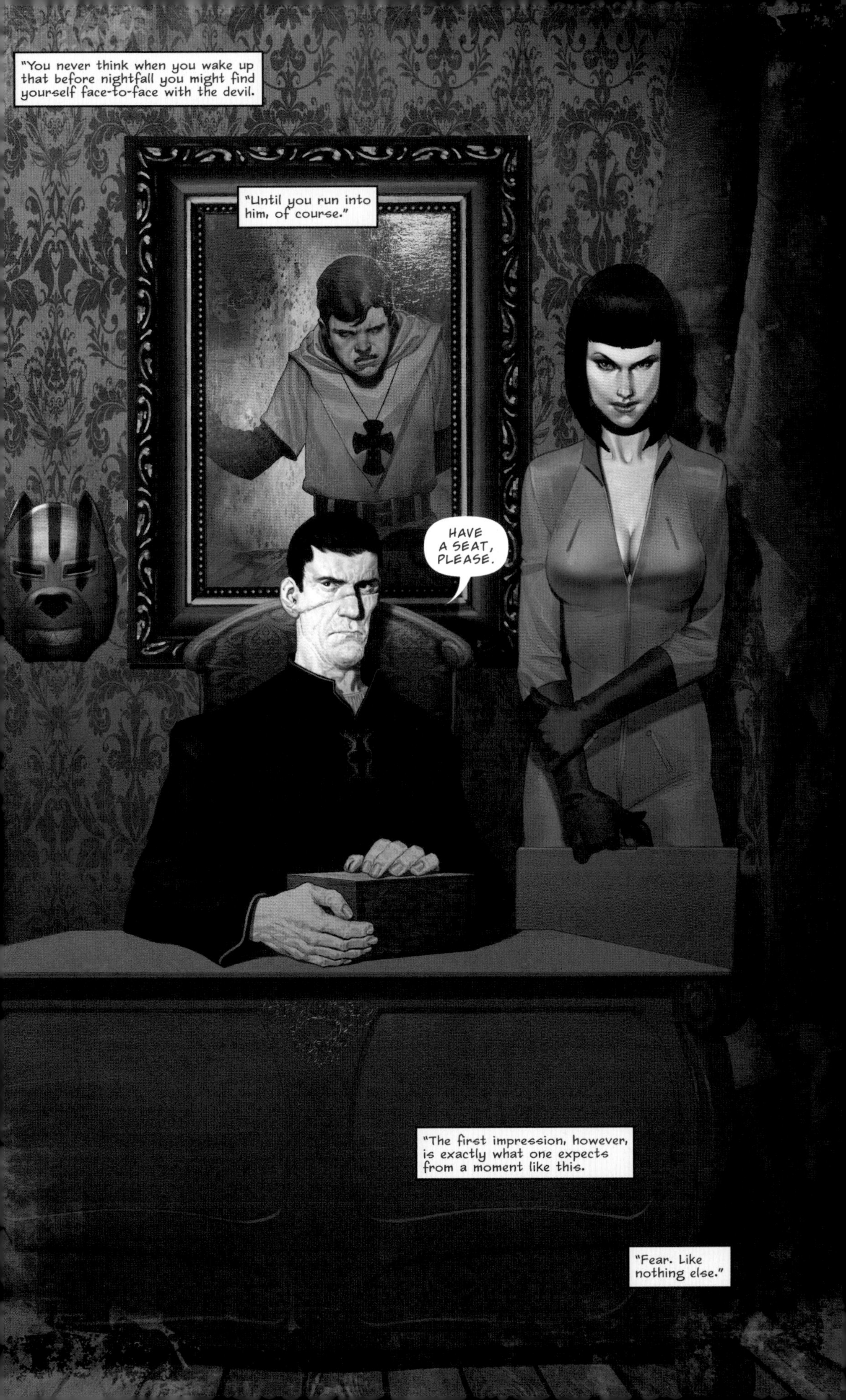
"You never think when you wake up that before nightfall you might find yourself face-to-face with the devil.
"Until you run into him, of course."
HAVE A SEAT, PLEASE.
"The first impression, however, is exactly what one expects from a moment like this.
"Fear. Like nothing else."

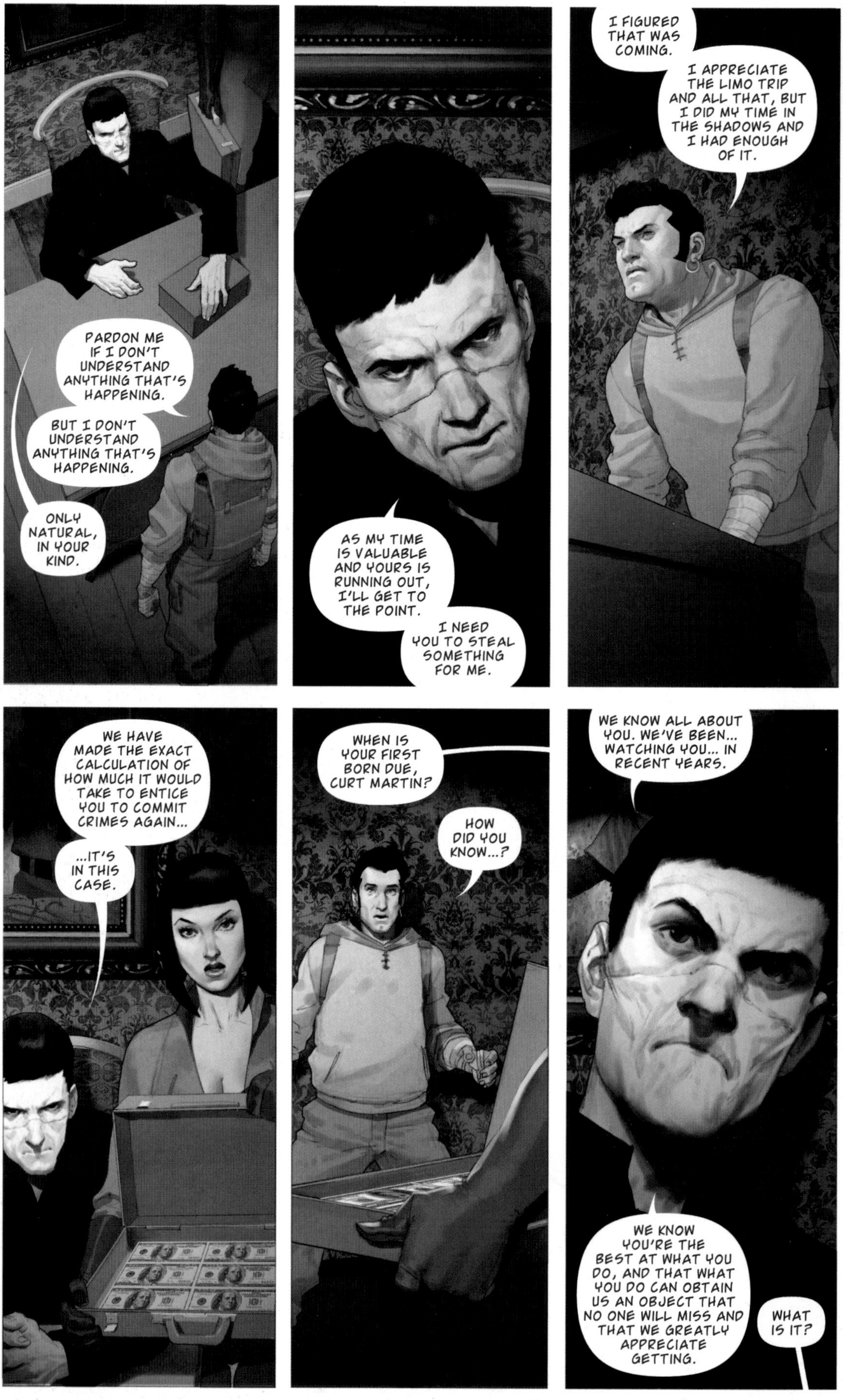
PARDON ME IF I DON'T UNDERSTAND ANYTHING THAT'S HAPPENING.
BUT I DON'T UNDERSTAND ANYTHING THAT'S HAPPENING.
ONLY NATURAL, IN YOUR KIND.
AS MY TIME IS VALUABLE AND YOURS IS RUNNING OUT, I'LL GET TO THE POINT.
I NEED YOU TO STEAL SOMETHING FOR ME.
I FIGURED THAT WAS COMING.
I APPRECIATE THE LIMO TRIP AND ALL THAT, BUT I DID MY TIME IN THE SHADOWS AND I HAD ENOUGH OF IT.
WE HAVE MADE THE EXACT CALCULATION OF HOW MUCH IT WOULD TAKE TO ENTICE YOU TO COMMIT CRIMES AGAIN...
...IT'S IN THIS CASE.
WHEN IS YOUR FIRST BORN DUE, CURT MARTIN?
HOW DID YOU KNOW...?
WE KNOW ALL ABOUT YOU. WE'VE BEEN... WATCHING YOU... IN RECENT YEARS.
WE KNOW YOU'RE THE BEST AT WHAT YOU DO, AND THAT WHAT YOU DO CAN OBTAIN US AN OBJECT THAT NO ONE WILL MISS AND THAT WE GREATLY APPRECIATE GETTING.
WHAT IS IT?

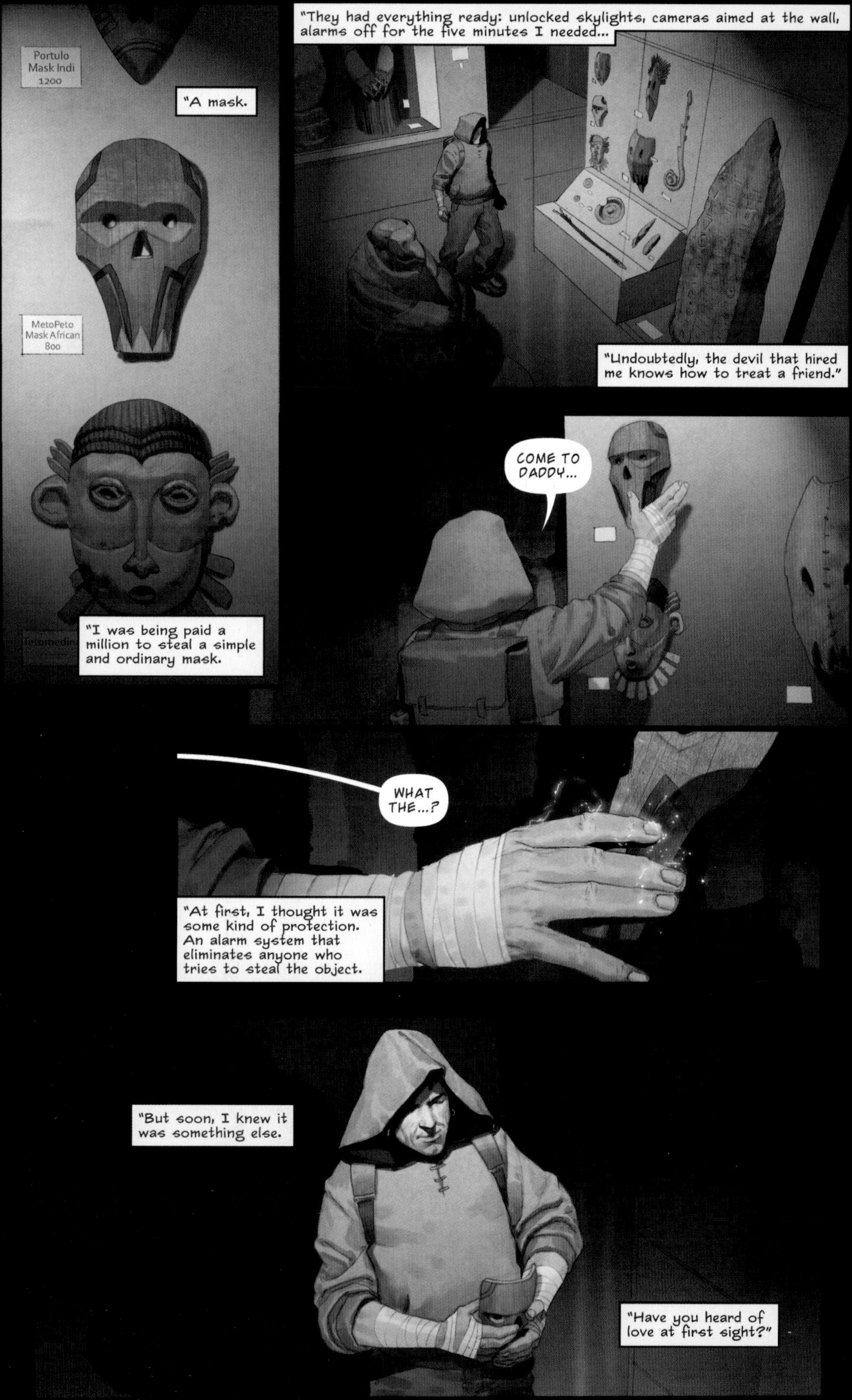
Portulo
Mask Indi
1200
"A mask.
MetoPeto
Mask African
800
"I was being paid a million to steal a simple and ordinary mask.
"They had everything ready: unlocked skylights, cameras aimed at the wall, alarms off for the five minutes I needed...
"Undoubtedly, the devil that hired me knows how to treat a friend."
COME TO DADDY...
WHAT THE...?
"At first, I thought it was some kind of protection. An alarm system that eliminates anyone who tries to steal the object.
"But soon, I knew it was something else.
"Have you heard of love at first sight?"

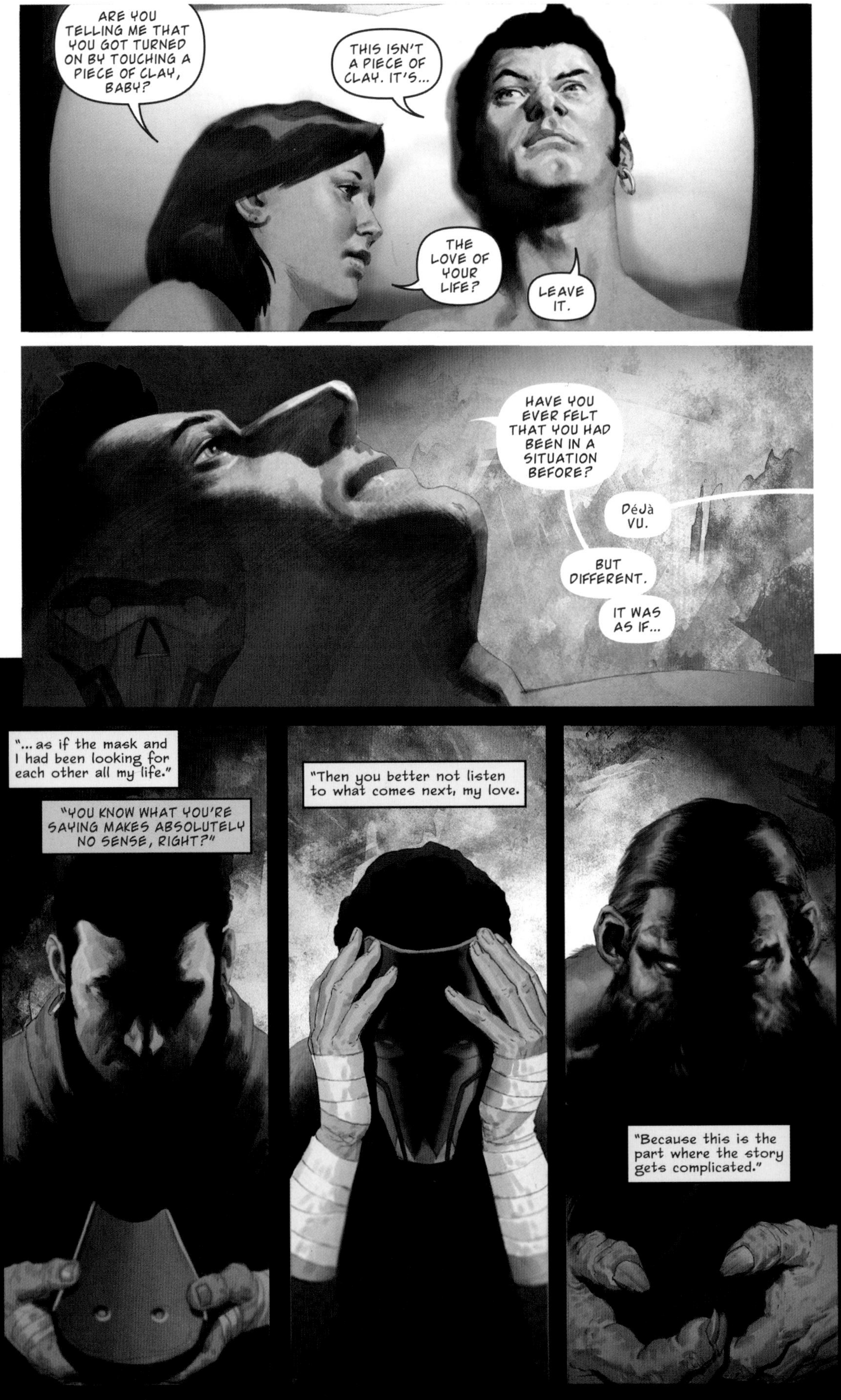
ARE YOU TELLING ME THAT YOU GOT TURNED ON BY TOUCHING A PIECE OF CLAY, BABY?
THIS ISN'T A PIECE OF CLAY. IT'S...
THE LOVE OF YOUR LIFE?
LEAVE IT.
HAVE YOU EVER FELT THAT YOU HAD BEEN IN A SITUATION BEFORE?
DéJà VU.
BUT DIFFERENT.
IT WAS AS IF...
"...as if the mask and I had been looking for each other all my life."
"YOU KNOW WHAT YOU'RE SAYING MAKES ABSOLUTELY NO SENSE, RIGHT?"
"Then you better not listen to what comes next, my love.
"Because this is the part where the story gets complicated."

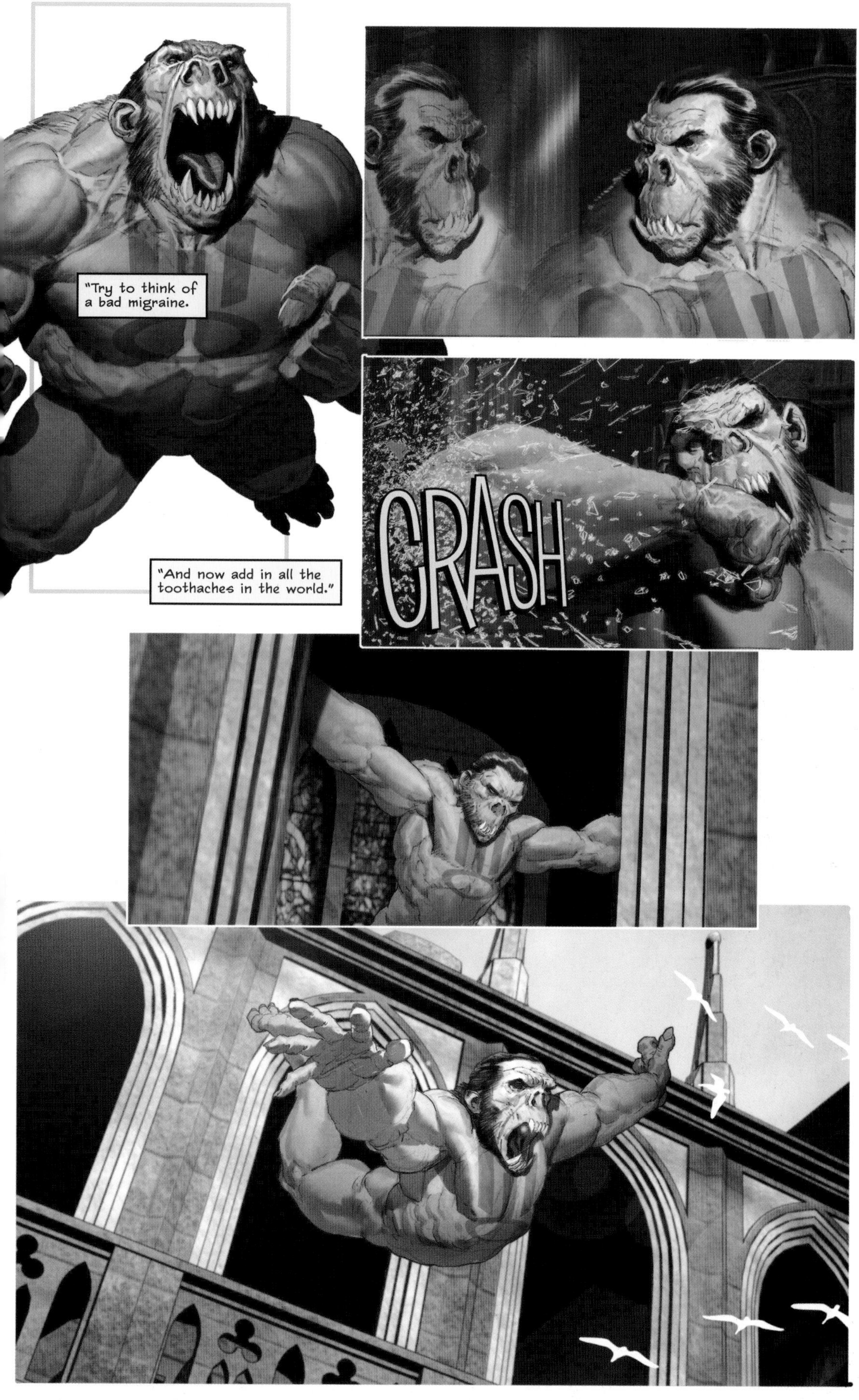
"Try to think of a bad migraine.
"And now add in all the toothaches in the world."
CRASH

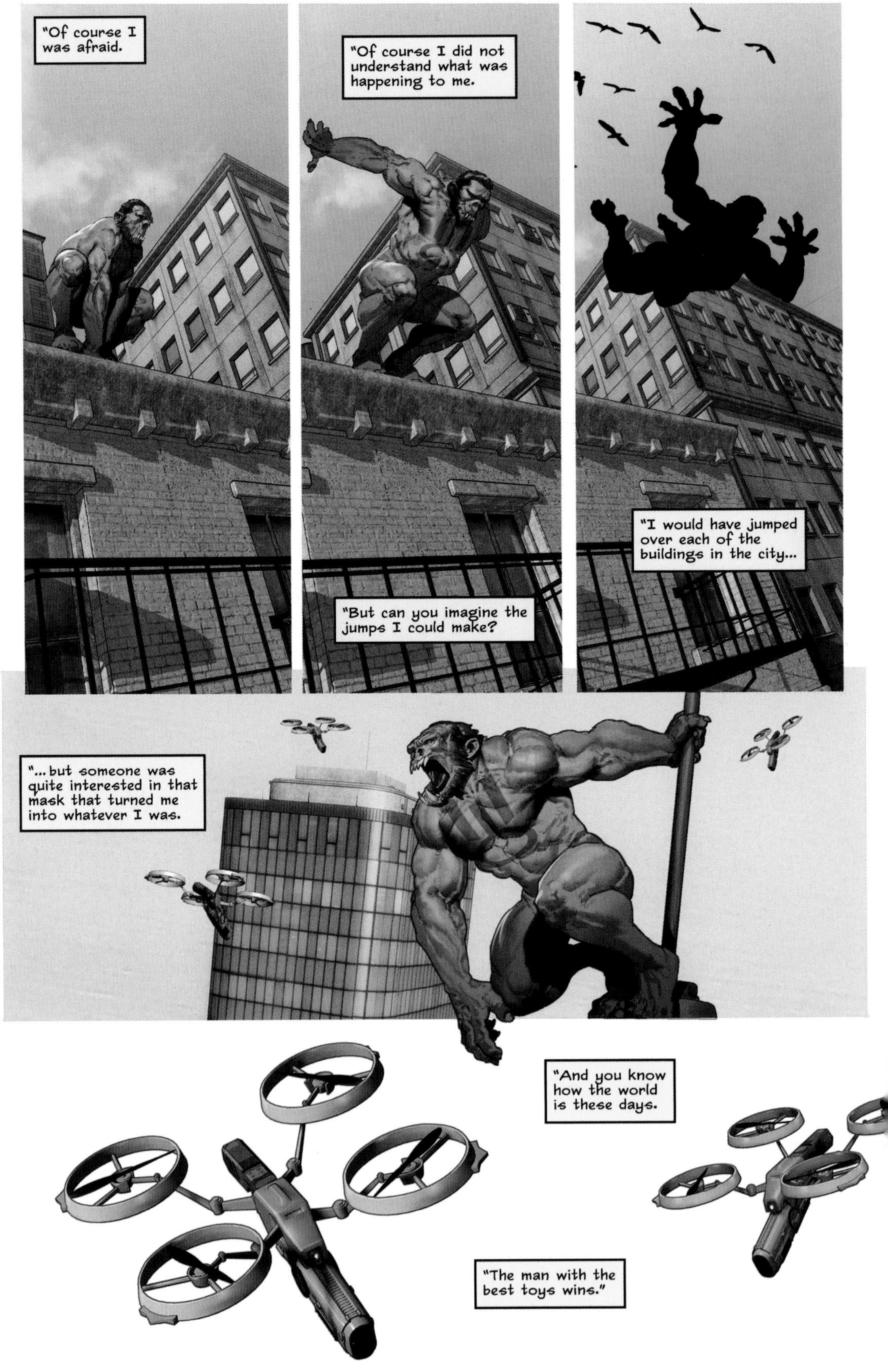
"Of course I was afraid.
"Of course I did not understand what was happening to me.
"But can you imagine the jumps I could make?
"I would have jumped over each of the buildings in the city...
"...but someone was quite interested in that mask that turned me into whatever I was.
"And you know how the world is these days.
"The man with the best toys wins."

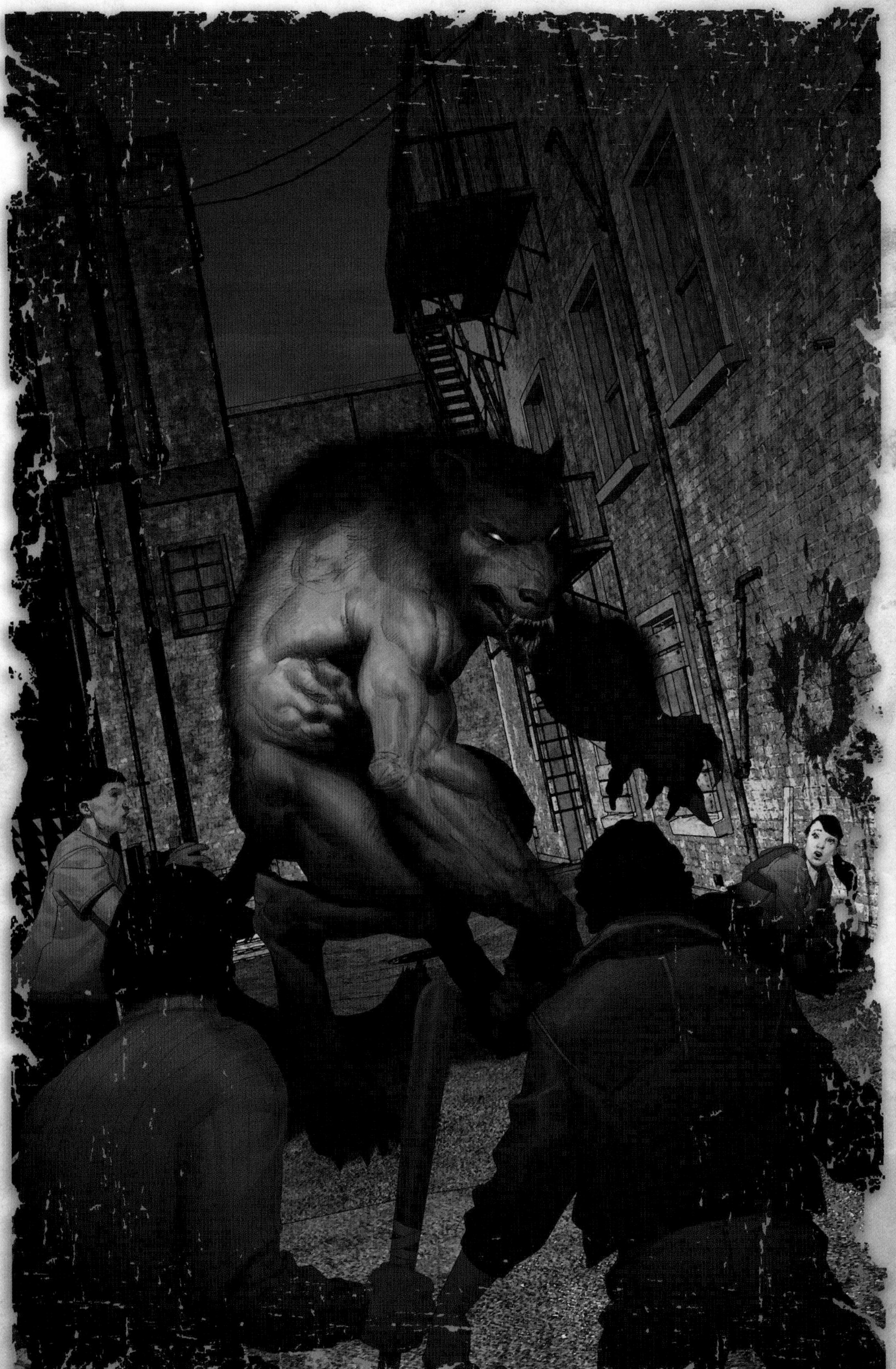

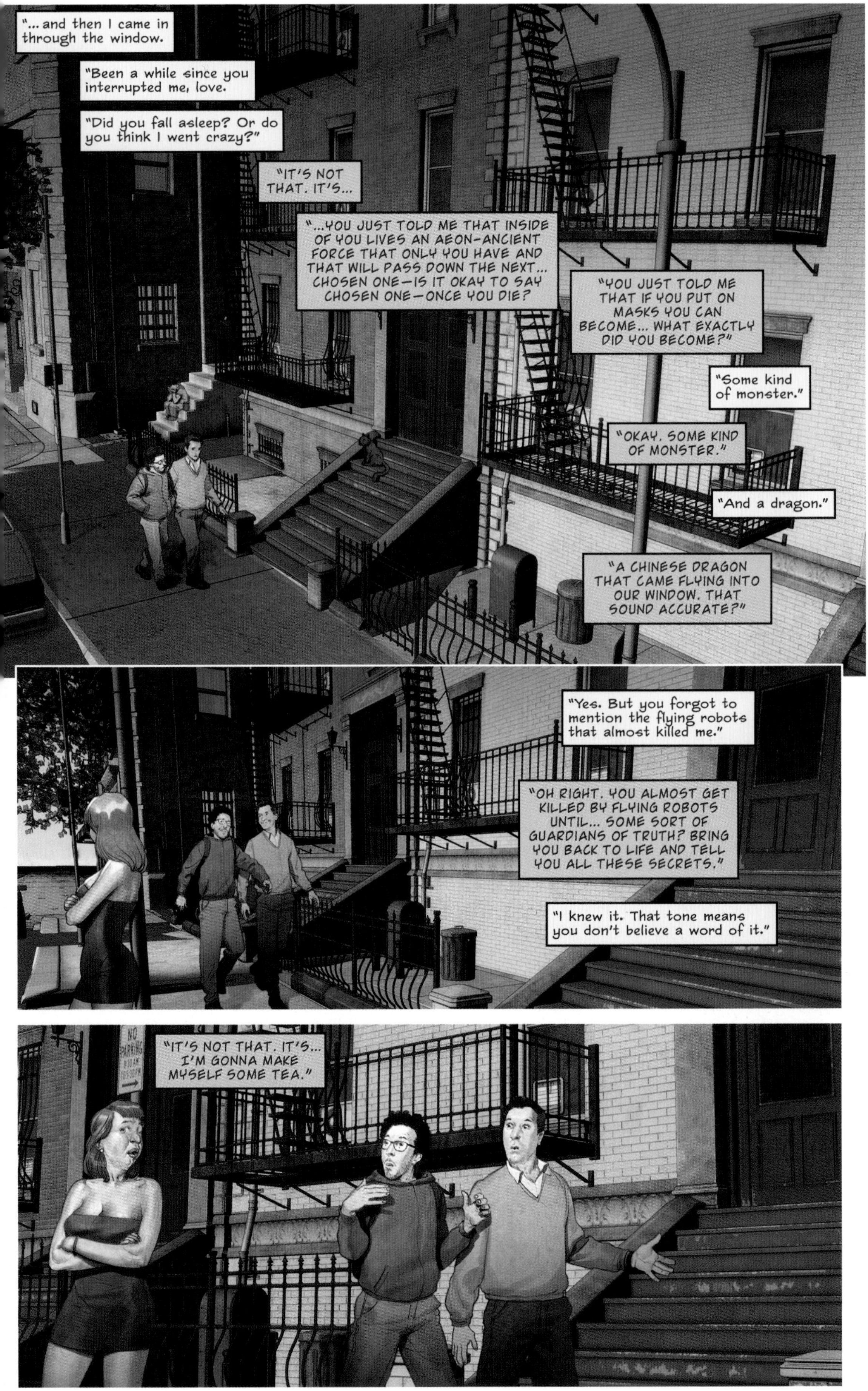
"... and then I came in through the window.
"Been a while since you interrupted me, love.
"Did you fall asleep? Or do you think I went crazy?"
"IT'S NOT THAT. IT'S...
"...YOU JUST TOLD ME THAT INSIDE OF YOU LIVES AN AEON-ANCIENT FORCE THAT ONLY YOU HAVE AND THAT WILL PASS DOWN THE NEXT... CHOSEN ONE—IS IT OKAY TO SAY CHOSEN ONE—ONCE YOU DIE?
"YOU JUST TOLD ME THAT IF YOU PUT ON MASKS YOU CAN BECOME... WHAT EXACTLY DID YOU BECOME?"
"Some kind of monster."
"OKAY. SOME KIND OF MONSTER."
"And a dragon."
"A CHINESE DRAGON THAT CAME FLYING INTO OUR WINDOW. THAT SOUND ACCURATE?"
"Yes. But you forgot to mention the flying robots that almost killed me."
"OH RIGHT. YOU ALMOST GET KILLED BY FLYING ROBOTS UNTIL... SOME SORT OF GUARDIANS OF TRUTH? BRING YOU BACK TO LIFE AND TELL YOU ALL THESE SECRETS."
"I knew it. That tone means you don't believe a word of it."
NO PARKING
"IT'S NOT THAT. IT'S... I'M GONNA MAKE MYSELF SOME TEA."

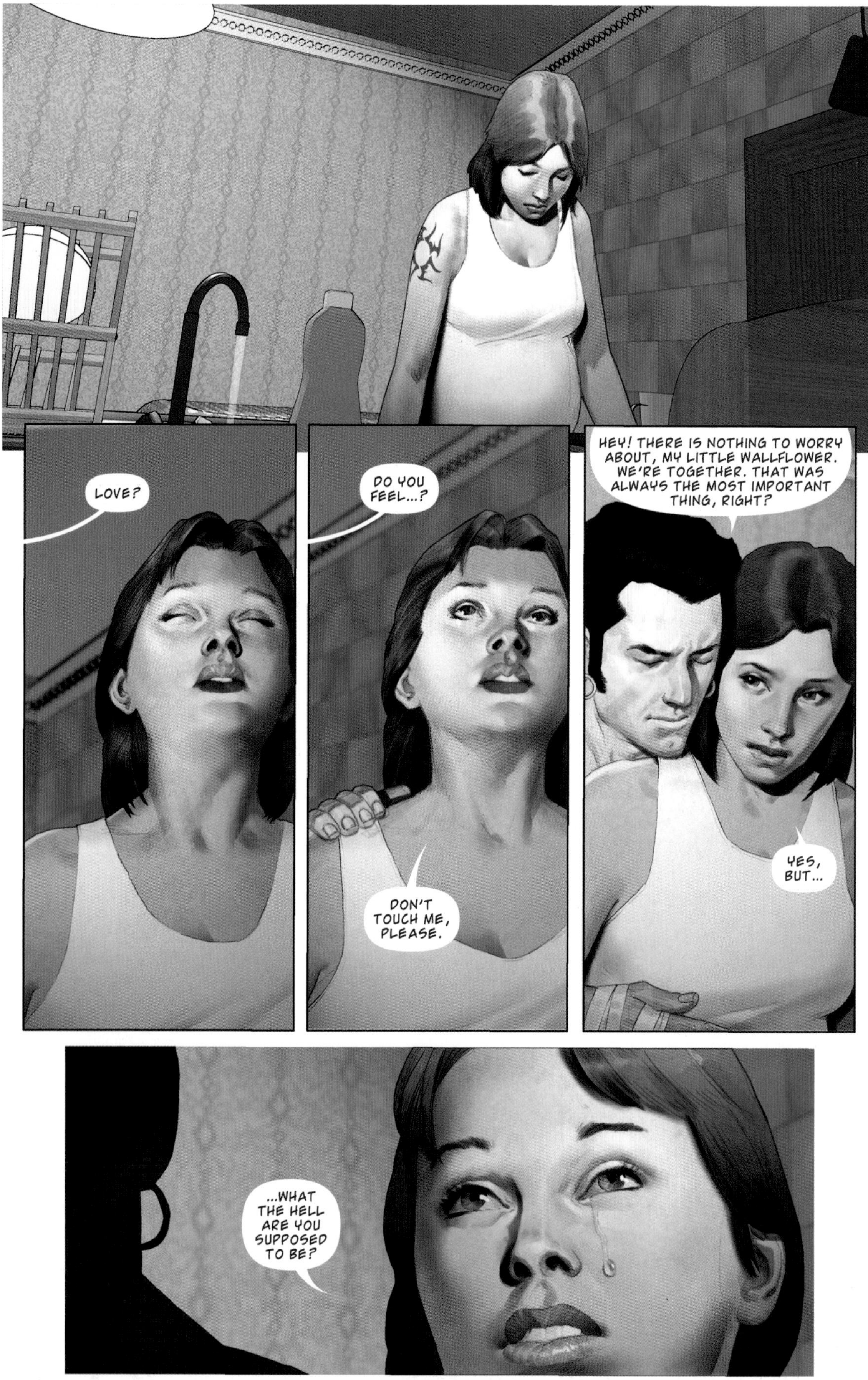

LOVE?
DO YOU FEEL...?
DON'T TOUCH ME, PLEASE.
HEY! THERE IS NOTHING TO WORRY ABOUT, MY LITTLE WALLFLOWER. WE'RE TOGETHER. THAT WAS ALWAYS THE MOST IMPORTANT THING, RIGHT?
YES, BUT...
...WHAT THE HELL ARE YOU SUPPOSED TO BE?

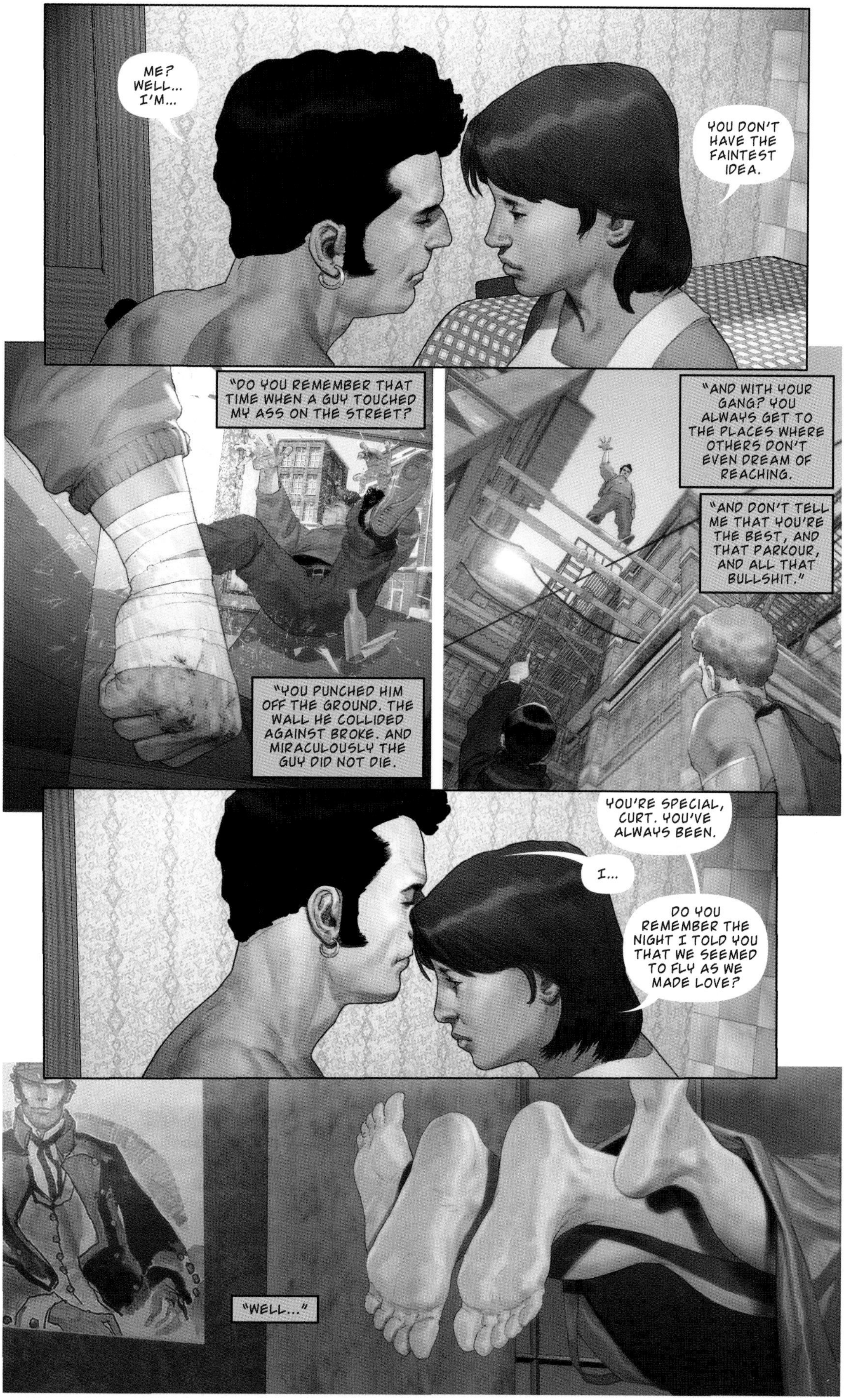

ME? WELL... I'M...
YOU DON'T HAVE THE FAINTEST IDEA.
"DO YOU REMEMBER THAT TIME WHEN A GUY TOUCHED MY ASS ON THE STREET?
"YOU PUNCHED HIM OFF THE GROUND. THE WALL HE COLLIDED AGAINST BROKE. AND MIRACULOUSLY THE GUY DID NOT DIE.
"AND WITH YOUR GANG? YOU ALWAYS GET TO THE PLACES WHERE OTHERS DON'T EVEN DREAM OF REACHING.
"AND DON'T TELL ME THAT YOU'RE THE BEST, AND THAT PARKOUR, AND ALL THAT BULLSHIT."
YOU'RE SPECIAL, CURT. YOU'VE ALWAYS BEEN.
I...
DO YOU REMEMBER THE NIGHT I TOLD YOU THAT WE SEEMED TO FLY AS WE MADE LOVE?
"WELL..."

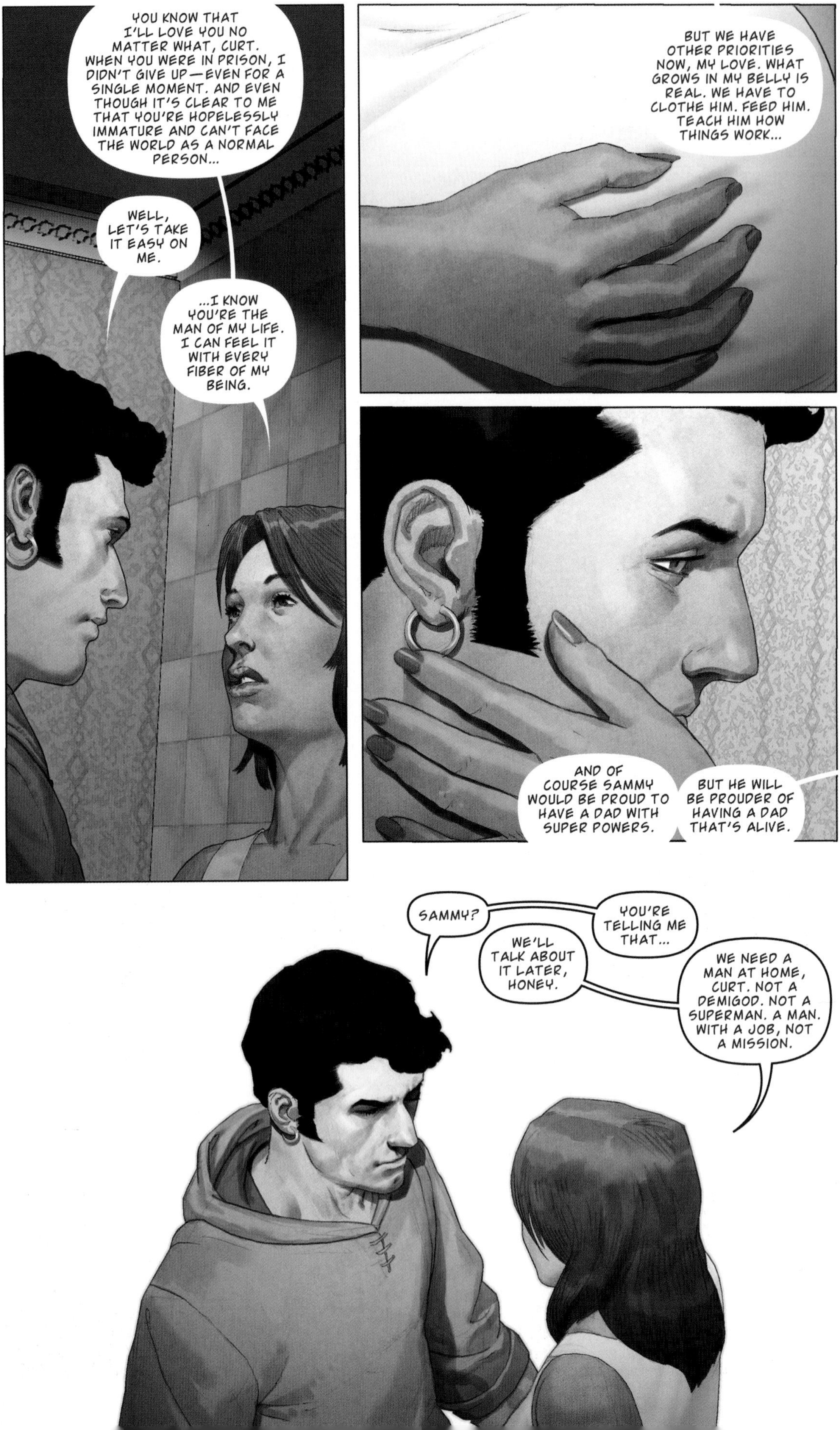
YOU KNOW THAT I'LL LOVE YOU NO MATTER WHAT, CURT. WHEN YOU WERE IN PRISON, I DIDN'T GIVE UP—EVEN FOR A SINGLE MOMENT. AND EVEN THOUGH IT'S CLEAR TO ME THAT YOU'RE HOPELESSLY IMMATURE AND CAN'T FACE THE WORLD AS A NORMAL PERSON...
WELL, LET'S TAKE IT EASY ON ME.
...I KNOW YOU'RE THE MAN OF MY LIFE. I CAN FEEL IT WITH EVERY FIBER OF MY BEING.
BUT WE HAVE OTHER PRIORITIES NOW, MY LOVE. WHAT GROWS IN MY BELLY IS REAL. WE HAVE TO CLOTHE HIM. FEED HIM. TEACH HIM HOW THINGS WORK...
AND OF COURSE SAMMY WOULD BE PROUD TO HAVE A DAD WITH SUPER POWERS.
BUT HE WILL BE PROUDER OF HAVING A DAD THAT'S ALIVE.
SAMMY?
WE'LL TALK ABOUT IT LATER, HONEY.
YOU'RE TELLING ME THAT...
WE NEED A MAN AT HOME, CURT. NOT A DEMIGOD. NOT A SUPERMAN. A MAN. WITH A JOB, NOT A MISSION.

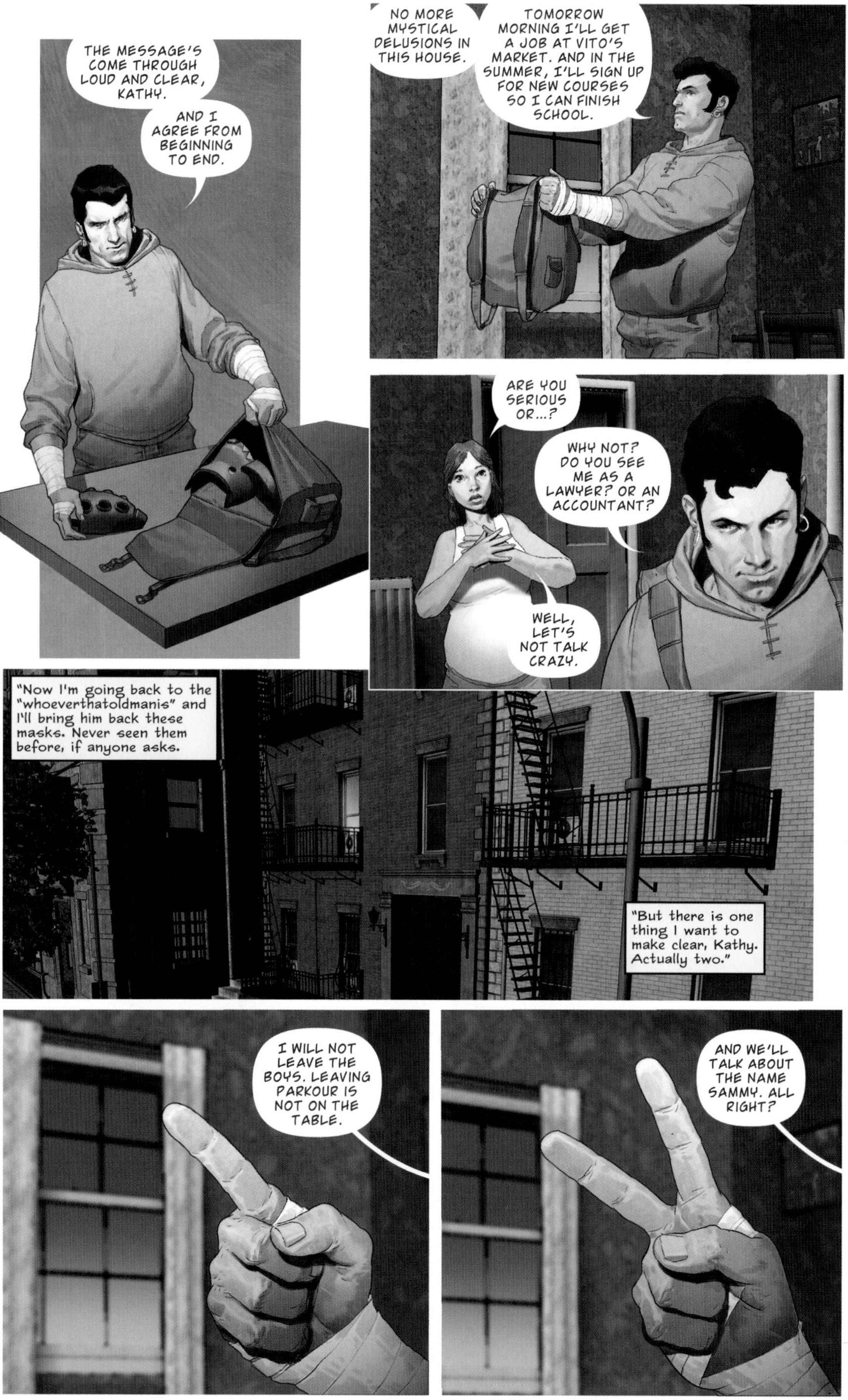
THE MESSAGE'S COME THROUGH LOUD AND CLEAR, KATHY.
AND I AGREE FROM BEGINNING TO END.
NO MORE MYSTICAL DELUSIONS IN THIS HOUSE.
TOMORROW MORNING I'LL GET A JOB AT VITO'S MARKET. AND IN THE SUMMER, I'LL SIGN UP FOR NEW COURSES SO I CAN FINISH SCHOOL.
ARE YOU SERIOUS OR...?
WHY NOT? DO YOU SEE ME AS A LAWYER? OR AN ACCOUNTANT?
WELL, LET'S NOT TALK CRAZY.
"Now I'm going back to the "whoeverthatoldmanis" and I'll bring him back these masks. Never seen them before, if anyone asks.
"But there is one thing I want to make clear, Kathy. Actually two."
I WILL NOT LEAVE THE BOYS. LEAVING PARKOUR IS NOT ON THE TABLE.
AND WE'LL TALK ABOUT THE NAME SAMMY. ALL RIGHT?

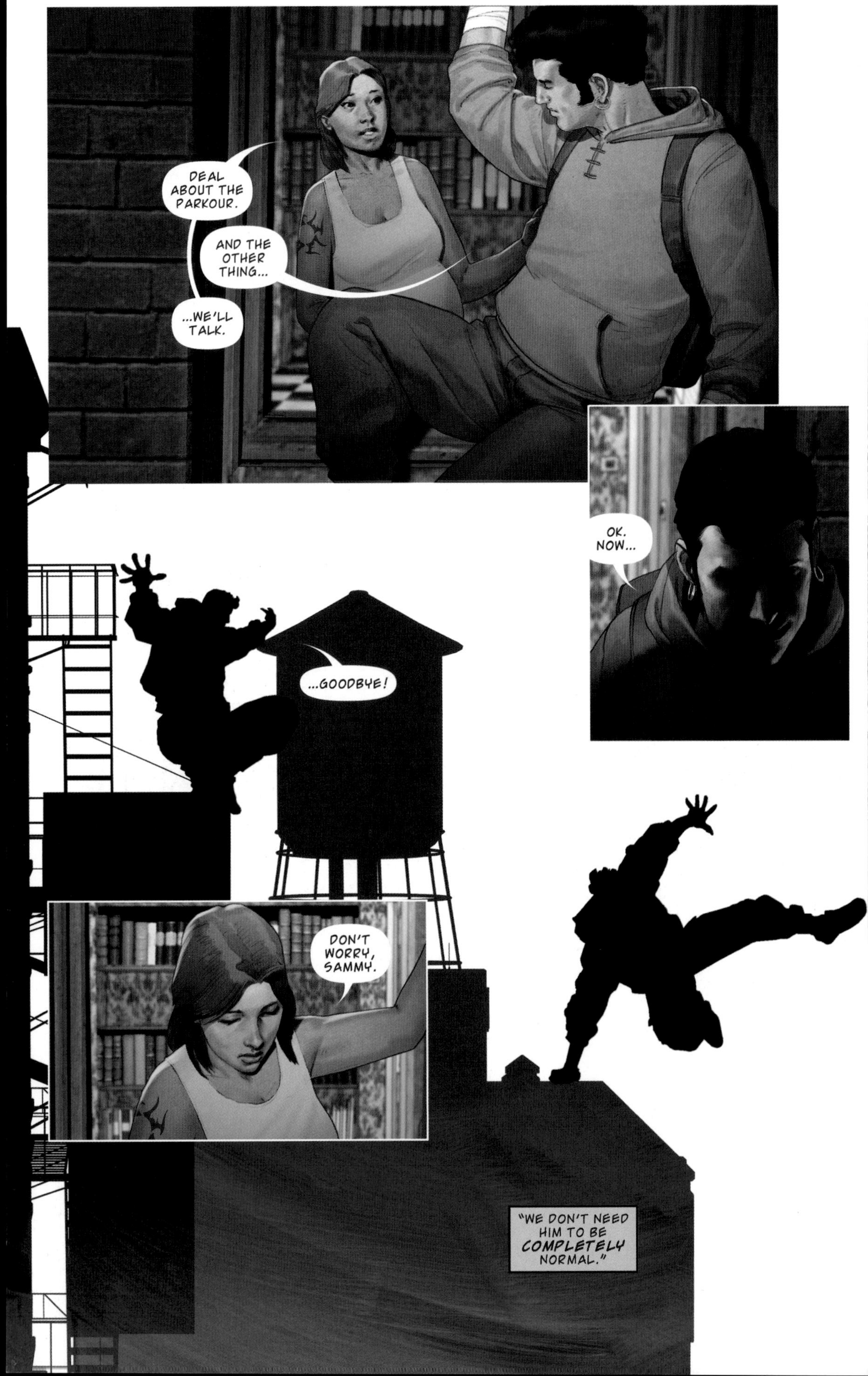
DEAL ABOUT THE PARKOUR.
AND THE OTHER THING...
...WE'LL TALK.
OK. NOW...
...GOODBYE!
DON'T WORRY, SAMMY.
"WE DON'T NEED HIM TO BE *COMPLETELY* NORMAL."

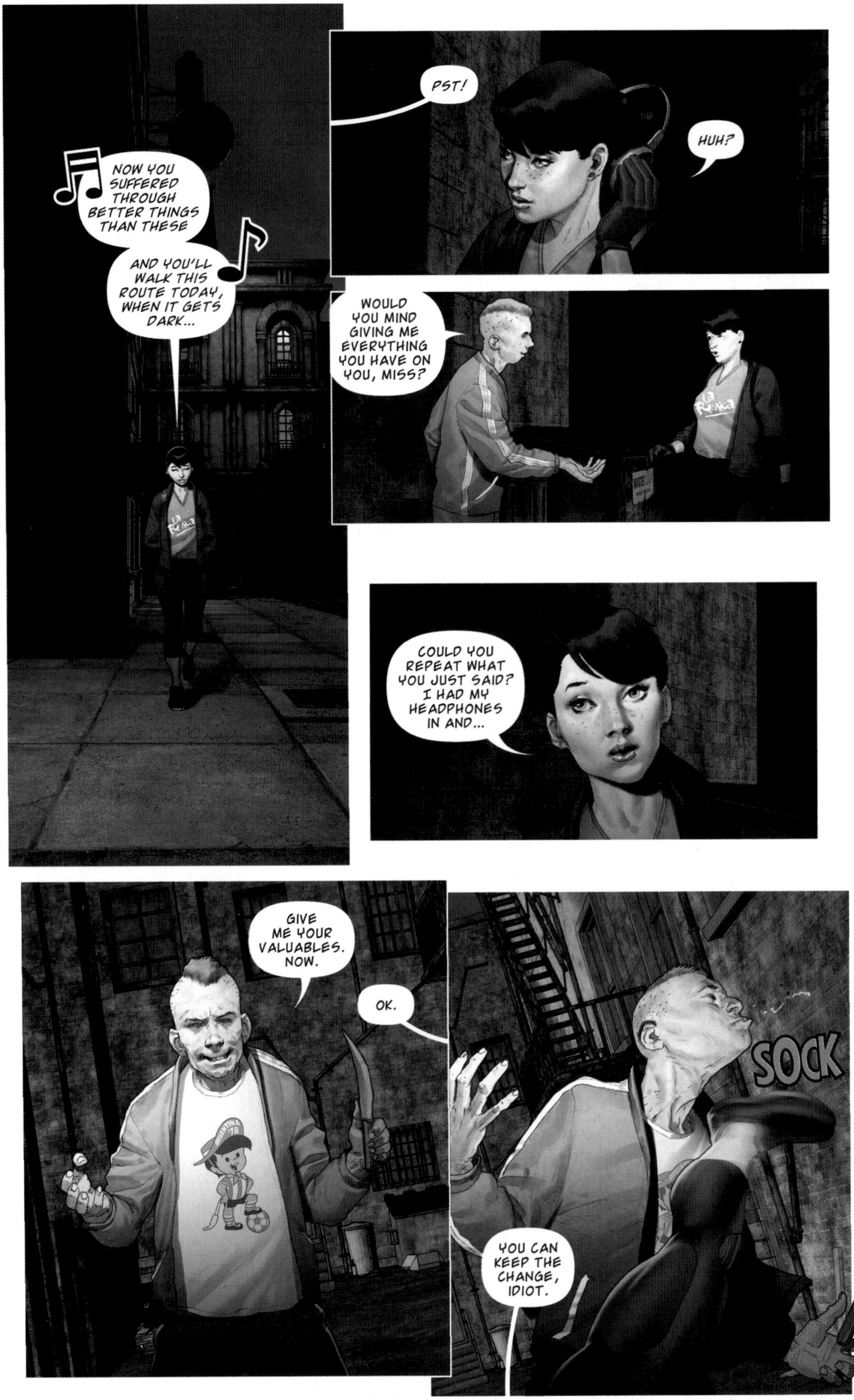
NOW YOU SUFFERED THROUGH BETTER THINGS THAN THESE
AND YOU'LL WALK THIS ROUTE TODAY, WHEN IT GETS DARK...
PST!
HUH?
WOULD YOU MIND GIVING ME EVERYTHING YOU HAVE ON YOU, MISS?
COULD YOU REPEAT WHAT YOU JUST SAID? I HAD MY HEADPHONES IN AND...
GIVE ME YOUR VALUABLES. NOW.
OK.
SOCK
YOU CAN KEEP THE CHANGE, IDIOT.

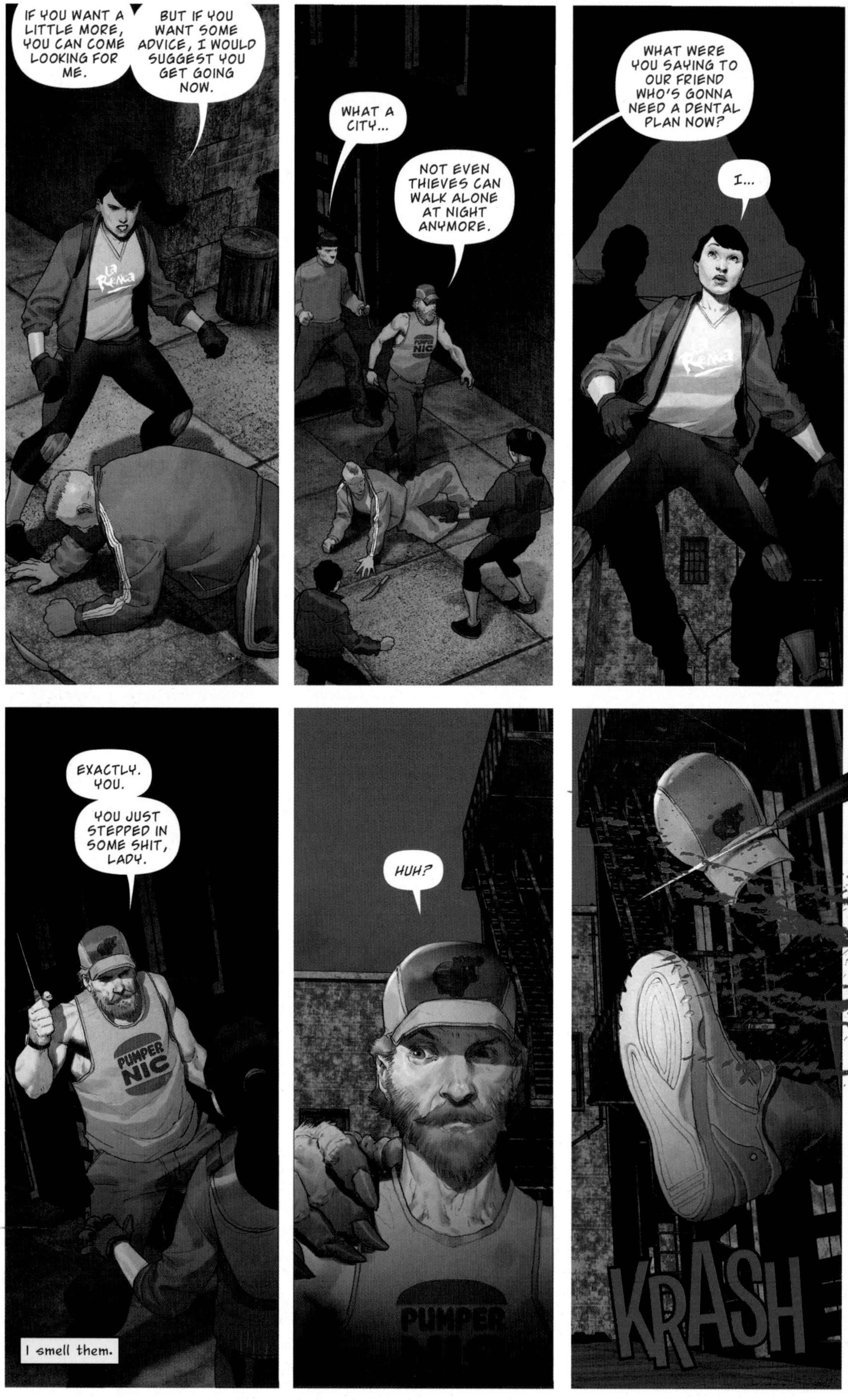
IF YOU WANT A LITTLE MORE, YOU CAN COME LOOKING FOR ME.
BUT IF YOU WANT SOME ADVICE, I WOULD SUGGEST YOU GET GOING NOW.
WHAT A CITY...
NOT EVEN THIEVES CAN WALK ALONE AT NIGHT ANYMORE.
WHAT WERE YOU SAYING TO OUR FRIEND WHO'S GONNA NEED A DENTAL PLAN NOW?
I...
EXACTLY. YOU.
YOU JUST STEPPED IN SOME SHIT, LADY.
I smell them.
HUH?
KRASH

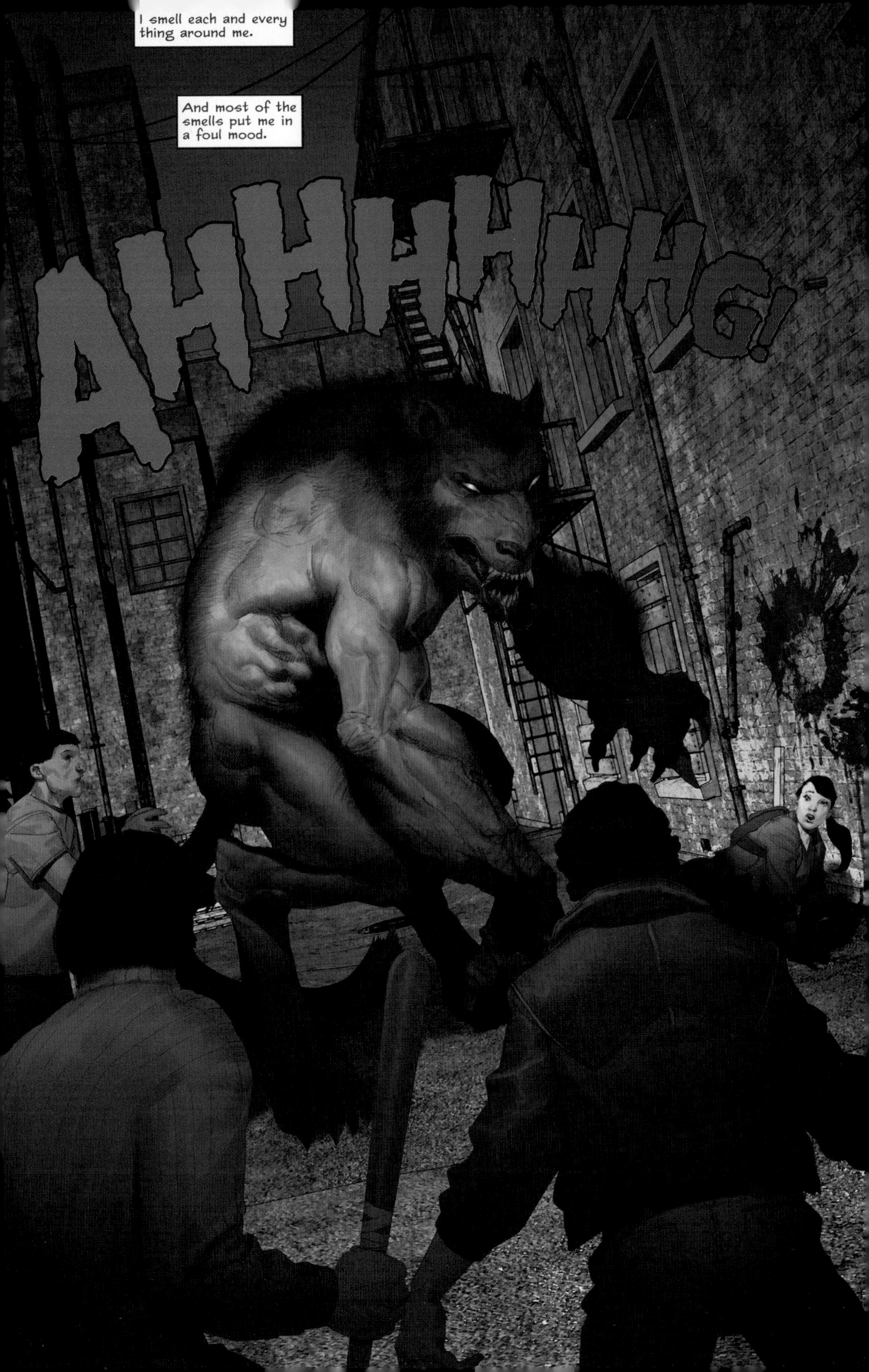
I smell each and every thing around me.
And most of the smells put me in a foul mood.
AHHHHHHG!

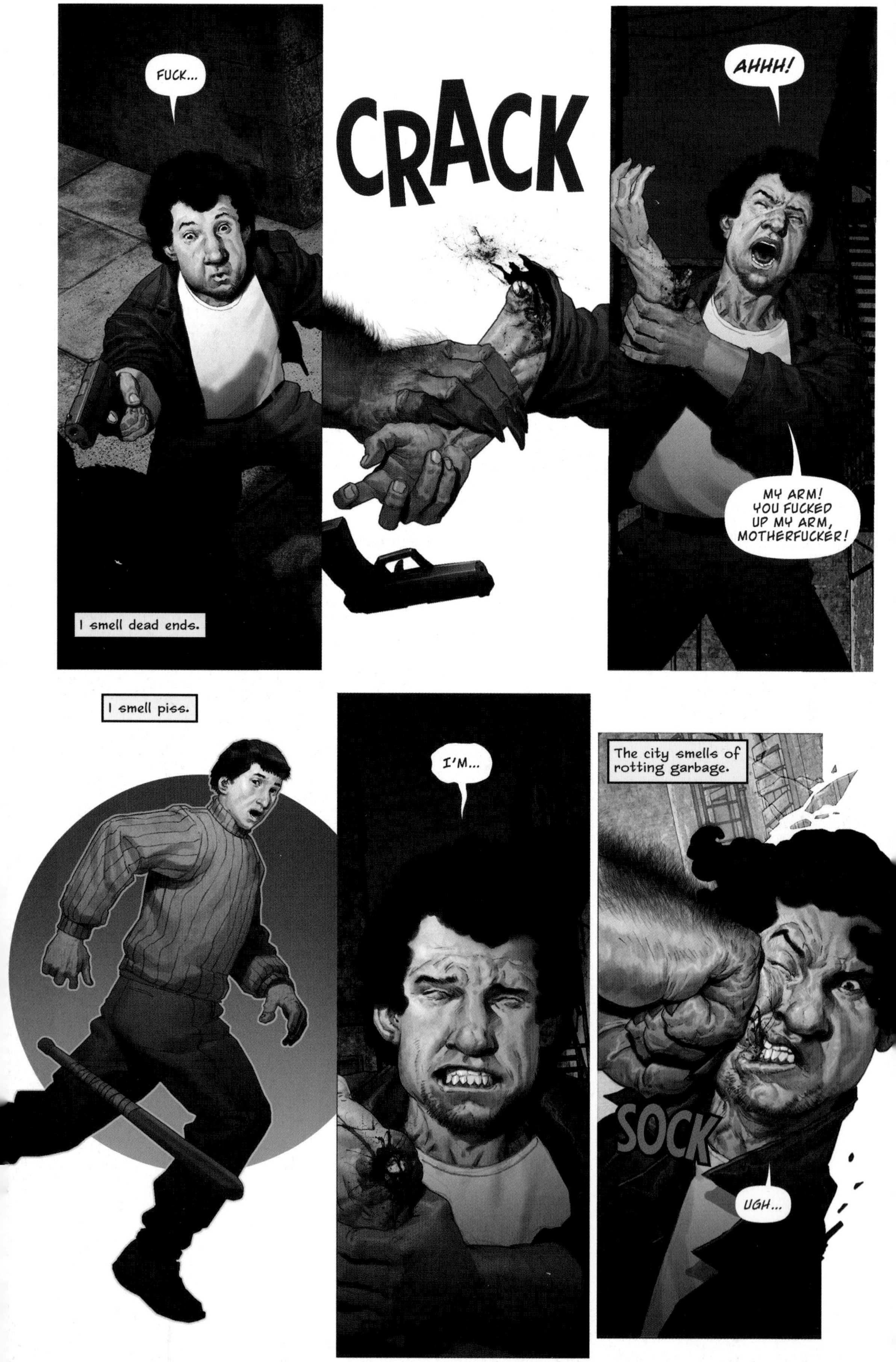
FUCK...
I smell dead ends.
CRACK
AHHH!
MY ARM! YOU FUCKED UP MY ARM, MOTHERFUCKER!
I smell piss.
I'M...
The city smells of rotting garbage.
SOCK
UGH...

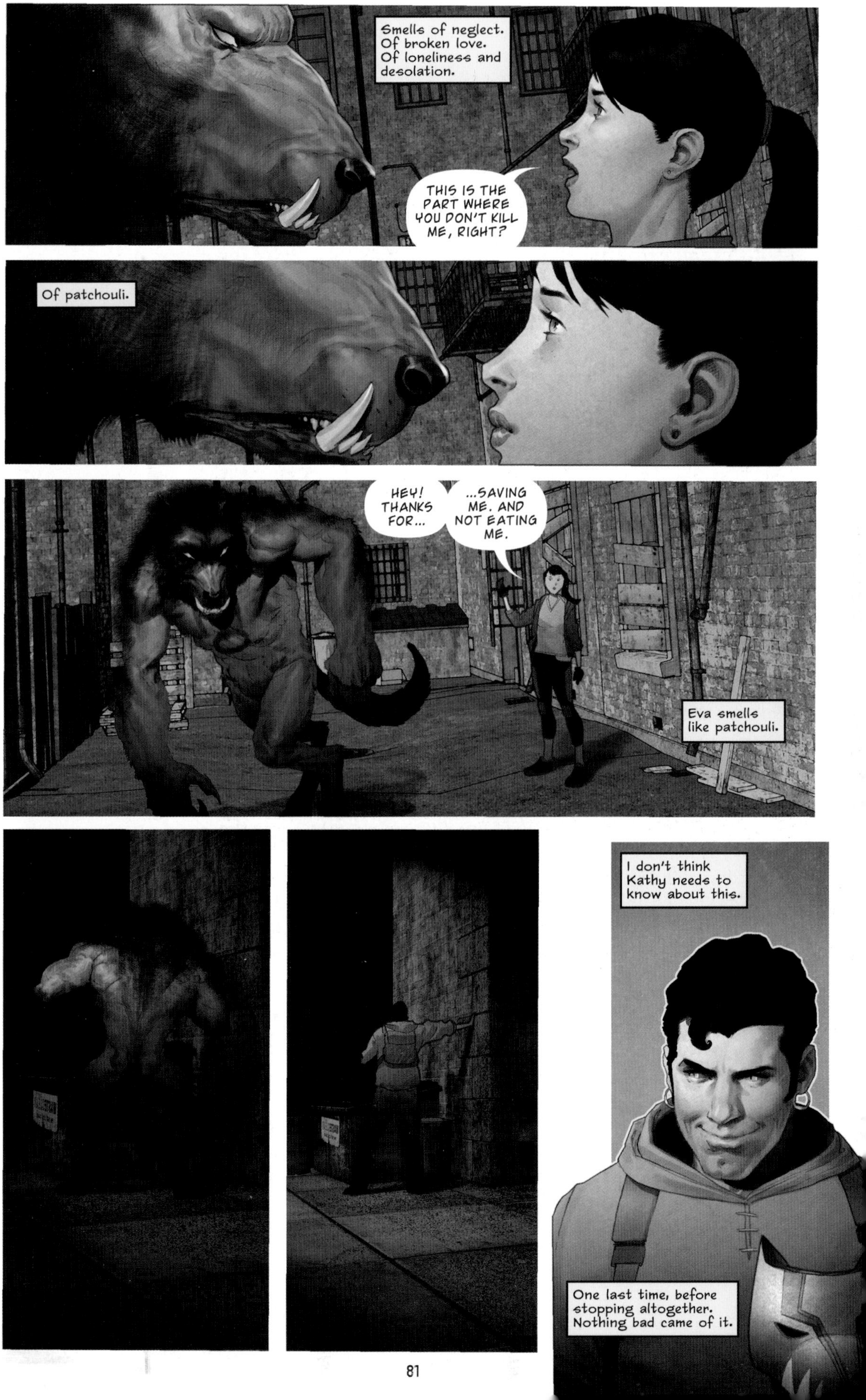

Smells of neglect. Of broken love. Of loneliness and desolation.
THIS IS THE PART WHERE YOU DON'T KILL ME, RIGHT?
Of patchouli.
HEY! THANKS FOR...
...SAVING ME. AND NOT EATING ME.
Eva smells like patchouli.
I don't think Kathy needs to know about this.
One last time, before stopping altogether. Nothing bad came of it.

...AND IF YOU LOOK CAREFULLY, THE MASKS DON'T HAVE A SCRATCH ON THEM.

NO.

EXCUSE ME?

I SAID NO.

YOU CANNOT GIVE UP BEING ICH.

OF COURSE I CAN. I'M DOING IT RIGHT NOW, RIGHT?

UNTIL TWO DAYS AGO, I HADN'T THE FOGGIEST IDEA OF THIS WHOLE MYSTICAL CHARADE OF MASKS AND BEASTS, AND NOW I JUST WANNA GO BACK TO THAT PEACEFUL IGNORANCE AS IF NOTHING EVER HAPPENED.

UNTIL TWO DAYS AGO, YOU DID NOT HAVE THE FOGGIEST IDEA THAT YOU WERE ICH, BOY.

HOWEVER, YOU WERE. AS YOU REMAIN TODAY. AND TOMORROW. AND SO ON UNTIL THE DAY YOU ARE GONE AND WHAT YOU HAVE INSIDE PASSES ON TO THE NEXT.

BECAUSE THAT'S THE WAY THINGS WORK IN THE REAL WORLD.

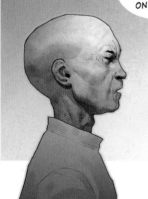

WELL, THEN IT'LL HAVE TO REMAIN INSIDE ME AS IT WAS BEFORE. CALM AND HIDDEN.

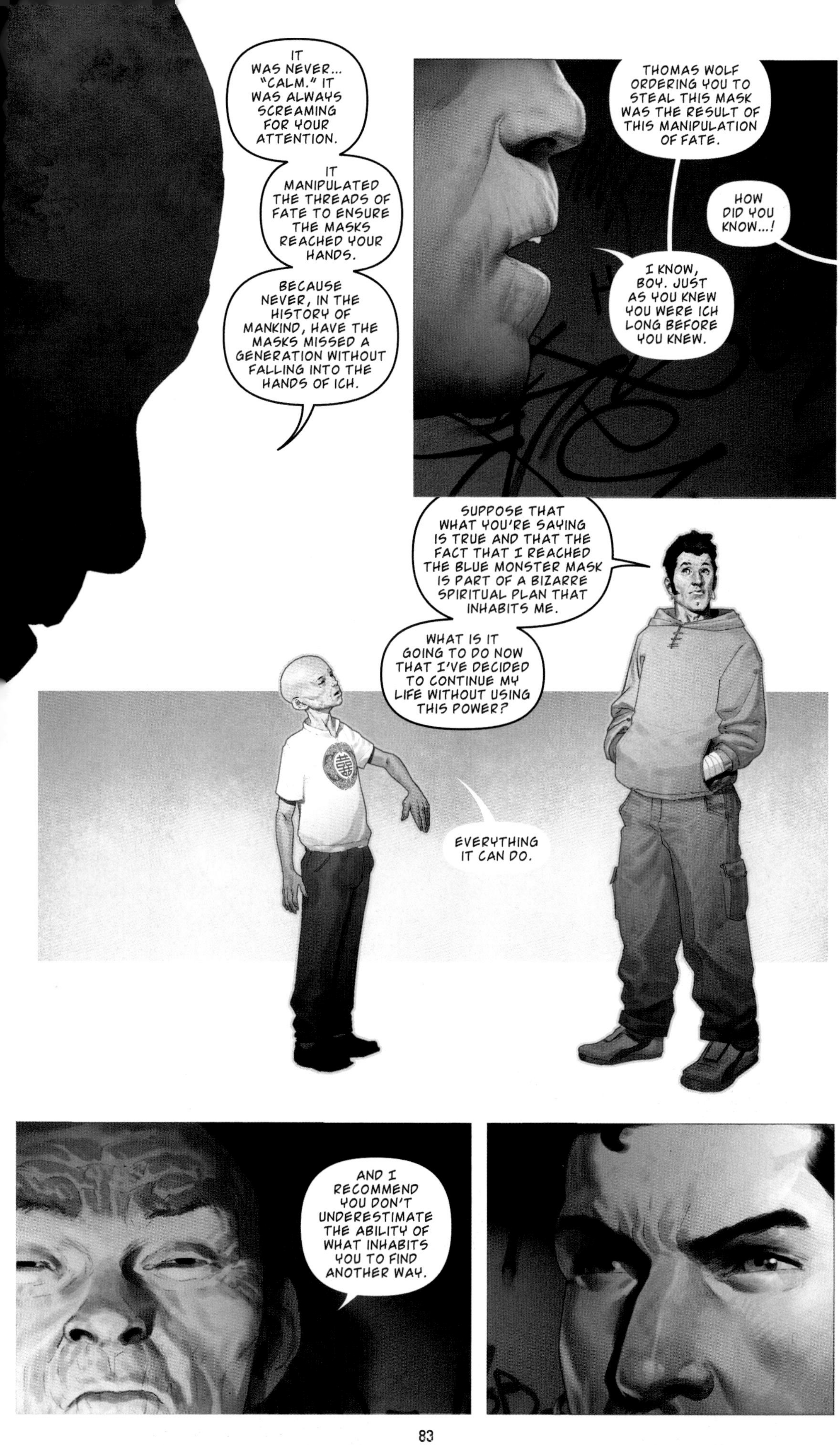
IT WAS NEVER... "CALM." IT WAS ALWAYS SCREAMING FOR YOUR ATTENTION.
IT MANIPULATED THE THREADS OF FATE TO ENSURE THE MASKS REACHED YOUR HANDS.
BECAUSE NEVER, IN THE HISTORY OF MANKIND, HAVE THE MASKS MISSED A GENERATION WITHOUT FALLING INTO THE HANDS OF ICH.
THOMAS WOLF ORDERING YOU TO STEAL THIS MASK WAS THE RESULT OF THIS MANIPULATION OF FATE.
HOW DID YOU KNOW...!
I KNOW, BOY. JUST AS YOU KNEW YOU WERE ICH LONG BEFORE YOU KNEW.
SUPPOSE THAT WHAT YOU'RE SAYING IS TRUE AND THAT THE FACT THAT I REACHED THE BLUE MONSTER MASK IS PART OF A BIZARRE SPIRITUAL PLAN THAT INHABITS ME.
WHAT IS IT GOING TO DO NOW THAT I'VE DECIDED TO CONTINUE MY LIFE WITHOUT USING THIS POWER?
EVERYTHING IT CAN DO.
AND I RECOMMEND YOU DON'T UNDERESTIMATE THE ABILITY OF WHAT INHABITS YOU TO FIND ANOTHER WAY.

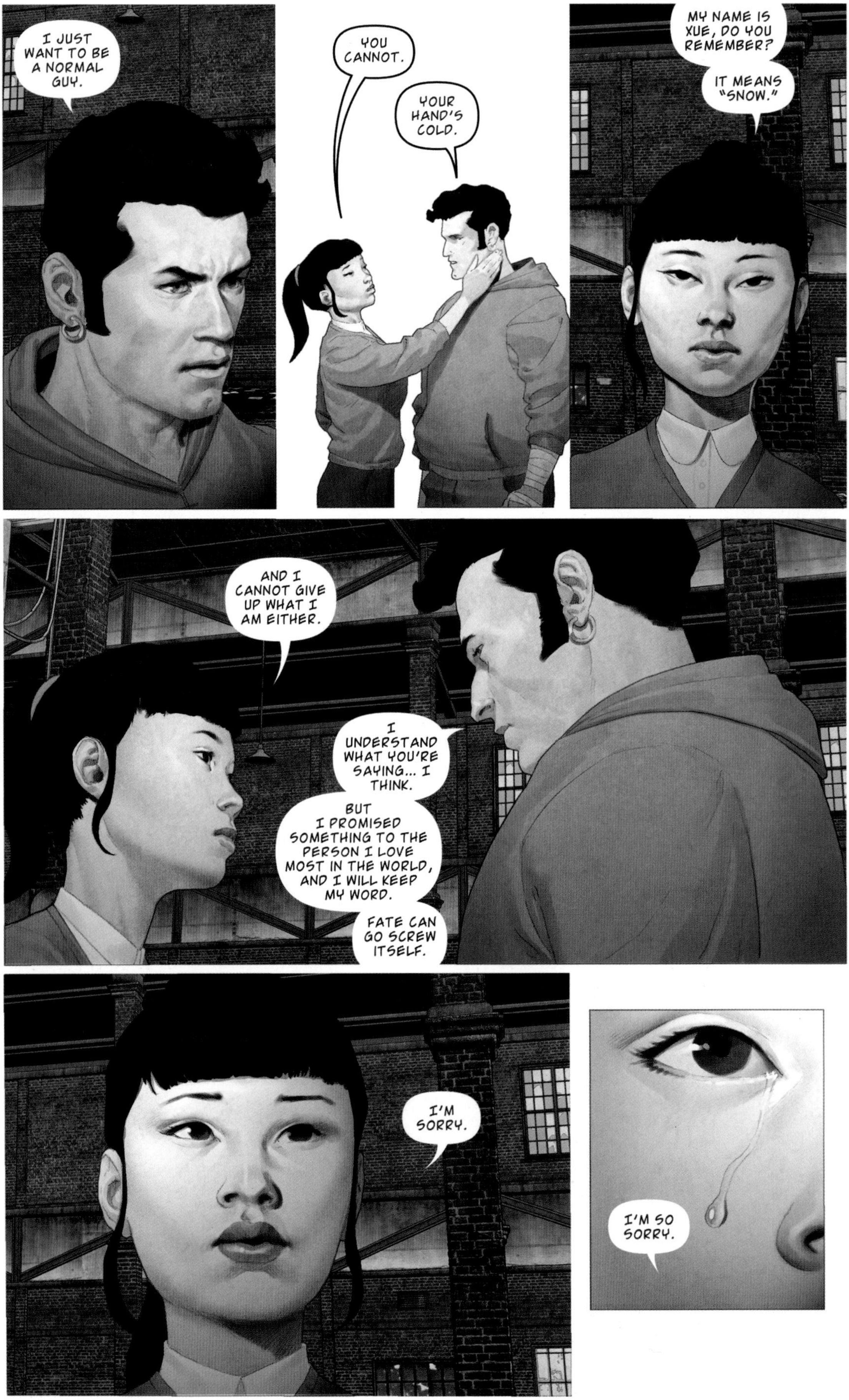
I JUST WANT TO BE A NORMAL GUY.
YOU CANNOT.
YOUR HAND'S COLD.
MY NAME IS XUE, DO YOU REMEMBER?
IT MEANS "SNOW."
AND I CANNOT GIVE UP WHAT I AM EITHER.
I UNDERSTAND WHAT YOU'RE SAYING... I THINK.
BUT I PROMISED SOMETHING TO THE PERSON I LOVE MOST IN THE WORLD, AND I WILL KEEP MY WORD.
FATE CAN GO SCREW ITSELF.
I'M SORRY.
I'M SO SORRY.

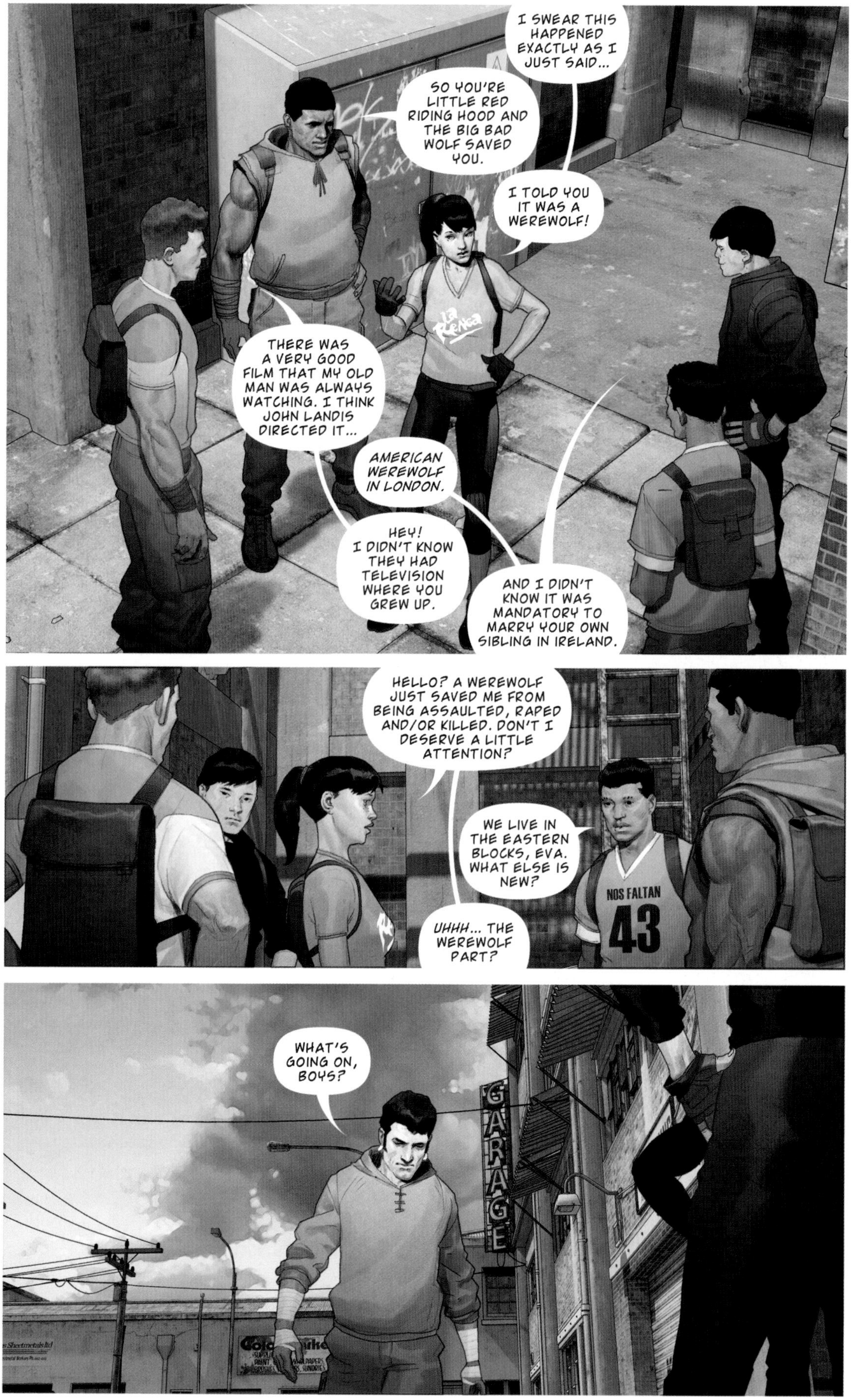
I SWEAR THIS HAPPENED EXACTLY AS I JUST SAID...
SO YOU'RE LITTLE RED RIDING HOOD AND THE BIG BAD WOLF SAVED YOU.
I TOLD YOU IT WAS A WEREWOLF!
La Renga
THERE WAS A VERY GOOD FILM THAT MY OLD MAN WAS ALWAYS WATCHING. I THINK JOHN LANDIS DIRECTED IT...
AMERICAN WEREWOLF IN LONDON.
HEY! I DIDN'T KNOW THEY HAD TELEVISION WHERE YOU GREW UP.
AND I DIDN'T KNOW IT WAS MANDATORY TO MARRY YOUR OWN SIBLING IN IRELAND.
HELLO? A WEREWOLF JUST SAVED ME FROM BEING ASSAULTED, RAPED AND/OR KILLED. DON'T I DESERVE A LITTLE ATTENTION?
WE LIVE IN THE EASTERN BLOCKS, EVA. WHAT ELSE IS NEW?
NOS FALTAN 43
UHHH... THE WEREWOLF PART?
WHAT'S GOING ON, BOYS?
GARAGE

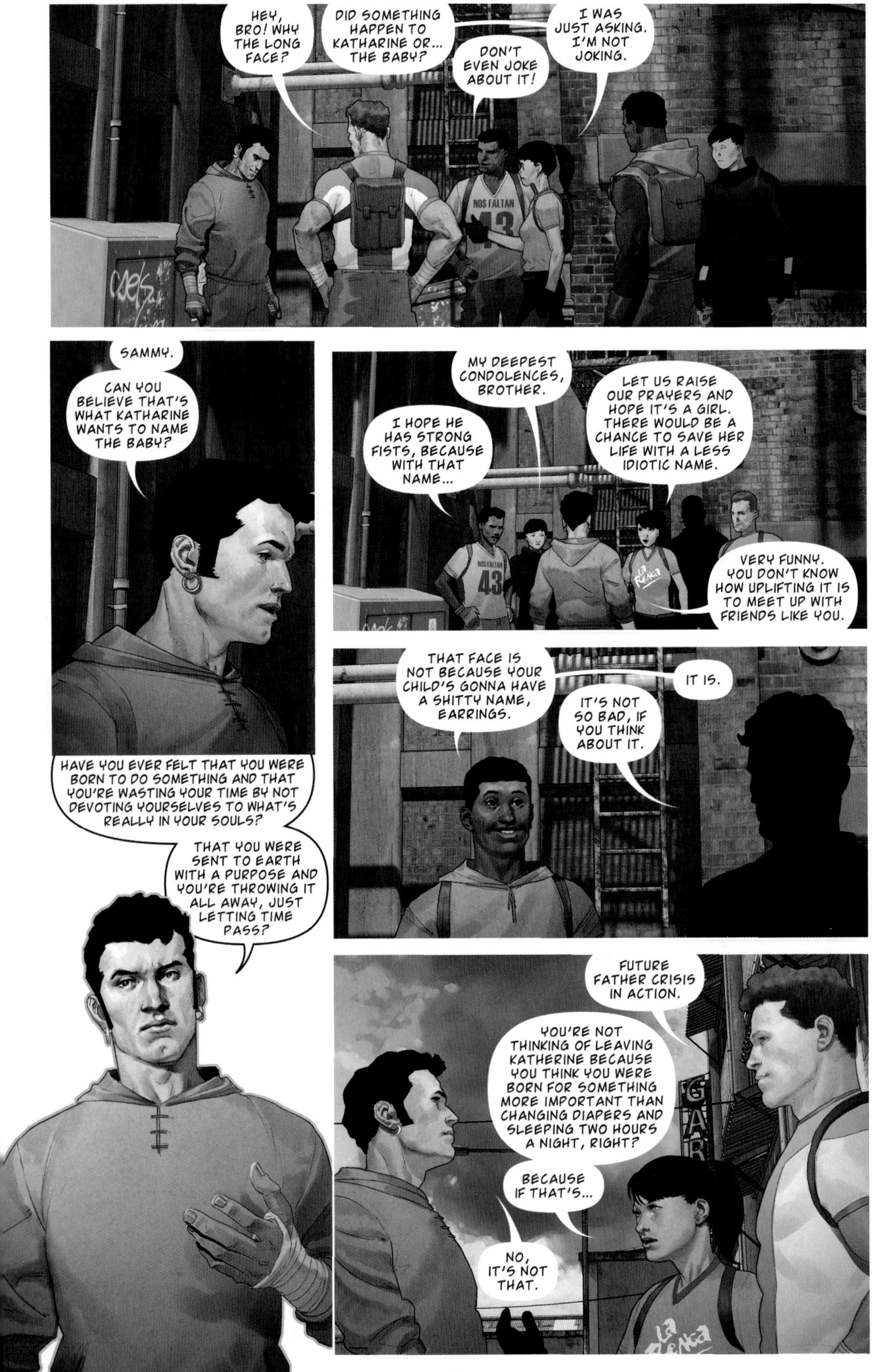
HEY, BRO! WHY THE LONG FACE?
DID SOMETHING HAPPEN TO KATHARINE OR... THE BABY?
DON'T EVEN JOKE ABOUT IT!
I WAS JUST ASKING. I'M NOT JOKING.
NOS FALTAN 43
SAMMY.
CAN YOU BELIEVE THAT'S WHAT KATHARINE WANTS TO NAME THE BABY?
I HOPE HE HAS STRONG FISTS, BECAUSE WITH THAT NAME...
MY DEEPEST CONDOLENCES, BROTHER.
LET US RAISE OUR PRAYERS AND HOPE IT'S A GIRL. THERE WOULD BE A CHANCE TO SAVE HER LIFE WITH A LESS IDIOTIC NAME.
VERY FUNNY. YOU DON'T KNOW HOW UPLIFTING IT IS TO MEET UP WITH FRIENDS LIKE YOU.
THAT FACE IS NOT BECAUSE YOUR CHILD'S GONNA HAVE A SHITTY NAME, EARRINGS.
IT IS.
IT'S NOT SO BAD, IF YOU THINK ABOUT IT.
HAVE YOU EVER FELT THAT YOU WERE BORN TO DO SOMETHING AND THAT YOU'RE WASTING YOUR TIME BY NOT DEVOTING YOURSELVES TO WHAT'S REALLY IN YOUR SOULS?
THAT YOU WERE SENT TO EARTH WITH A PURPOSE AND YOU'RE THROWING IT ALL AWAY, JUST LETTING TIME PASS?
FUTURE FATHER CRISIS IN ACTION.
YOU'RE NOT THINKING OF LEAVING KATHERINE BECAUSE YOU THINK YOU WERE BORN FOR SOMETHING MORE IMPORTANT THAN CHANGING DIAPERS AND SLEEPING TWO HOURS A NIGHT, RIGHT?
BECAUSE IF THAT'S...
NO, IT'S NOT THAT.

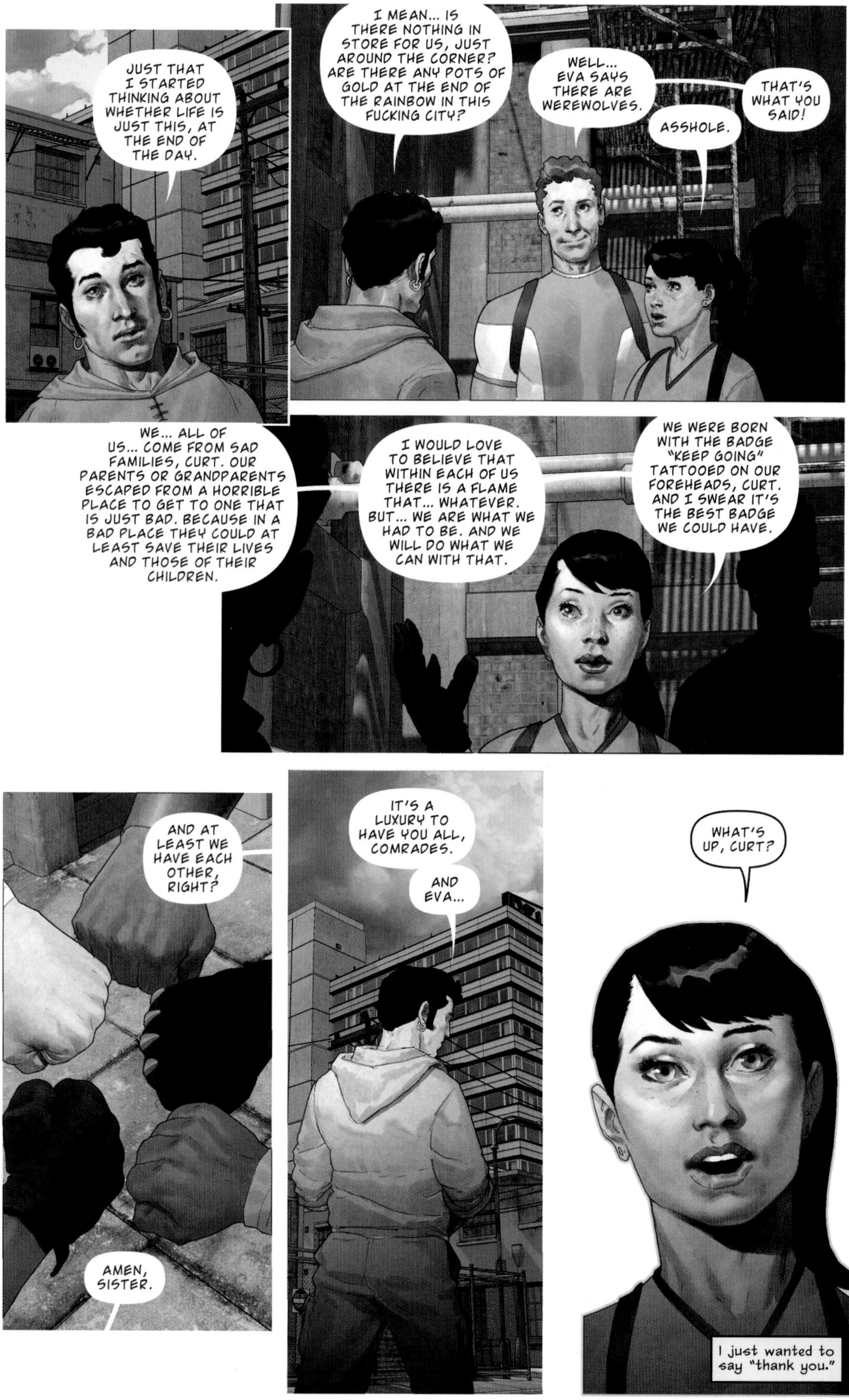
JUST THAT I STARTED THINKING ABOUT WHETHER LIFE IS JUST THIS, AT THE END OF THE DAY.
I MEAN... IS THERE NOTHING IN STORE FOR US, JUST AROUND THE CORNER? ARE THERE ANY POTS OF GOLD AT THE END OF THE RAINBOW IN THIS FUCKING CITY?
WELL... EVA SAYS THERE ARE WEREWOLVES.
THAT'S WHAT YOU SAID!
ASSHOLE.
WE... ALL OF US... COME FROM SAD FAMILIES, CURT. OUR PARENTS OR GRANDPARENTS ESCAPED FROM A HORRIBLE PLACE TO GET TO ONE THAT IS JUST BAD. BECAUSE IN A BAD PLACE THEY COULD AT LEAST SAVE THEIR LIVES AND THOSE OF THEIR CHILDREN.
I WOULD LOVE TO BELIEVE THAT WITHIN EACH OF US THERE IS A FLAME THAT... WHATEVER. BUT... WE ARE WHAT WE HAD TO BE. AND WE WILL DO WHAT WE CAN WITH THAT.
WE WERE BORN WITH THE BADGE "KEEP GOING" TATTOOED ON OUR FOREHEADS, CURT. AND I SWEAR IT'S THE BEST BADGE WE COULD HAVE.
AND AT LEAST WE HAVE EACH OTHER, RIGHT?
AMEN, SISTER.
IT'S A LUXURY TO HAVE YOU ALL, COMRADES.
AND EVA...
WHAT'S UP, CURT?
I just wanted to say "thank you."

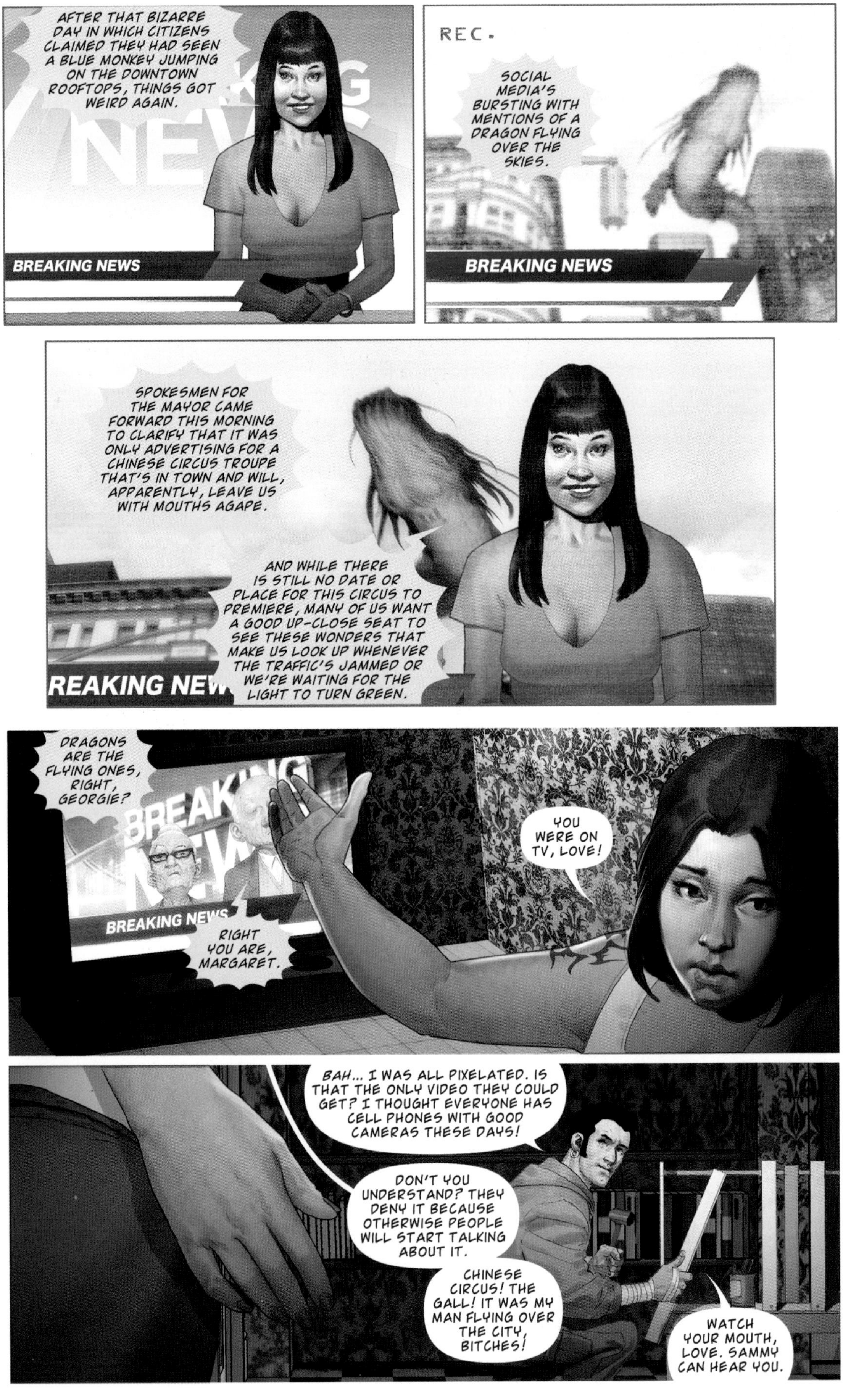
AFTER THAT BIZARRE DAY IN WHICH CITIZENS CLAIMED THEY HAD SEEN A BLUE MONKEY JUMPING ON THE DOWNTOWN ROOFTOPS, THINGS GOT WEIRD AGAIN.
BREAKING NEWS
REC.
SOCIAL MEDIA'S BURSTING WITH MENTIONS OF A DRAGON FLYING OVER THE SKIES.
BREAKING NEWS
SPOKESMEN FOR THE MAYOR CAME FORWARD THIS MORNING TO CLARIFY THAT IT WAS ONLY ADVERTISING FOR A CHINESE CIRCUS TROUPE THAT'S IN TOWN AND WILL, APPARENTLY, LEAVE US WITH MOUTHS AGAPE.
AND WHILE THERE IS STILL NO DATE OR PLACE FOR THIS CIRCUS TO PREMIERE, MANY OF US WANT A GOOD UP-CLOSE SEAT TO SEE THESE WONDERS THAT MAKE US LOOK UP WHENEVER THE TRAFFIC'S JAMMED OR WE'RE WAITING FOR THE LIGHT TO TURN GREEN.
REAKING NEW
DRAGONS ARE THE FLYING ONES, RIGHT, GEORGIE?
BREAKING NEWS
RIGHT YOU ARE, MARGARET.
YOU WERE ON TV, LOVE!
BAH... I WAS ALL PIXELATED. IS THAT THE ONLY VIDEO THEY COULD GET? I THOUGHT EVERYONE HAS CELL PHONES WITH GOOD CAMERAS THESE DAYS!
DON'T YOU UNDERSTAND? THEY DENY IT BECAUSE OTHERWISE PEOPLE WILL START TALKING ABOUT IT.
CHINESE CIRCUS! THE GALL! IT WAS MY MAN FLYING OVER THE CITY, BITCHES!
WATCH YOUR MOUTH, LOVE. SAMMY CAN HEAR YOU.

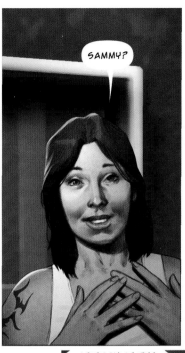

SAMMY?

DO YOU REALLY LIKE THE NAME?

WELL... I...

WE'LL PAINT HIS ROOM ORANGE. ORANGE IS NEUTRAL. IF THE BABY'S A GIRL, WE'LL PUT UP THAT BEAUTIFUL PINK VINYL THEY SELL AT THE MALL. AND IF IT'S A BOY, WE'LL PUT UP STARS.

AS SOON AS THE CRADLE'S FINISHED, WE'LL OPEN THE WINE BOTTLE VITO GAVE YOU... I STILL CAN'T BELIEVE HE GAVE YOU THAT JOB... WE'LL CELEBRATE!

SAMANTHA TOLD ME THAT IF I TAKE A FEW SIPS OF WINE, IT RELAXES THE BABY. JUST DON'T DRINK THE WHOLE GLASS, OR SOMETHING LIKE THAT. WE ARE TALKING ABOUT THE ROOM FOR OUR BABY, LOVE!

WELL... ACTUALLY, IT'S YOU TALKING NONSTOP WHILE I TRY TO FIGURE OUT HOW THE HELL THIS THING IS BUILT.

YOU KNOW WHAT I COULD USE RIGHT NOW, ACTUALLY?

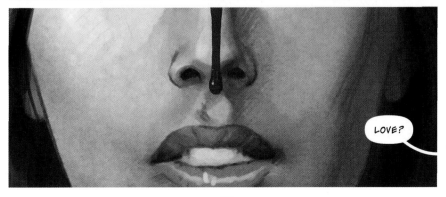

LOVE?

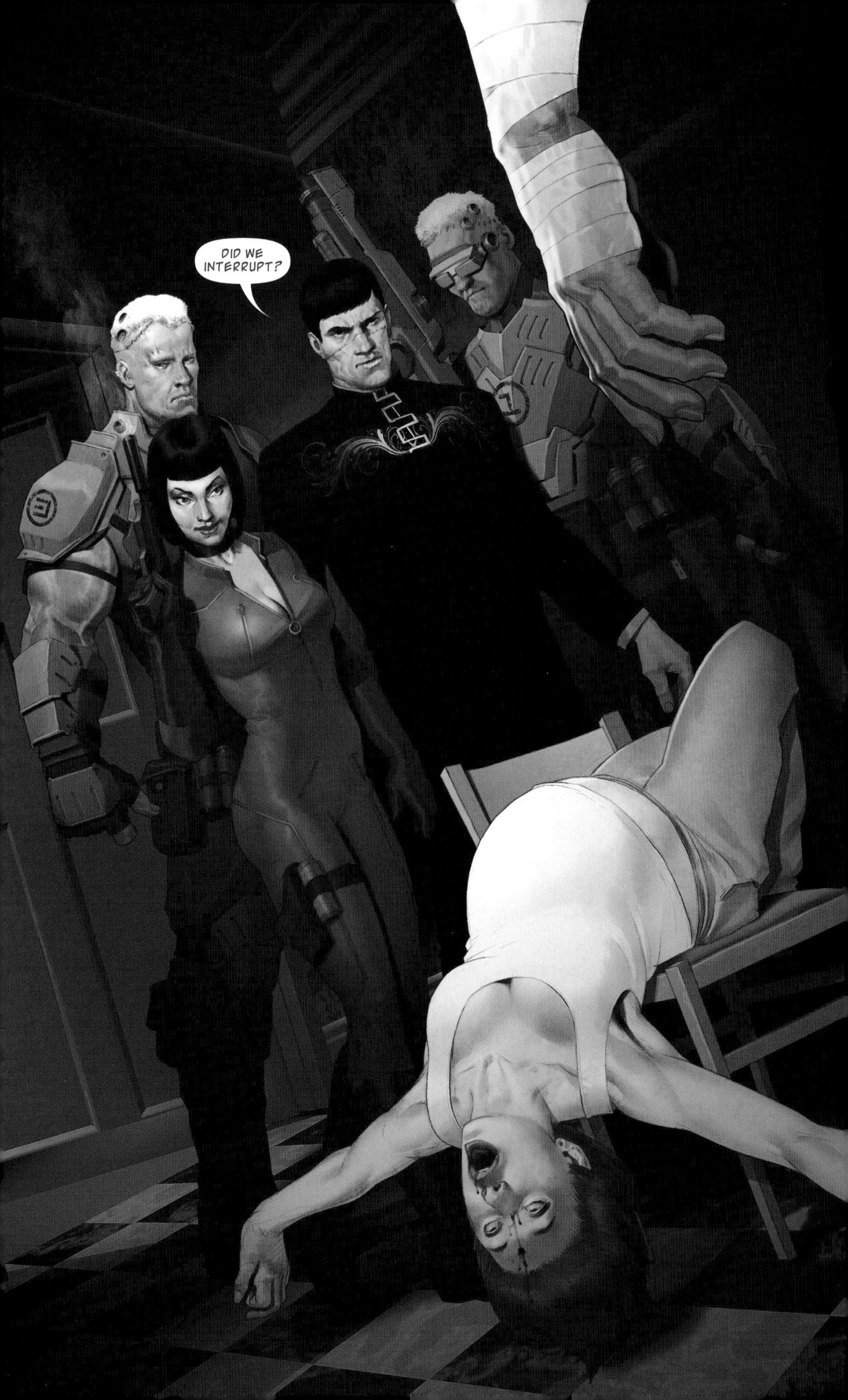
DID WE INTERRUPT?

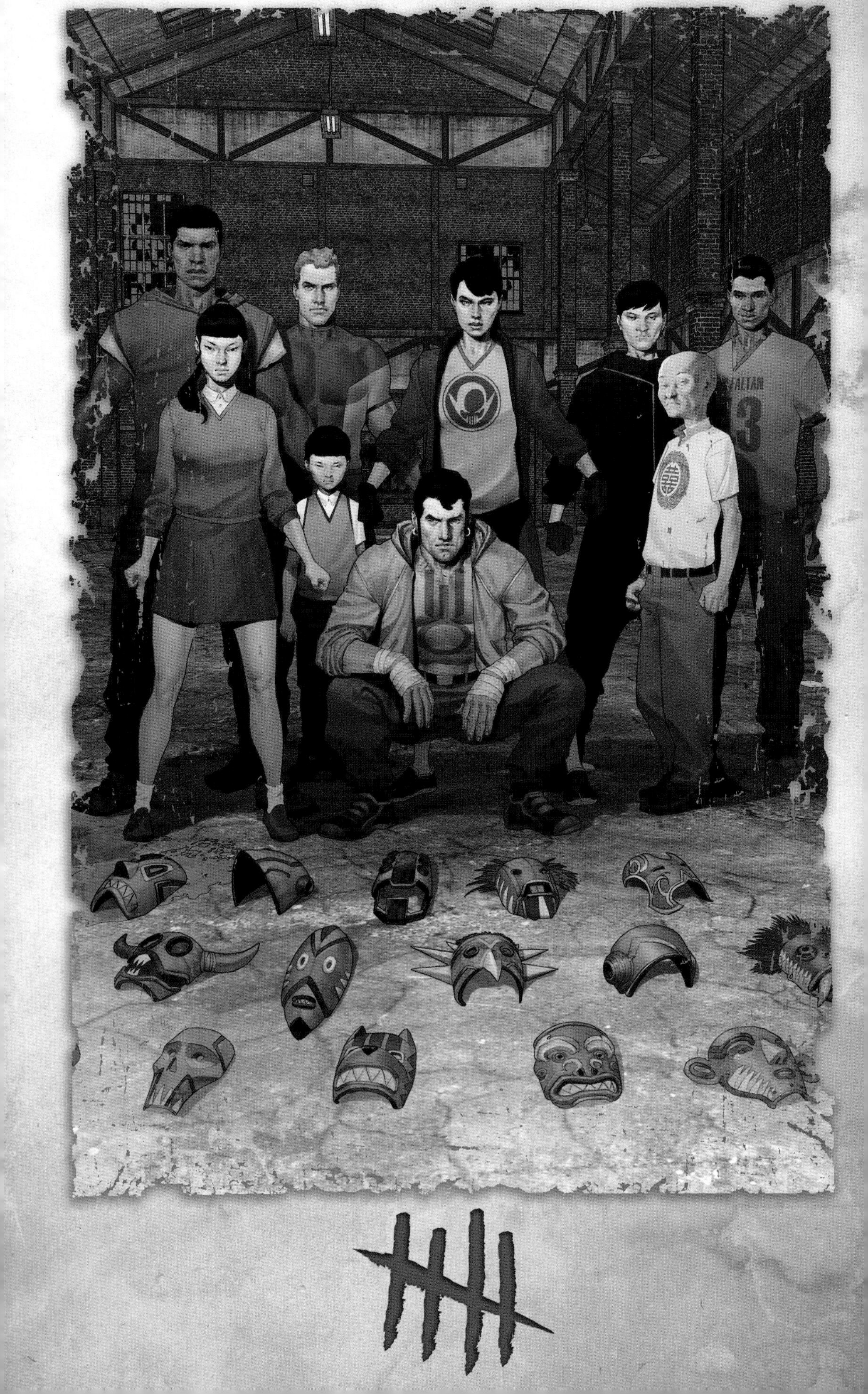
FALTAN

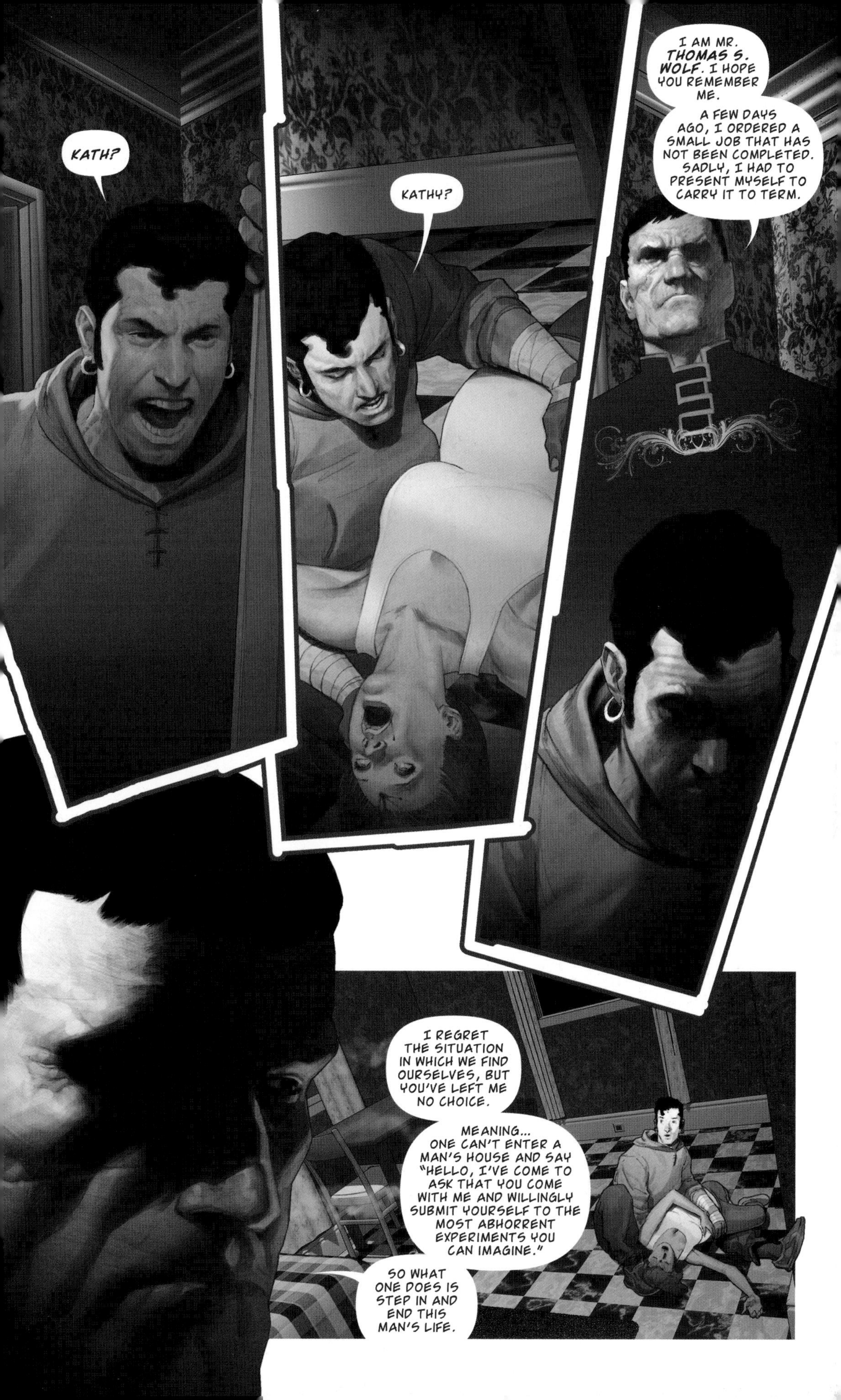
KATH?
KATHY?
I AM MR. THOMAS S. WOLF. I HOPE YOU REMEMBER ME.
A FEW DAYS AGO, I ORDERED A SMALL JOB THAT HAS NOT BEEN COMPLETED. SADLY, I HAD TO PRESENT MYSELF TO CARRY IT TO TERM.
I REGRET THE SITUATION IN WHICH WE FIND OURSELVES, BUT YOU'VE LEFT ME NO CHOICE.
MEANING... ONE CAN'T ENTER A MAN'S HOUSE AND SAY "HELLO, I'VE COME TO ASK THAT YOU COME WITH ME AND WILLINGLY SUBMIT YOURSELF TO THE MOST ABHORRENT EXPERIMENTS YOU CAN IMAGINE."
SO WHAT ONE DOES IS STEP IN AND END THIS MAN'S LIFE.

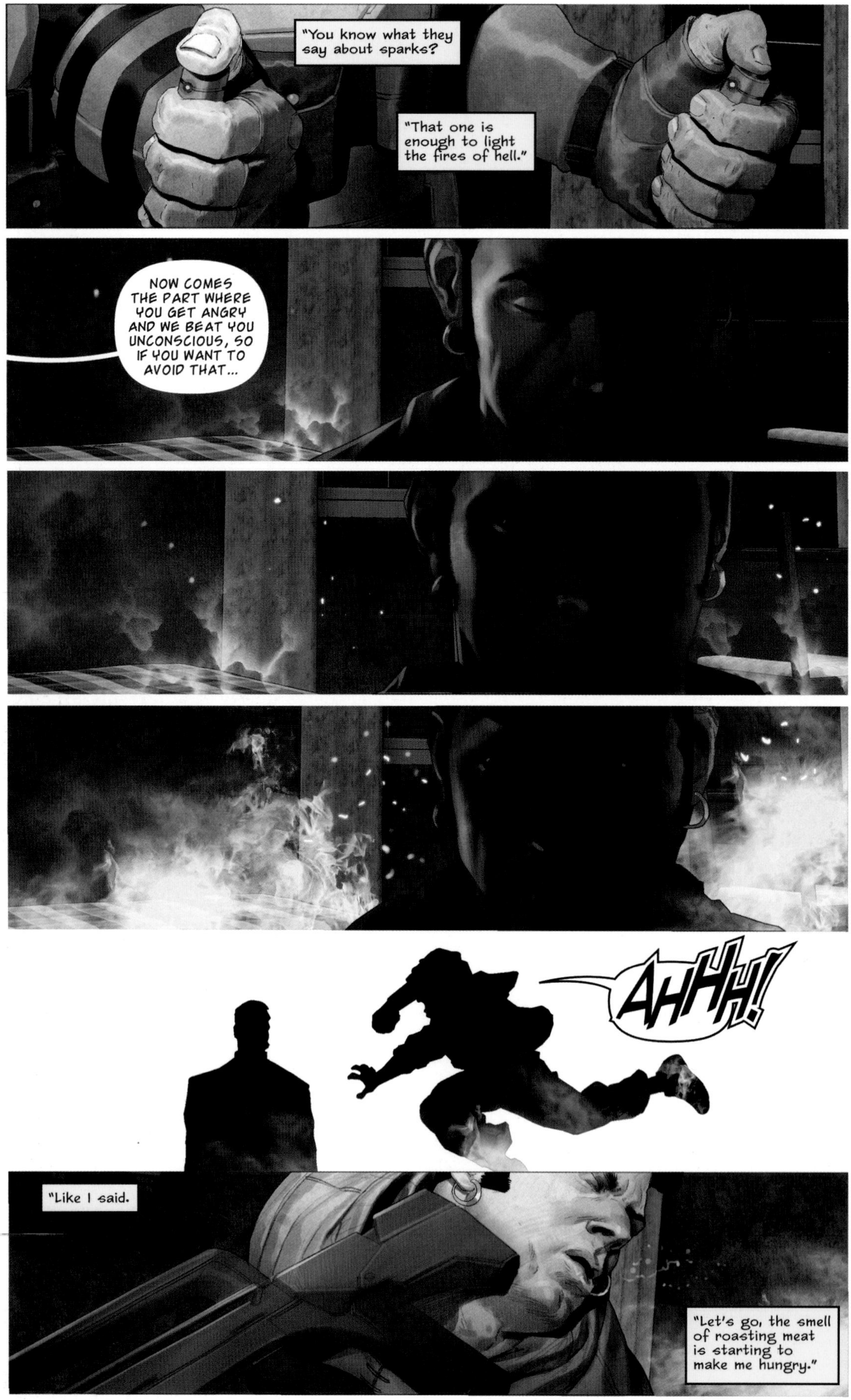
"You know what they say about sparks?
"That one is enough to light the fires of hell."
NOW COMES THE PART WHERE YOU GET ANGRY AND WE BEAT YOU UNCONSCIOUS, SO IF YOU WANT TO AVOID THAT...
AHHH!
"Like I said.
"Let's go, the smell of roasting meat is starting to make me hungry."

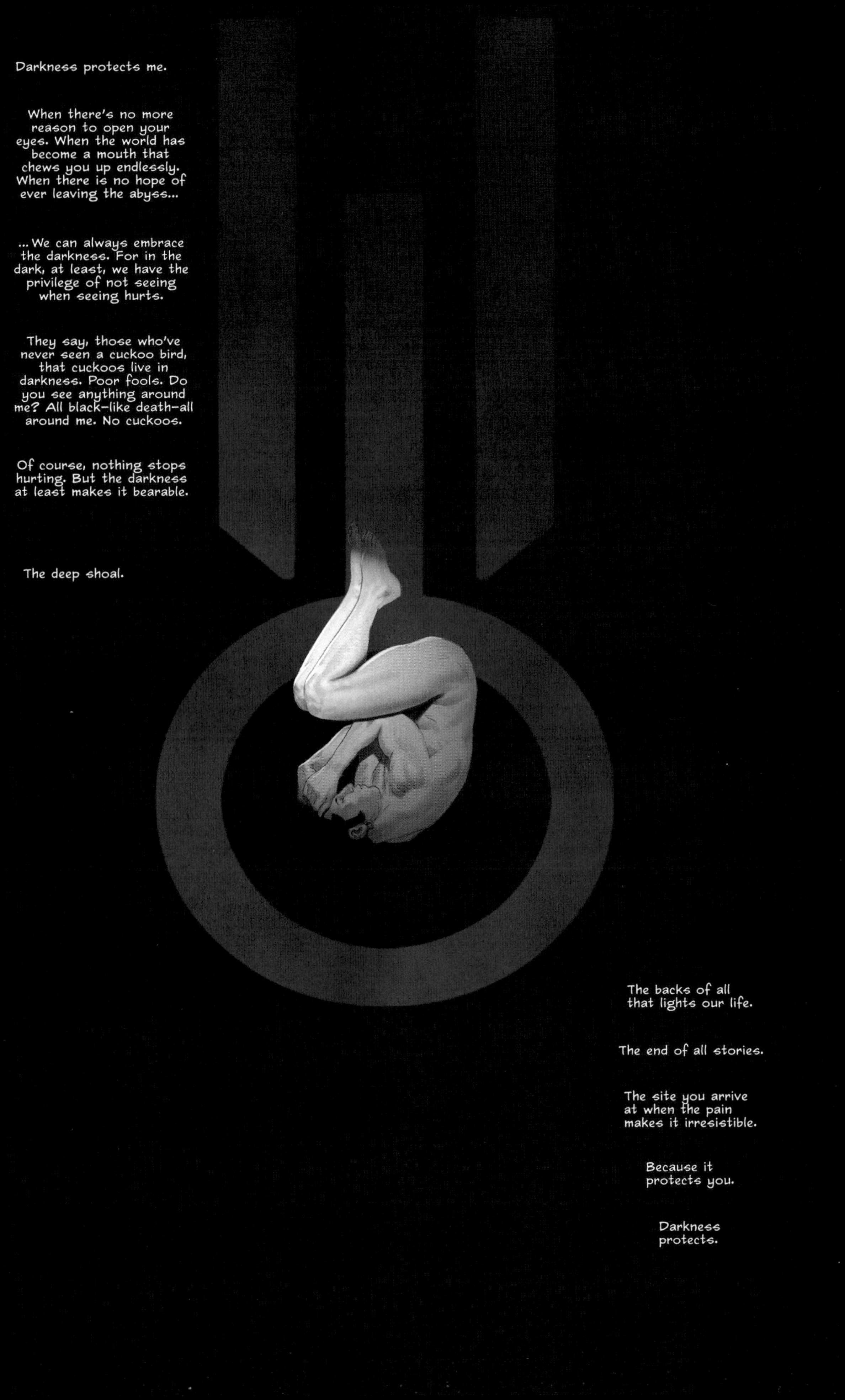

Darkness protects me.

When there's no more reason to open your eyes. When the world has become a mouth that chews you up endlessly. When there is no hope of ever leaving the abyss...

...We can always embrace the darkness. For in the dark, at least, we have the privilege of not seeing when seeing hurts.

They say, those who've never seen a cuckoo bird, that cuckoos live in darkness. Poor fools. Do you see anything around me? All black-like death-all around me. No cuckoos.

Of course, nothing stops hurting. But the darkness at least makes it bearable.

The deep shoal.

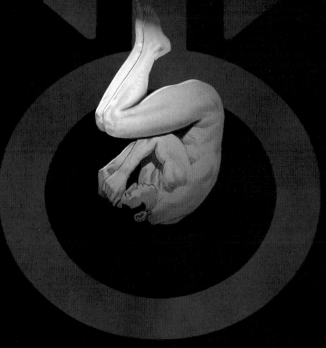

The backs of all that lights our life.

The end of all stories.

The site you arrive at when the pain makes it irresistible.

Because it protects you.

Darkness protects.

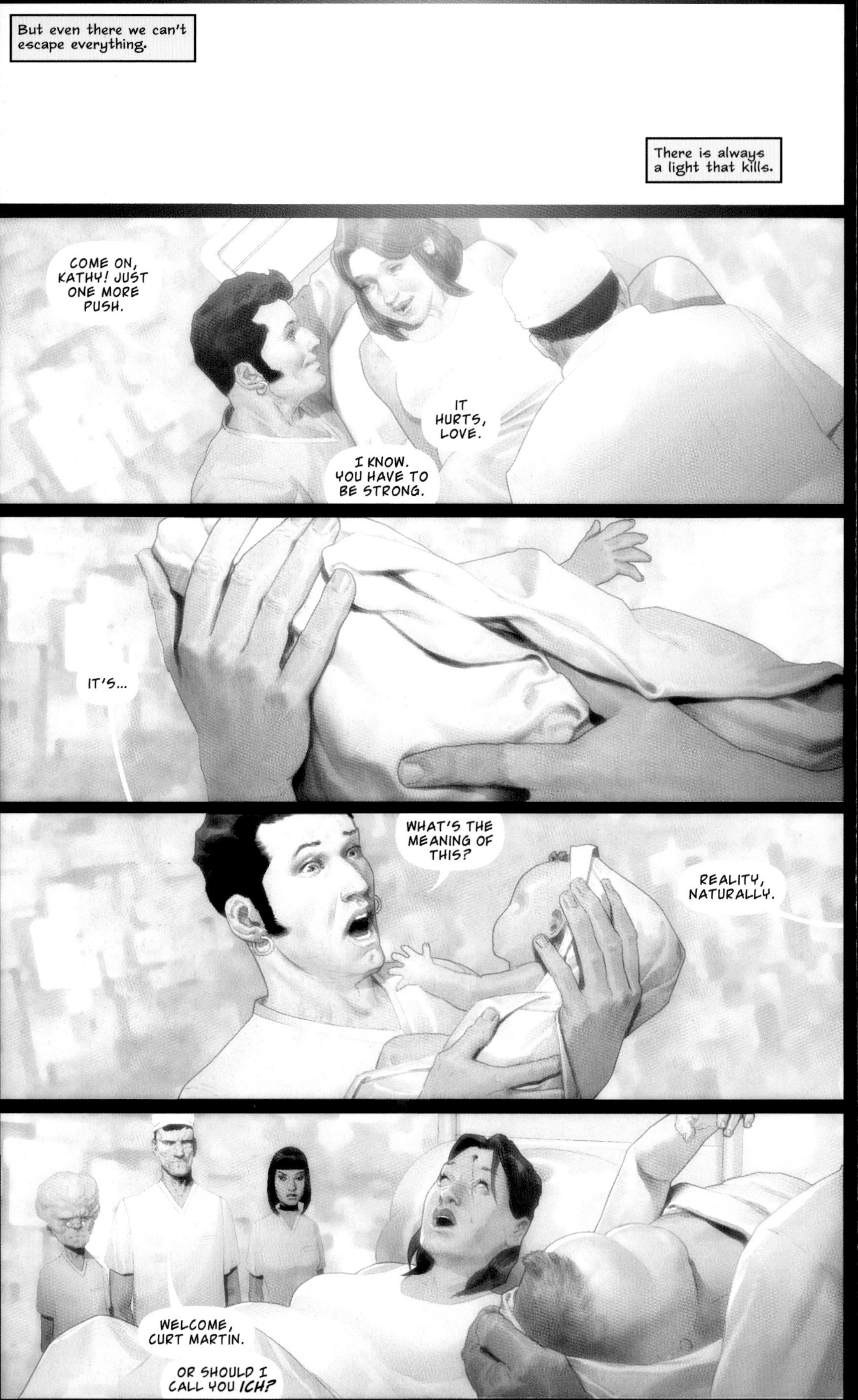
But even there we can't escape everything.
There is always a light that kills.
COME ON, KATHY! JUST ONE MORE PUSH.
IT HURTS, LOVE.
I KNOW. YOU HAVE TO BE STRONG.
IT'S...
WHAT'S THE MEANING OF THIS?
REALITY, NATURALLY.
WELCOME, CURT MARTIN.
OR SHOULD I CALL YOU *ICH?*

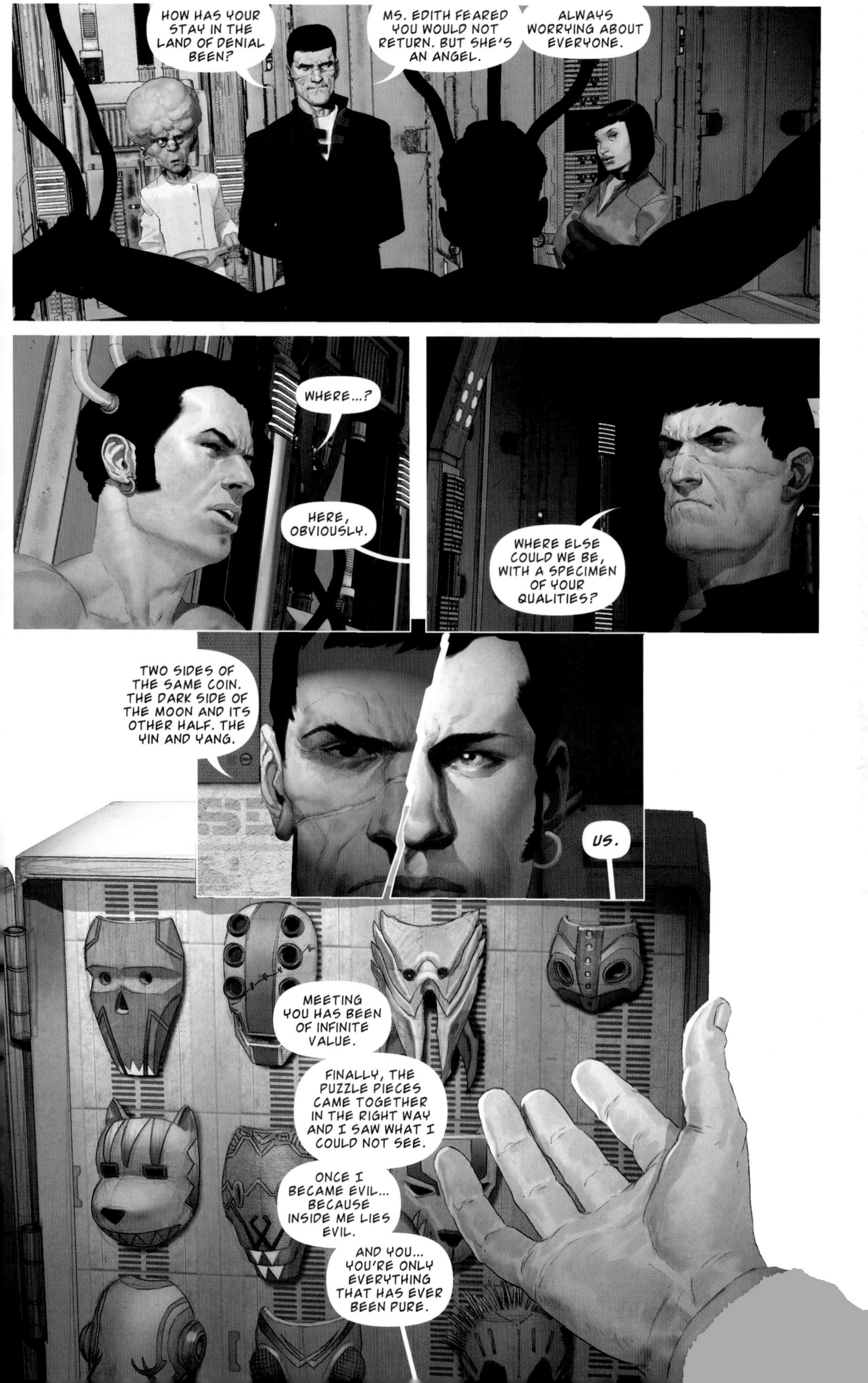
HOW HAS YOUR STAY IN THE LAND OF DENIAL BEEN?
MS. EDITH FEARED YOU WOULD NOT RETURN. BUT SHE'S AN ANGEL.
ALWAYS WORRYING ABOUT EVERYONE.
WHERE...?
HERE, OBVIOUSLY.
WHERE ELSE COULD WE BE, WITH A SPECIMEN OF YOUR QUALITIES?
TWO SIDES OF THE SAME COIN. THE DARK SIDE OF THE MOON AND ITS OTHER HALF. THE YIN AND YANG.
US.
MEETING YOU HAS BEEN OF INFINITE VALUE.
FINALLY, THE PUZZLE PIECES CAME TOGETHER IN THE RIGHT WAY AND I SAW WHAT I COULD NOT SEE.
ONCE I BECAME EVIL... BECAUSE INSIDE ME LIES EVIL.
AND YOU... YOU'RE ONLY EVERYTHING THAT HAS EVER BEEN PURE.

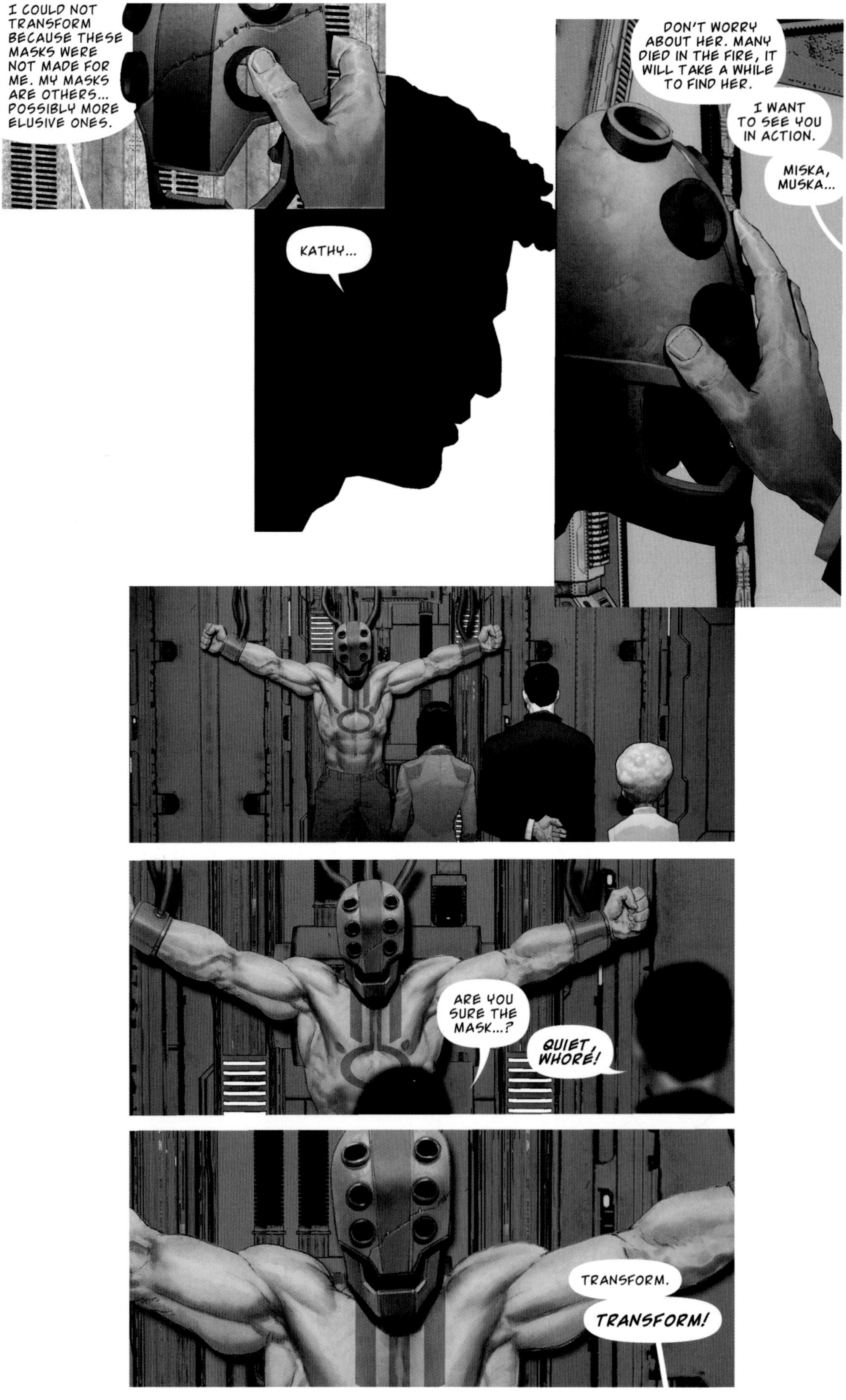
I COULD NOT TRANSFORM BECAUSE THESE MASKS WERE NOT MADE FOR ME. MY MASKS ARE OTHERS... POSSIBLY MORE ELUSIVE ONES.
KATHY...
DON'T WORRY ABOUT HER. MANY DIED IN THE FIRE, IT WILL TAKE A WHILE TO FIND HER.
I WANT TO SEE YOU IN ACTION.
MISKA, MUSKA...
ARE YOU SURE THE MASK...?
QUIET, WHORE!
TRANSFORM.
TRANSFORM!

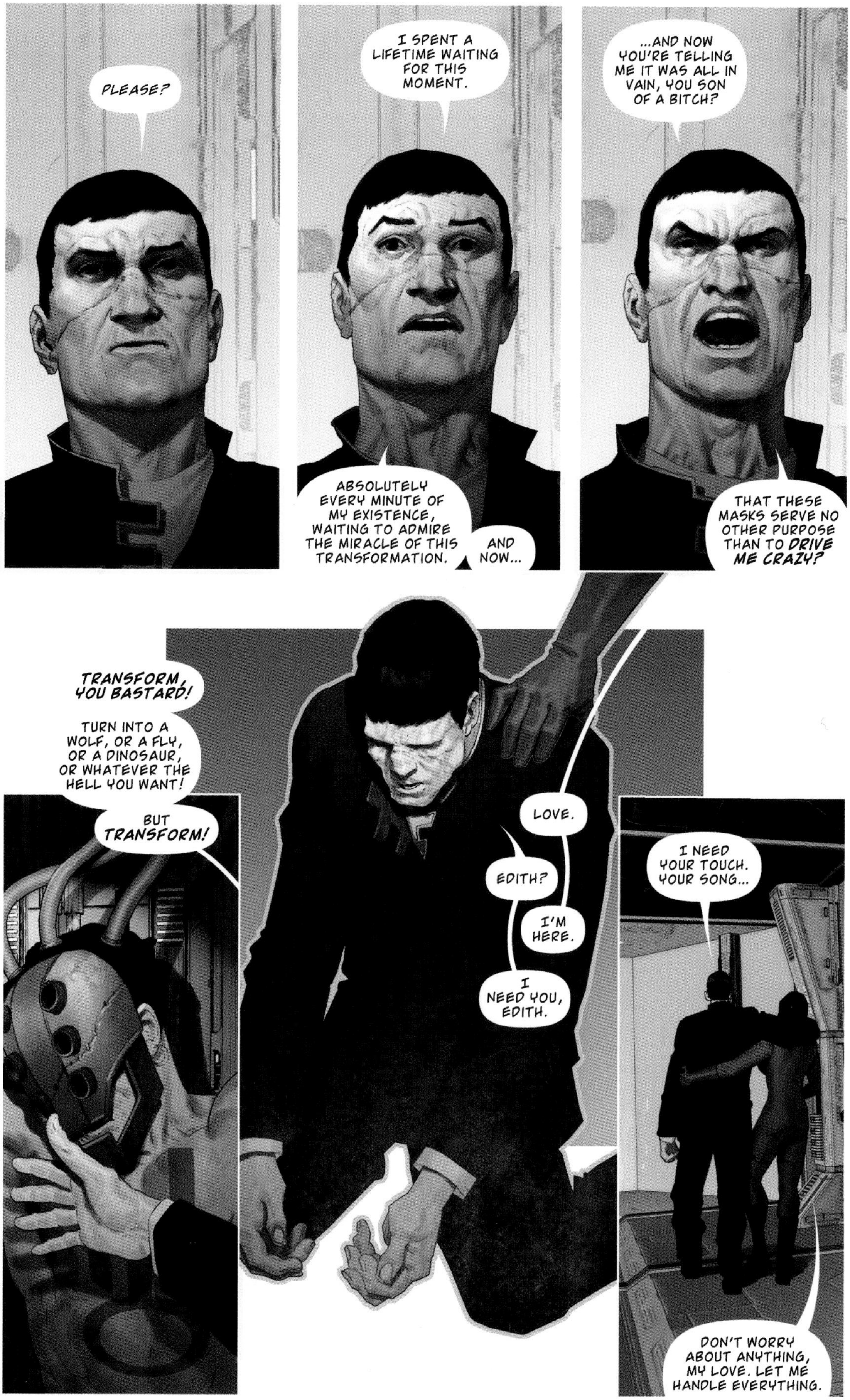
PLEASE?
I SPENT A LIFETIME WAITING FOR THIS MOMENT.
ABSOLUTELY EVERY MINUTE OF MY EXISTENCE, WAITING TO ADMIRE THE MIRACLE OF THIS TRANSFORMATION.
AND NOW...
...AND NOW YOU'RE TELLING ME IT WAS ALL IN VAIN, YOU SON OF A BITCH?
THAT THESE MASKS SERVE NO OTHER PURPOSE THAN TO DRIVE ME CRAZY?
TRANSFORM, YOU BASTARD!
TURN INTO A WOLF, OR A FLY, OR A DINOSAUR, OR WHATEVER THE HELL YOU WANT!
BUT TRANSFORM!
LOVE.
EDITH?
I'M HERE.
I NEED YOU, EDITH.
I NEED YOUR TOUCH. YOUR SONG...
DON'T WORRY ABOUT ANYTHING, MY LOVE. LET ME HANDLE EVERYTHING.

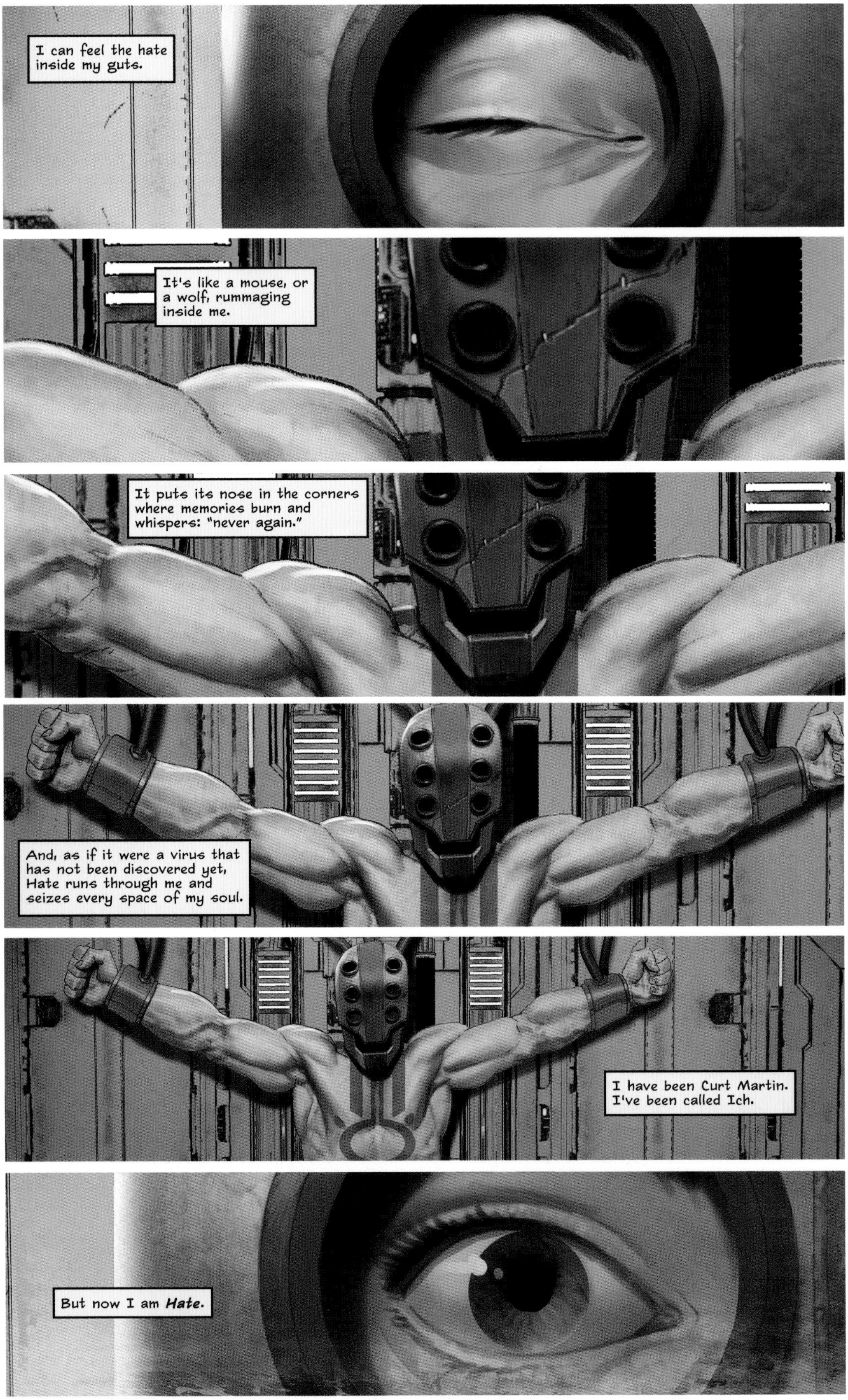

I can feel the hate inside my guts.
It's like a mouse, or a wolf, rummaging inside me.
It puts its nose in the corners where memories burn and whispers: "never again."
And, as if it were a virus that has not been discovered yet, Hate runs through me and seizes every space of my soul.
I have been Curt Martin. I've been called Ich.
But now I am *Hate*.

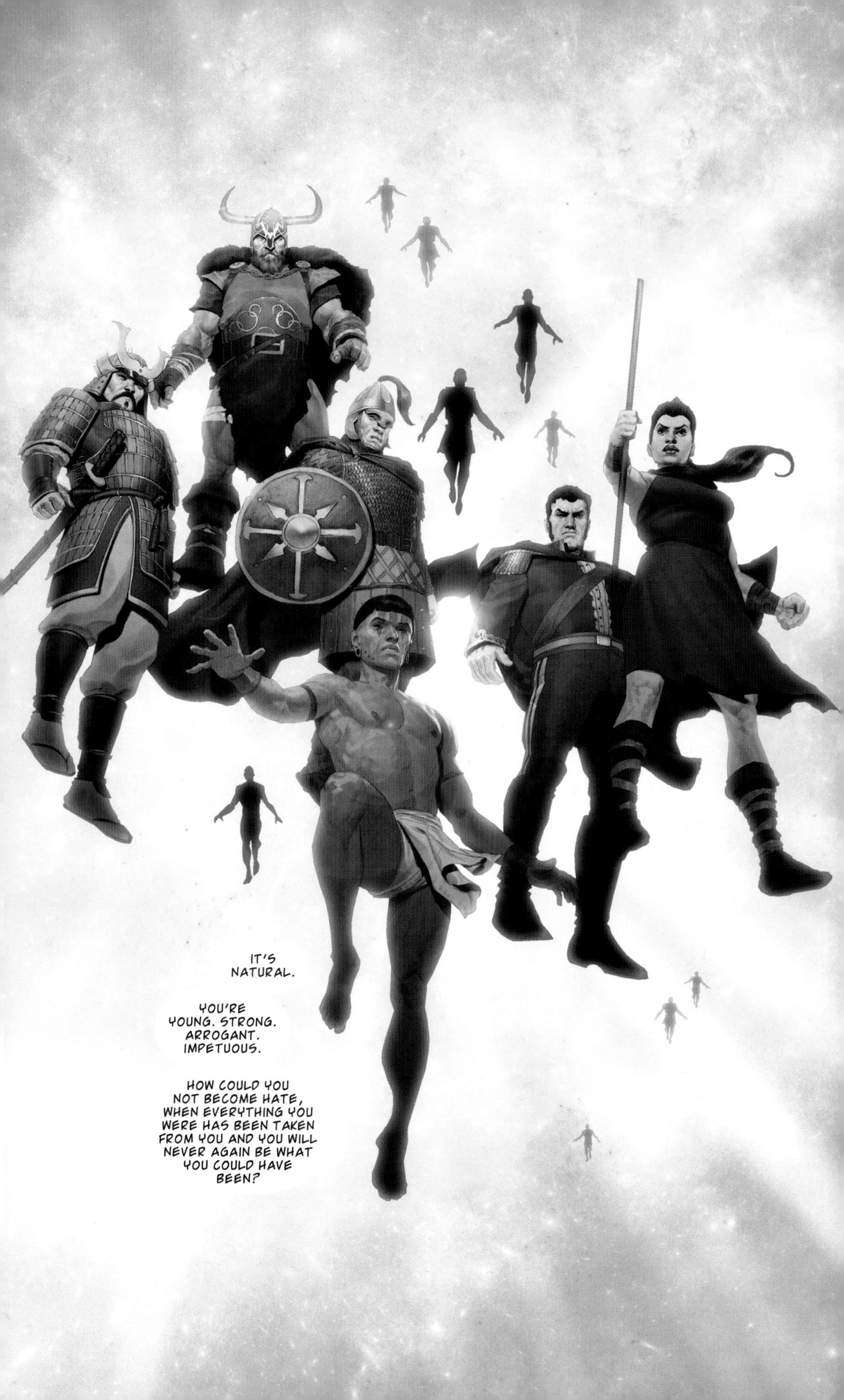
IT'S NATURAL.
YOU'RE YOUNG. STRONG. ARROGANT. IMPETUOUS.
HOW COULD YOU NOT BECOME HATE, WHEN EVERYTHING YOU WERE HAS BEEN TAKEN FROM YOU AND YOU WILL NEVER AGAIN BE WHAT YOU COULD HAVE BEEN?

ALL OF US HAVE LOST WHAT WAS OURS, ICH.

THEY HAVE BURNED OUR OFFSPRING.

THEY HAVE TORTURED EVERYONE WE LOVE.

THEY HAVE DENIED US OUR FREEDOM.

WE ALL TURNED OUR BACK ON THE STRENGTH THAT DWELLS WITHIN US.

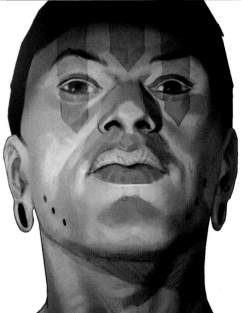

AND THE FORCE THAT LIVES WITHIN CAME BACK AGAIN, AGAIN AND AGAIN, UNTIL WE LEARNED TO ACCEPT IT.

WILL YOU ACCEPT THE POWER YOU HAVE INSIDE?

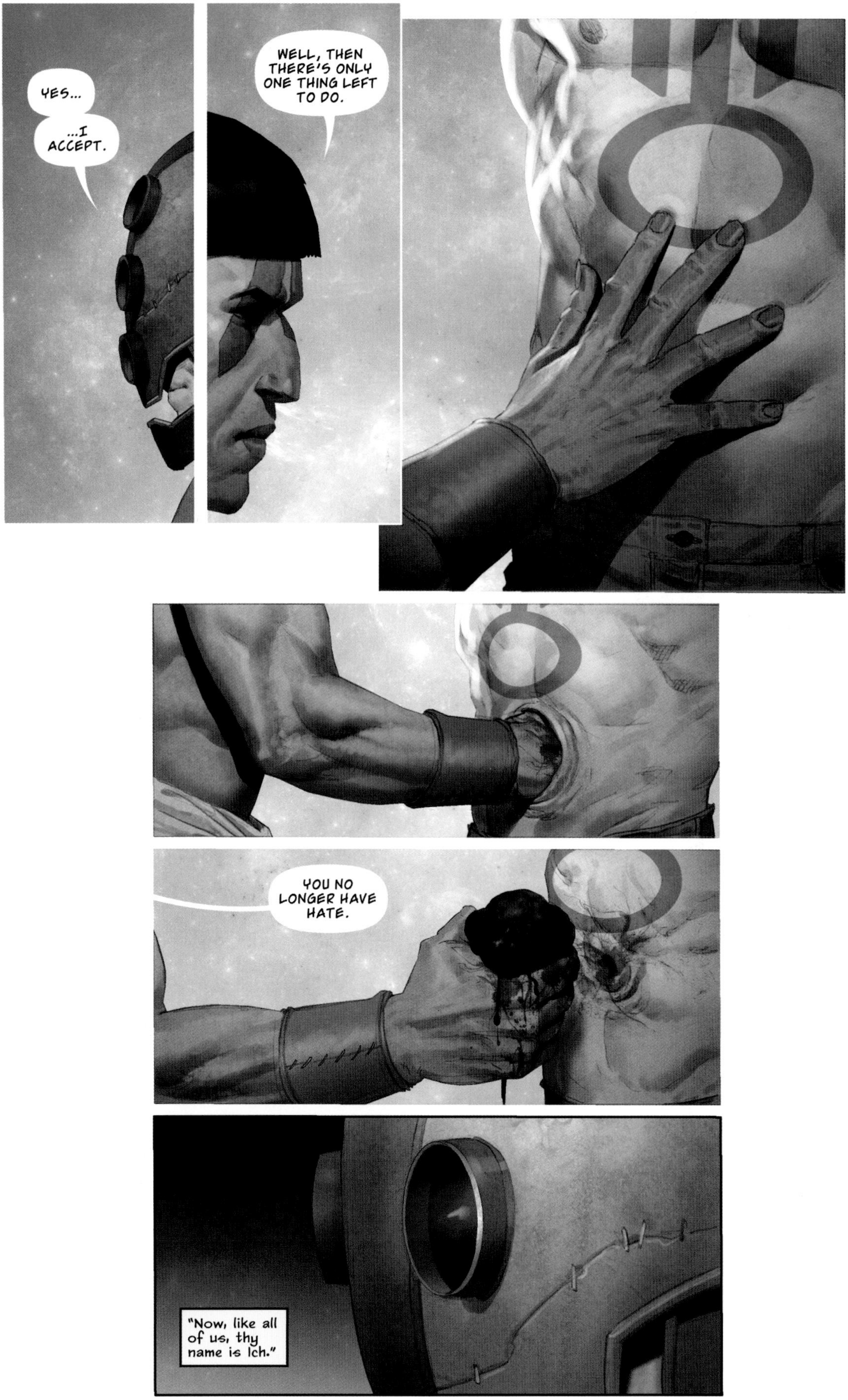
YES...
...I ACCEPT.
WELL, THEN THERE'S ONLY ONE THING LEFT TO DO.
YOU NO LONGER HAVE HATE.
"Now, like all of us, thy name is Ich."

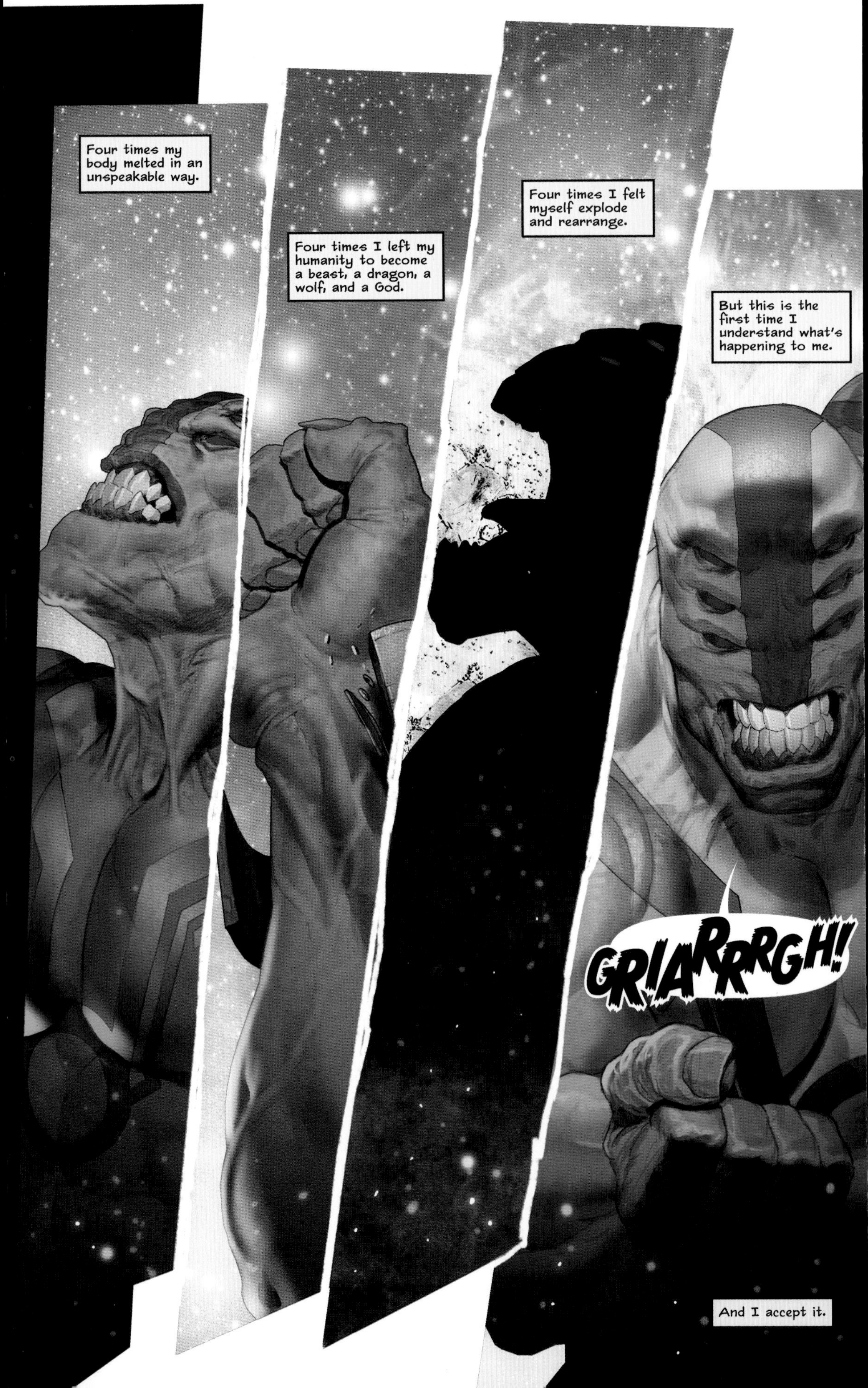
Four times my body melted in an unspeakable way.
Four times I left my humanity to become a beast, a dragon, a wolf, and a God.
Four times I felt myself explode and rearrange.
But this is the first time I understand what's happening to me.
GRIARRRGH!
And I accept it.

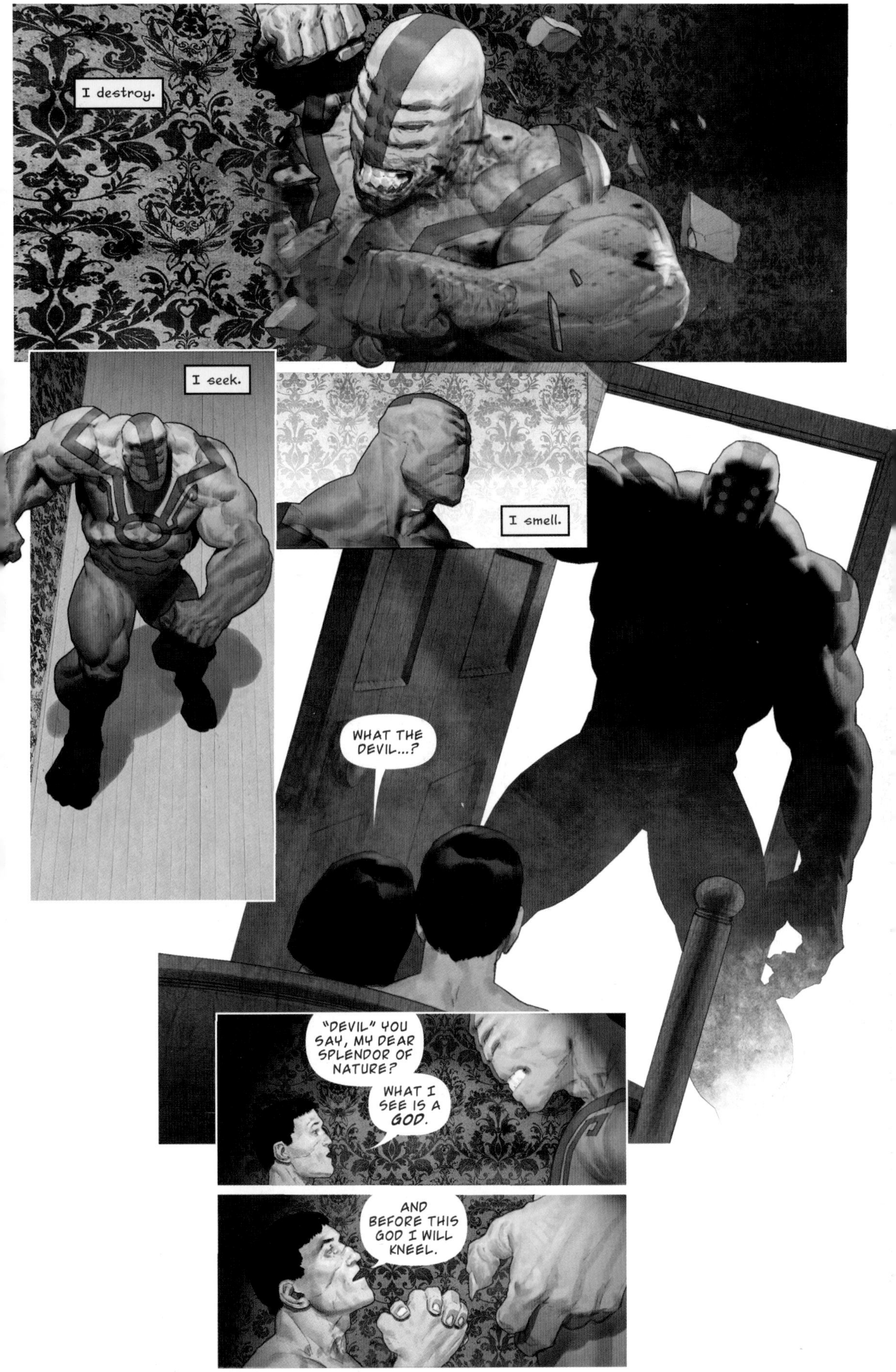

I destroy.
I seek.
I smell.
WHAT THE DEVIL...?
"DEVIL" YOU SAY, MY DEAR SPLENDOR OF NATURE?
WHAT I SEE IS A GOD.
AND BEFORE THIS GOD I WILL KNEEL.

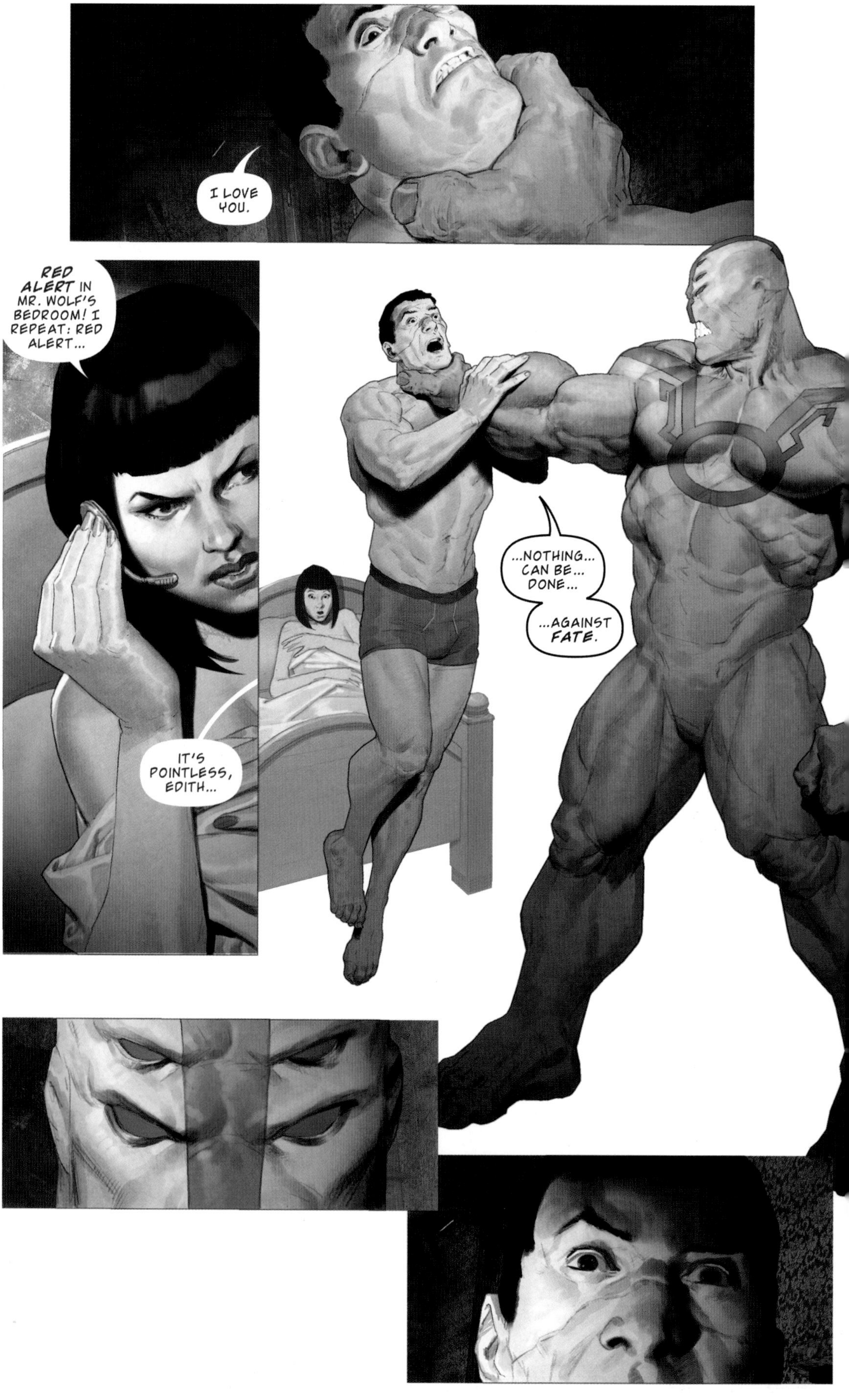
I LOVE YOU.
RED ALERT IN MR. WOLF'S BEDROOM! I REPEAT: RED ALERT...
...NOTHING... CAN BE... DONE...
...AGAINST FATE.
IT'S POINTLESS, EDITH...

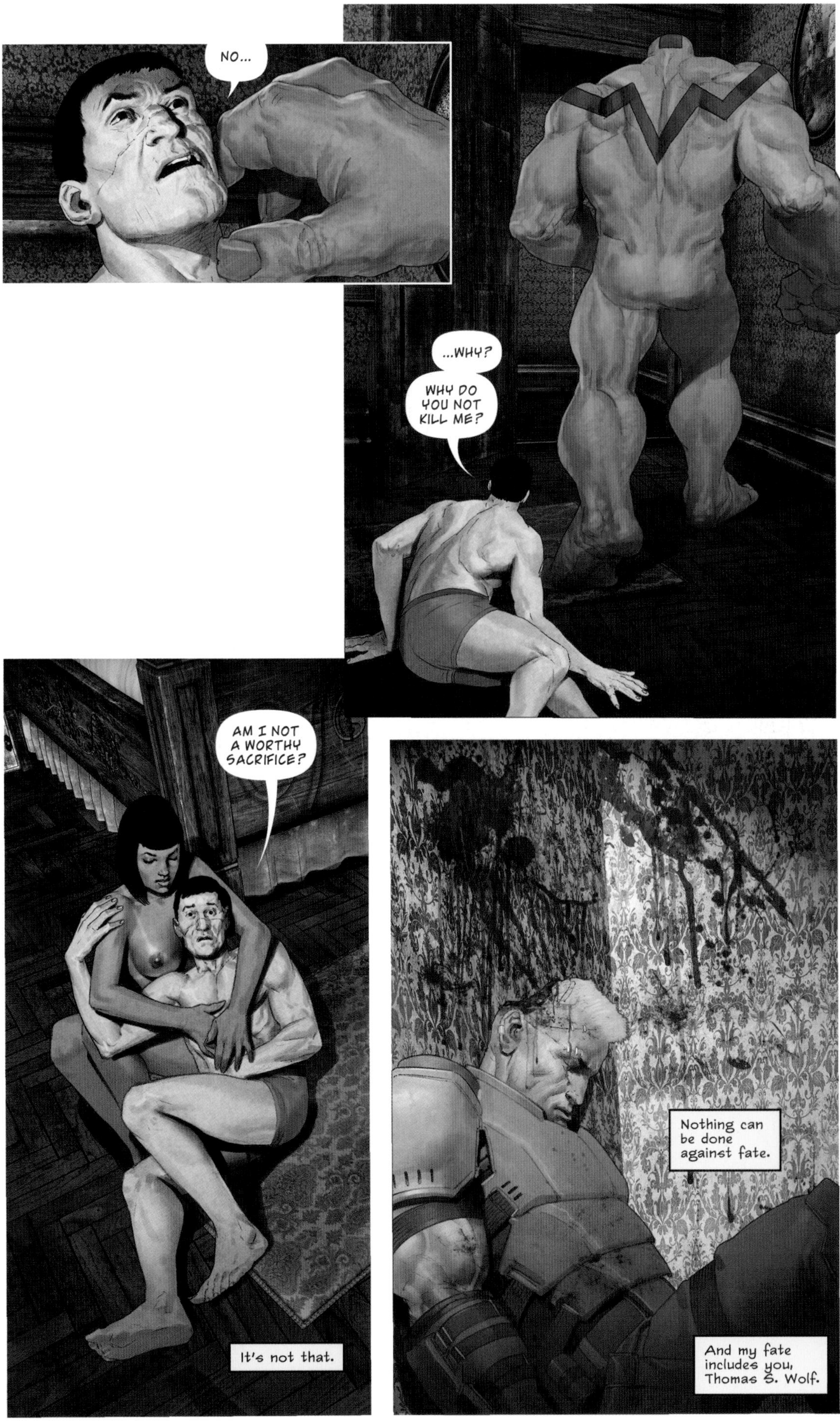
NO...
...WHY?
WHY DO YOU NOT KILL ME?
AM I NOT A WORTHY SACRIFICE?
It's not that.
Nothing can be done against fate.
And my fate includes you, Thomas S. Wolf.

It happens once and *only* once per generation.

There is a signal.

A feeling.

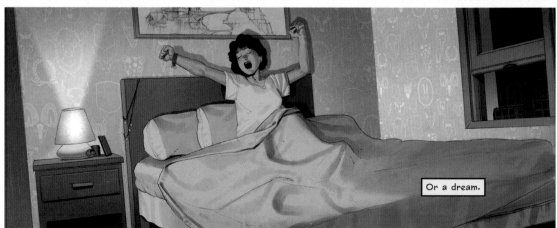

Or a dream.

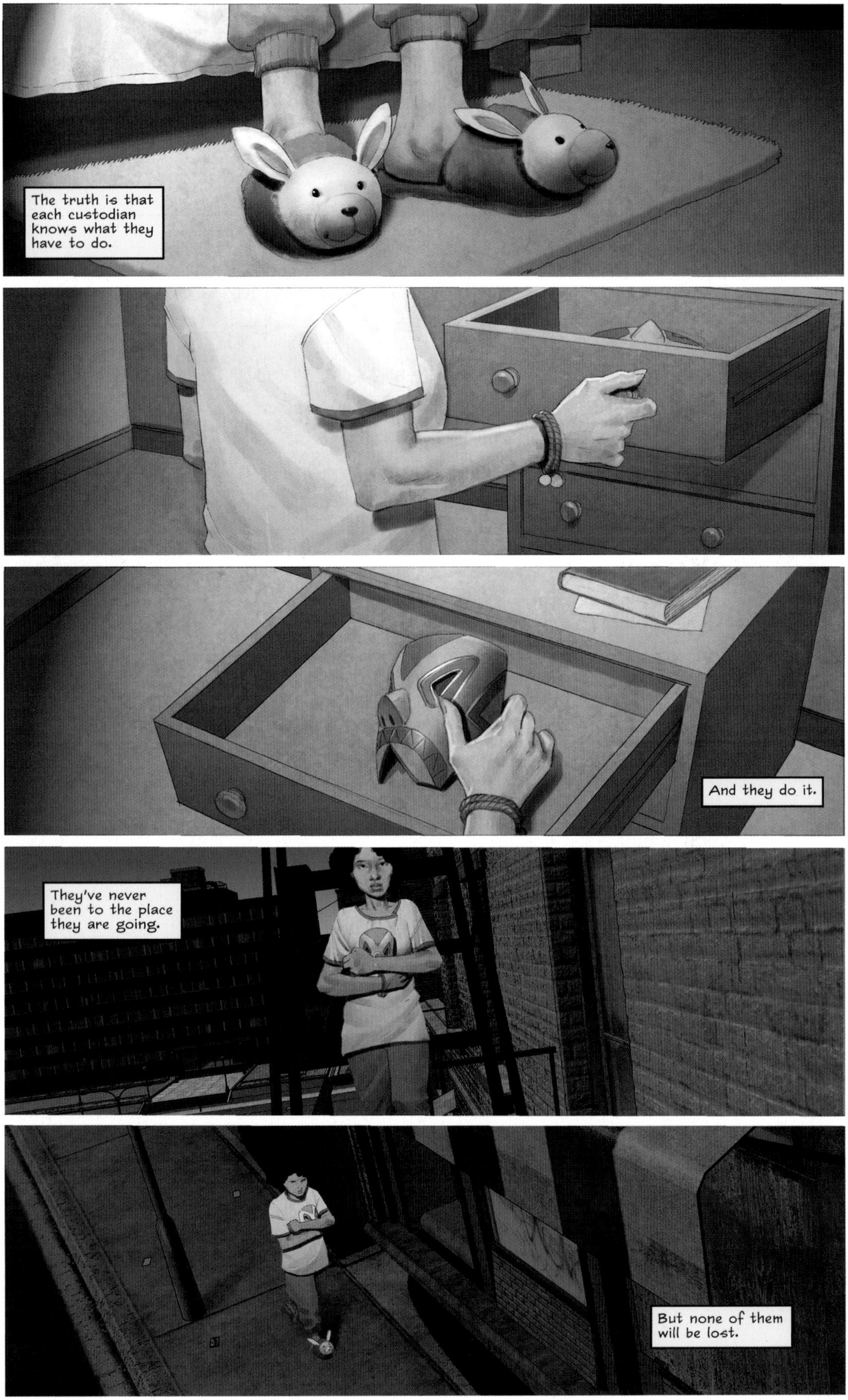
The truth is that each custodian knows what they have to do.
And they do it.
They've never been to the place they are going.
But none of them will be lost.

Everyone knows where to go.

They've gone countless times.

Although this is the first time.

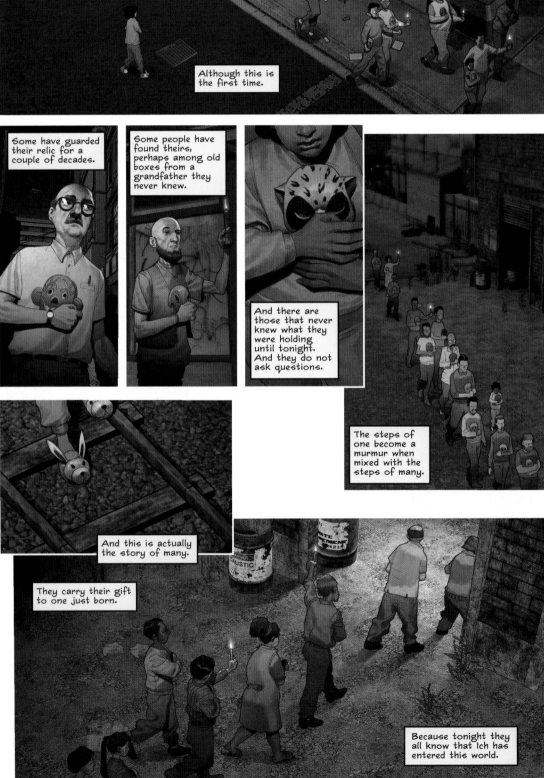

Some have guarded their relic for a couple of decades.

Some people have found theirs, perhaps among old boxes from a grandfather they never knew.

And there are those that never knew what they were holding until tonight. And they do not ask questions.

The steps of one become a murmur when mixed with the steps of many.

And this is actually the story of many.

They carry their gift to one just born.

Because tonight they all know that Ich has entered this world.

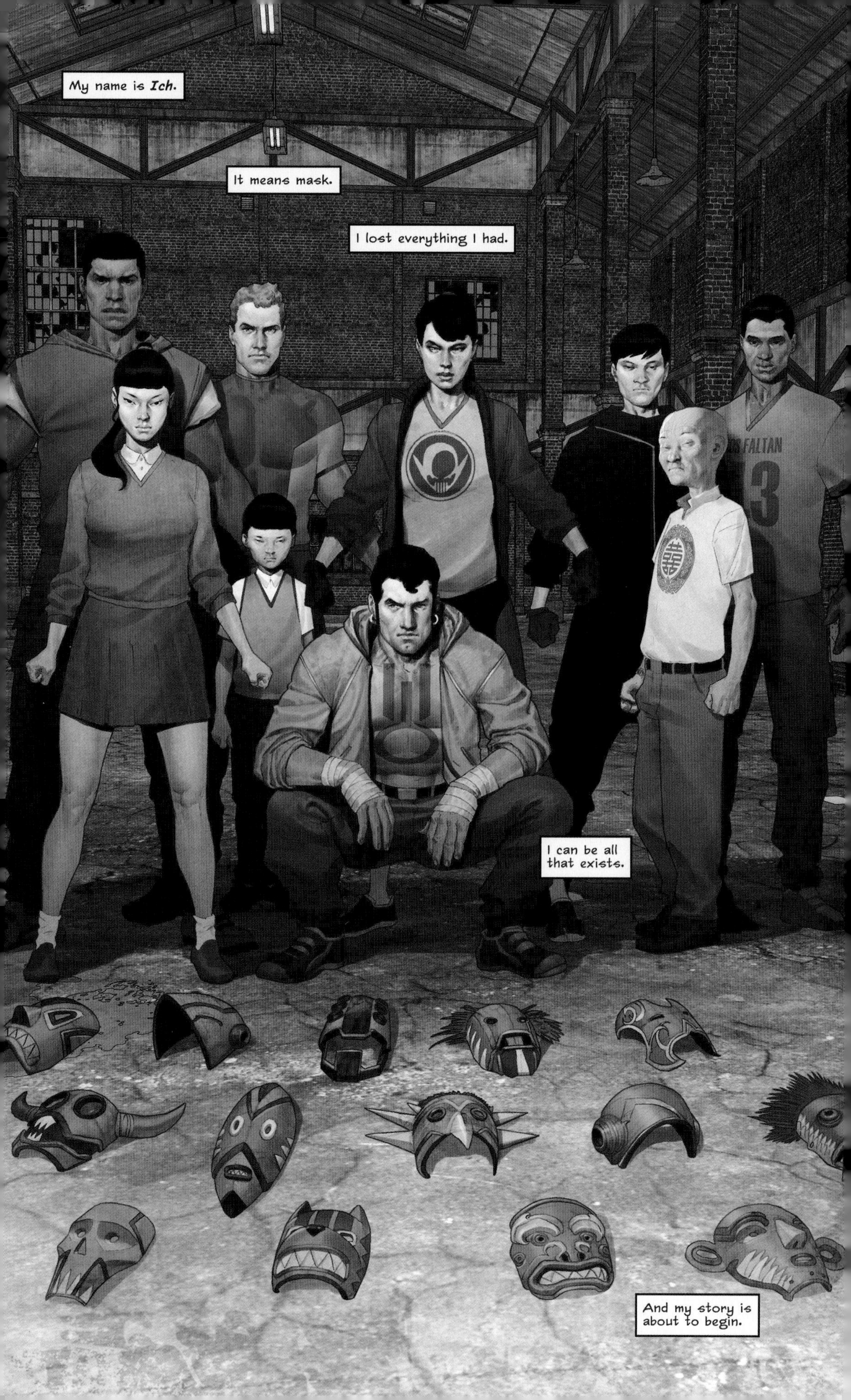
My name is *Ich*.
It means mask.
I lost everything I had.
I can be all that exists.
And my story is about to begin.

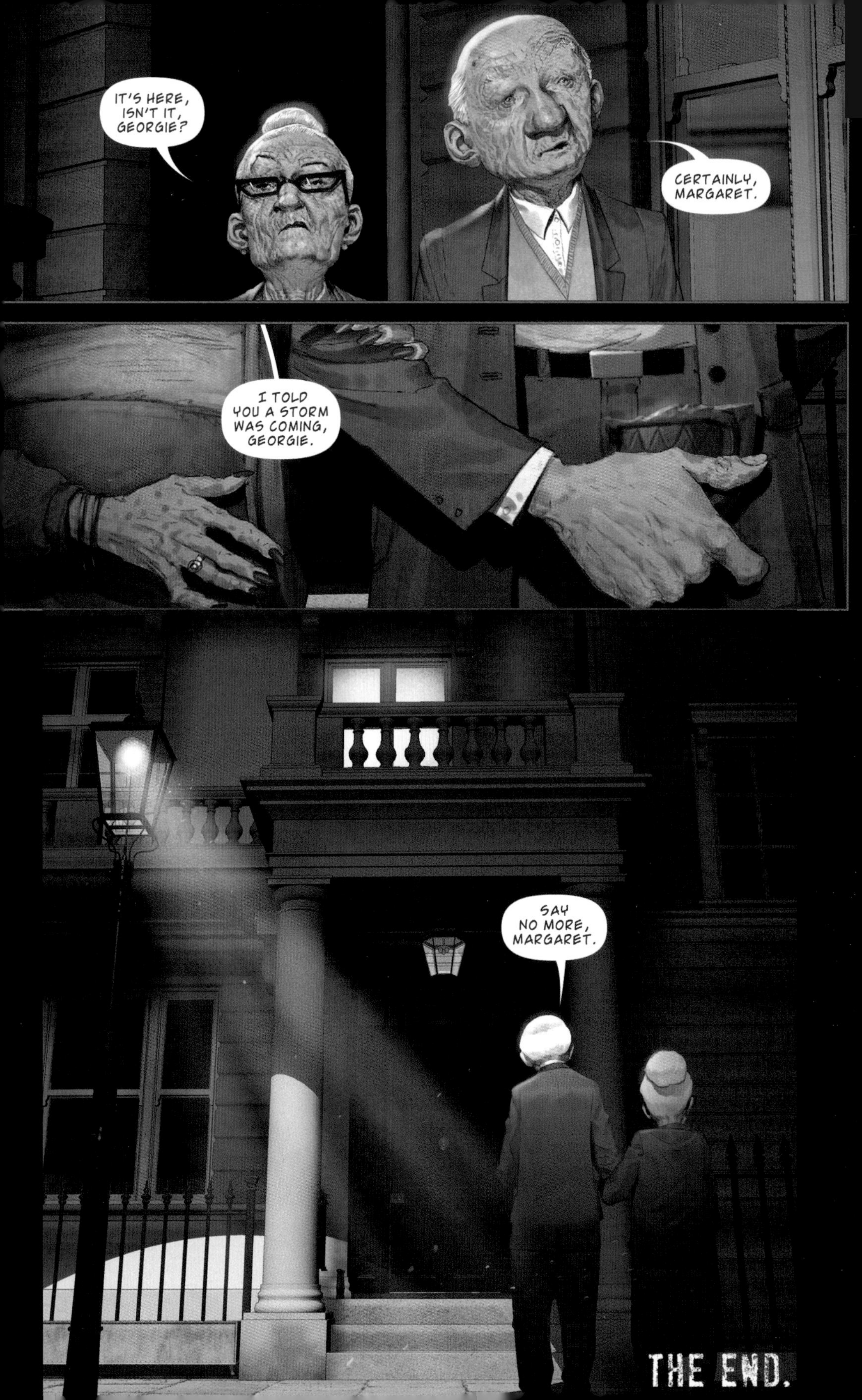
IT'S HERE, ISN'T IT, GEORGIE?
CERTAINLY, MARGARET.
I TOLD YOU A STORM WAS COMING, GEORGIE.
SAY NO MORE, MARGARET.
THE END.

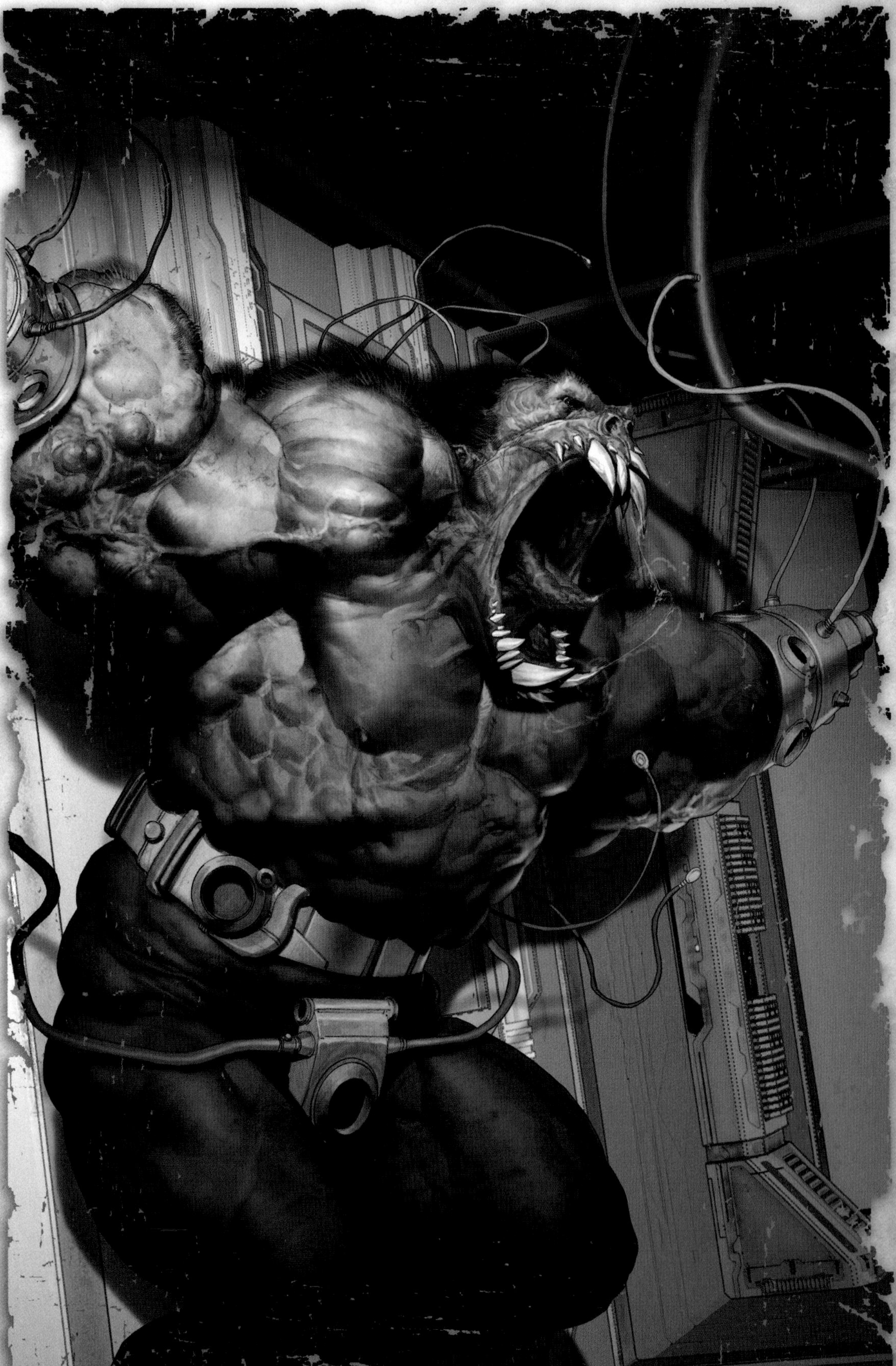

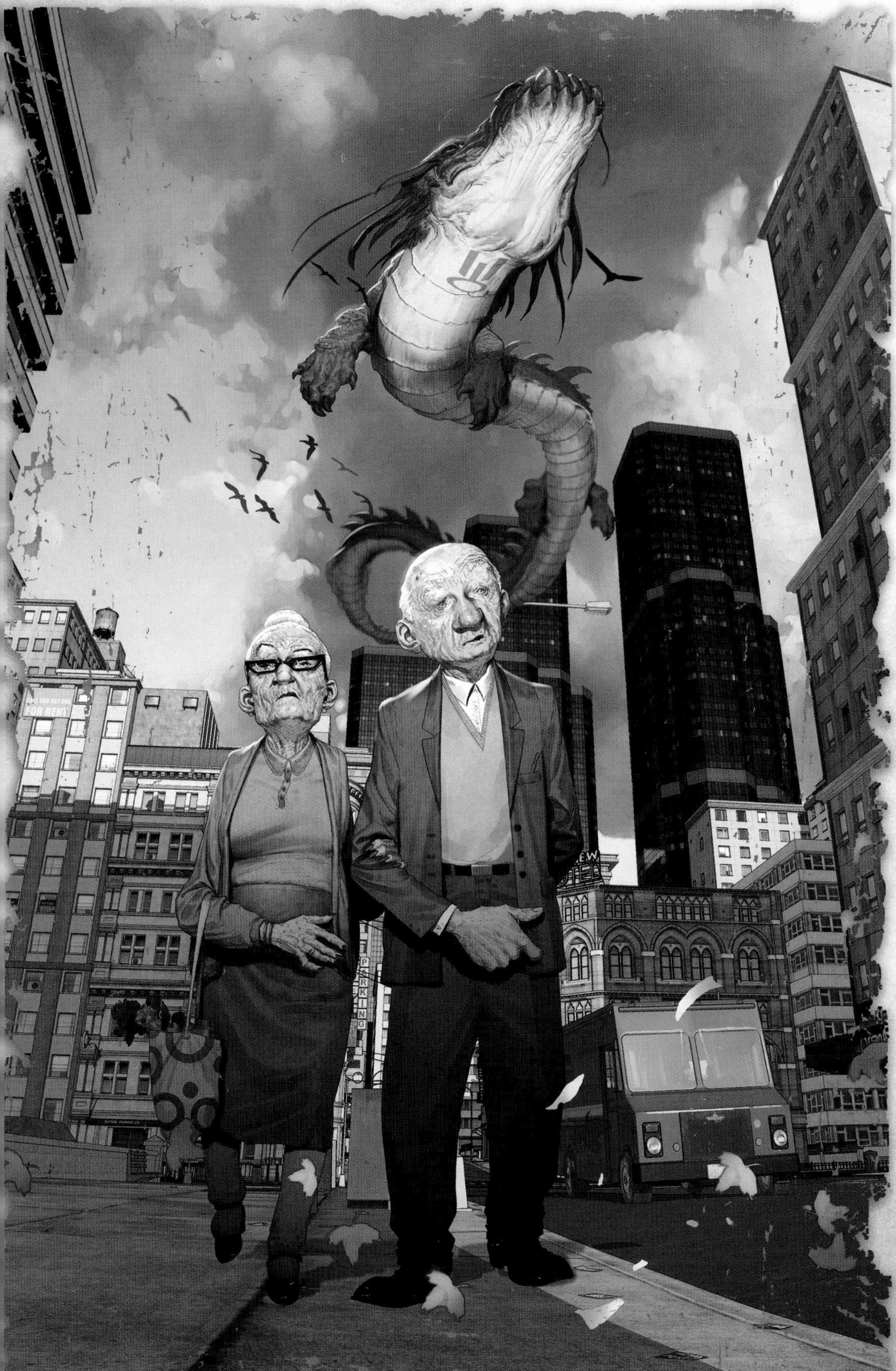
FOR RENT
PARKING

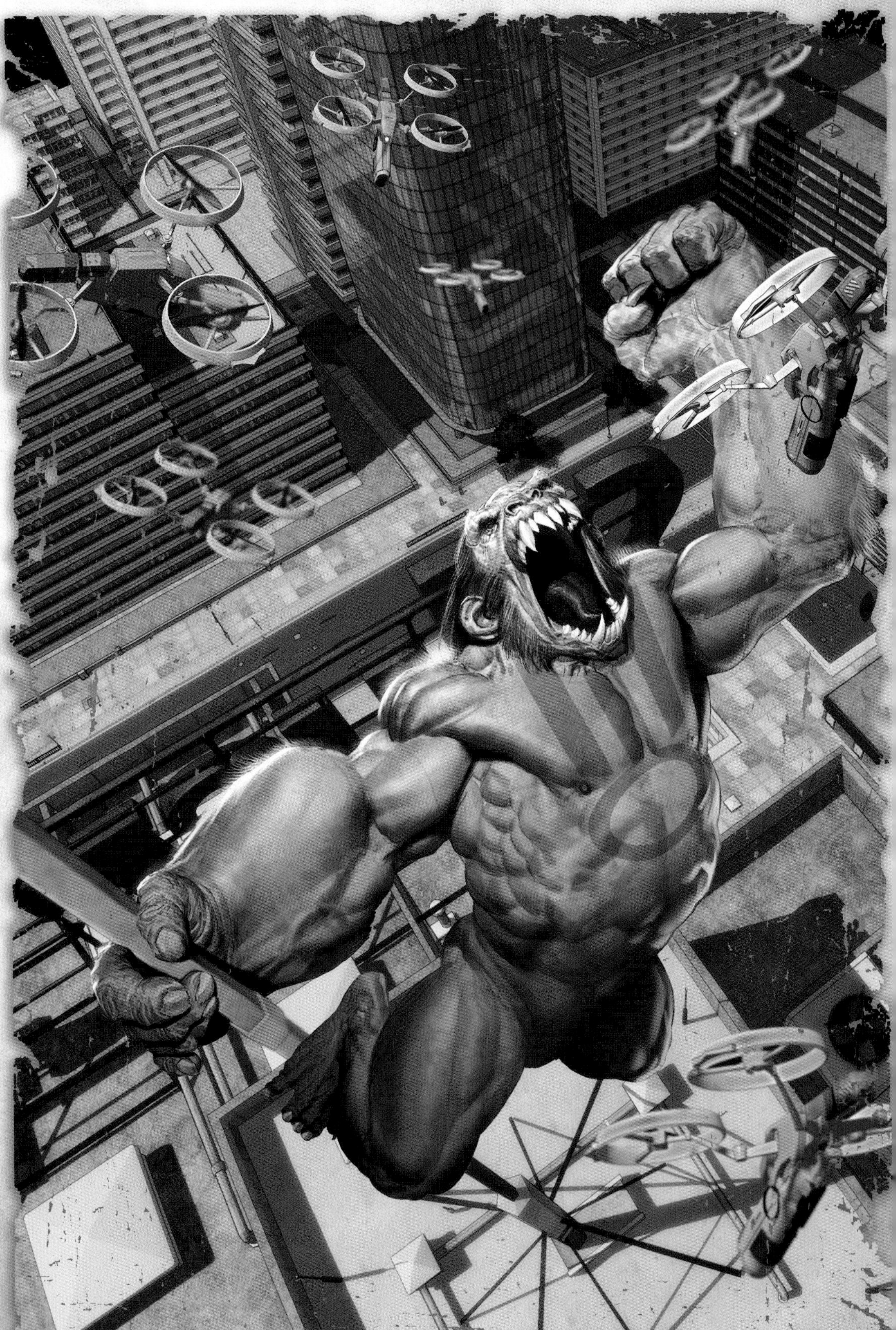

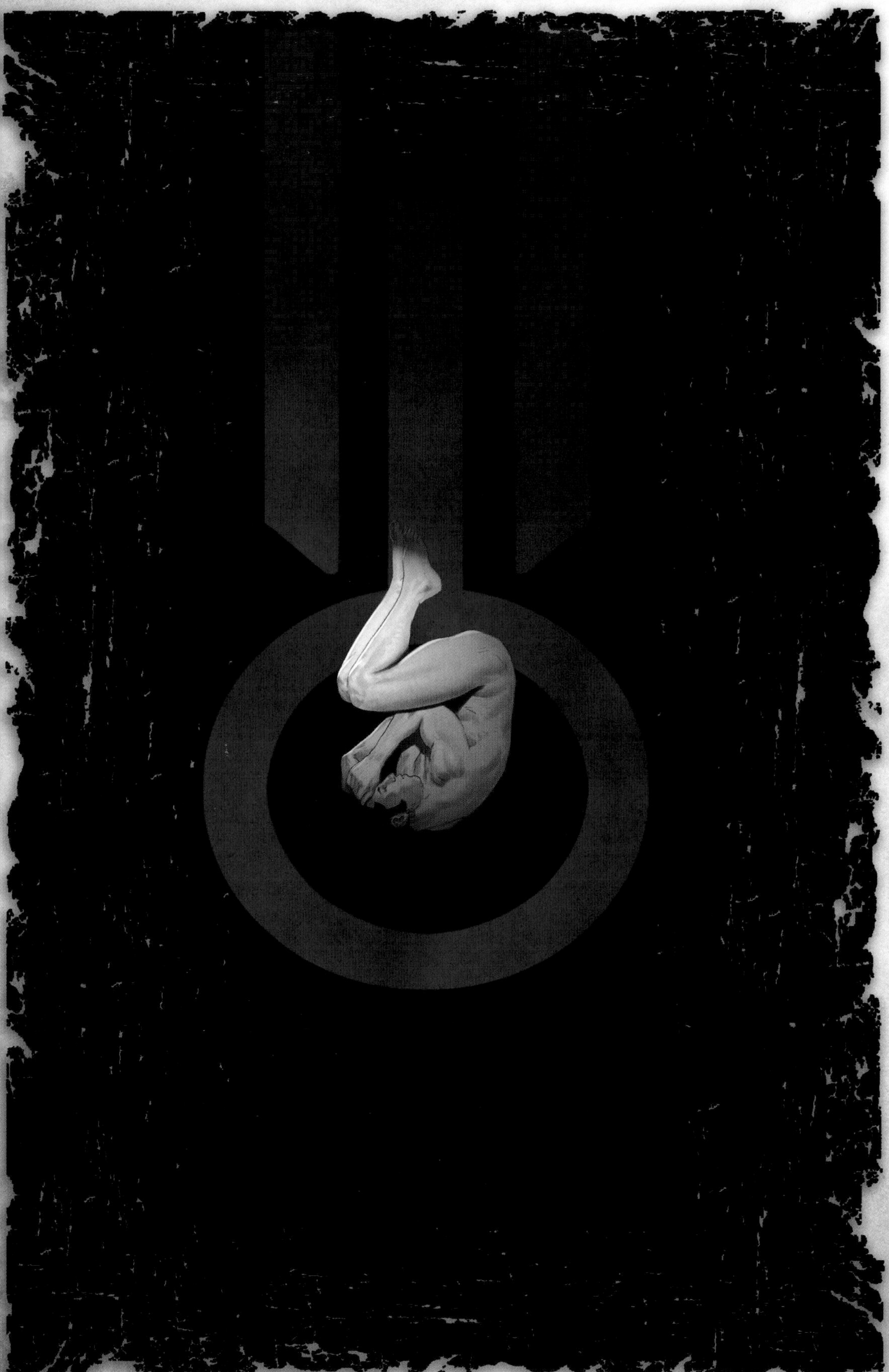

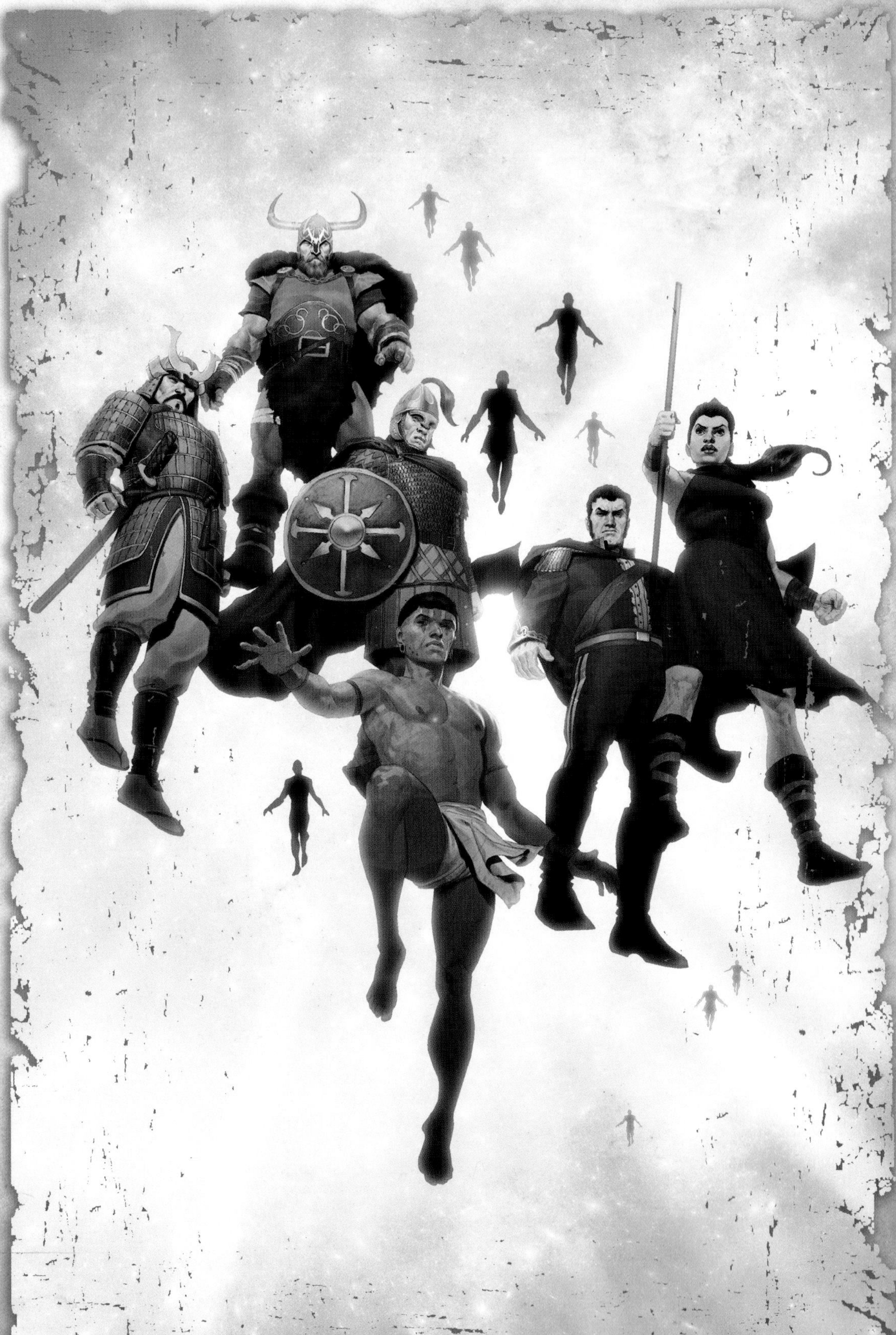

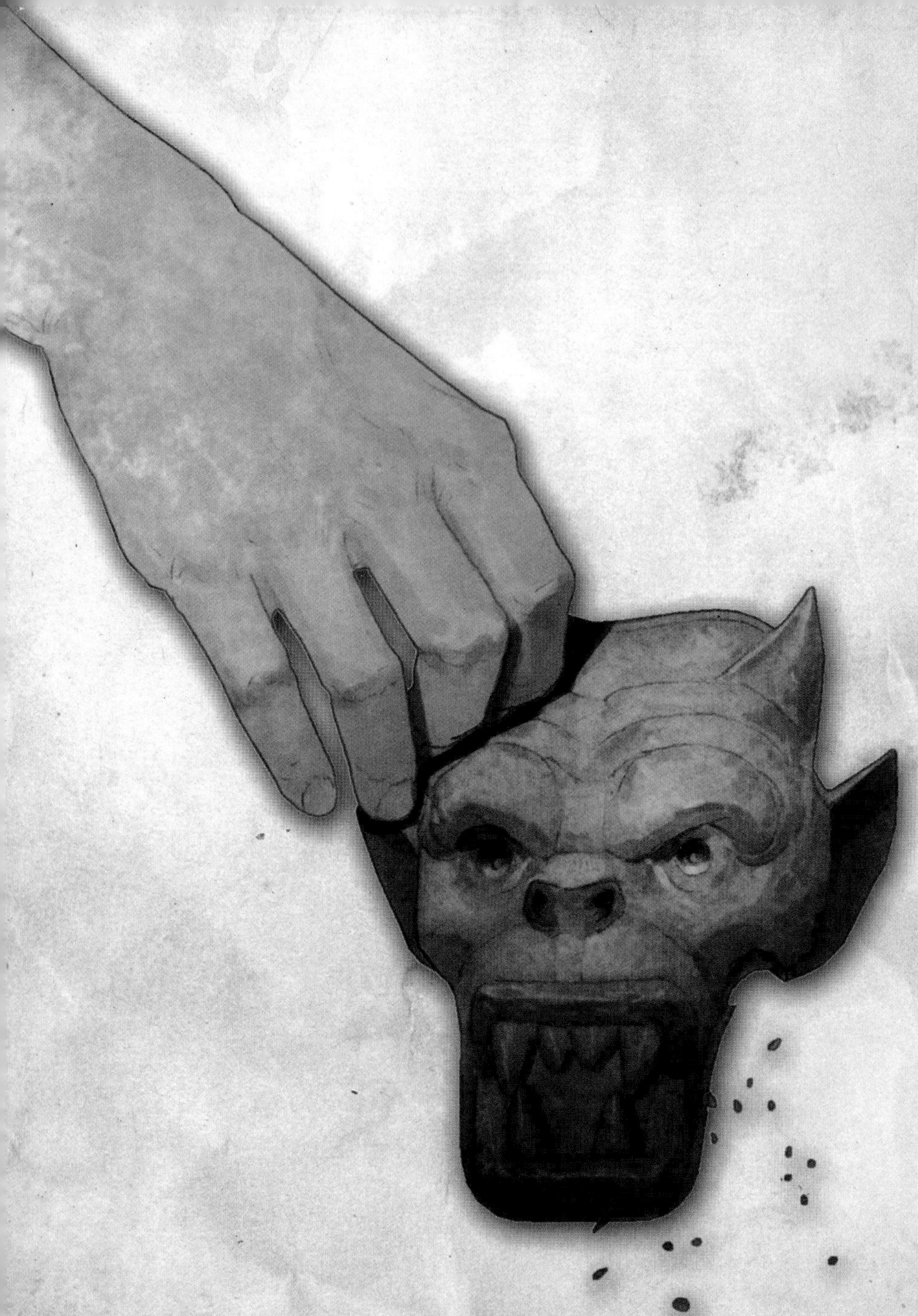

BRUTAL NATURE
CONCRETE FURY